TIME TO SPARE?

A HISTORY OF SUMMER FIELDS

G.I.F.M.

Dis Manibus

TIME TO SPARE?

A History of SUMMER FIELDS

NICHOLAS ALDRIDGE

WITH A FOREWORD BY THE
RT. HON. JULIAN AMERY M.P.

It seems like a fête-champêtre
With red caps everywhere,
Hay-castles in the meadow,
Happiness in the air.
Oh, all the fields were summer then,
And there was time to spare.
— C. DAY LEWIS,
First School

DAVID TALBOYS PUBLICATIONS
SUMMER FIELDS · OXFORD · 1989

First published in Great Britain 1989
by David Talboys Publications
Summer Fields, Oxford

ISBN 0 9514682 0 0

Printed in Great Britain by
Butler & Tanner Ltd
Frome, Somerset

PREFACE

BY THE RT. HON. JULIAN AMERY, M.P.

SUMMER FIELDS, Oxford, has now been in existence for a hundred and twenty-five years. It occupies a commanding position on the most important axis of English life: London, Windsor and Eton, Oxford University. The white cliffs of Dover and Hadrian's Wall have their importance; but it is in the Thames Valley that most of the political and intellectual life of Britain has had its roots.

A preparatory school by definition exists to prepare its pupils for the great public schools. Summer Fields has an enviable reputation for scoring a high number of successes in scholarships and entries to Eton. But it has been much more than just a crammer. It has tried, and with real success, not just to prepare pupils to get into Eton, but to prepare them to take the fullest advantage of it. The secret here has been to teach boys how to work: this is even more important than the particular subjects that they study.

When I was there, classics and divinity commanded most of the timetable. They are less fashionable today, though some knowledge of them is still essential to any understanding of European literature, art or indeed history. But it was the way we were taught that mattered. It was the ability to break up sentences and paragraphs into their component parts and to memorize and interpret the significance of longer passages that trained us in how to work.

This book sets out what is now a fairly long story. Some of it has been a revelation to me. As a small boy, I had dimly sensed that, somewhere in the stratosphere, there was a major conflict of philosophy between the classicists and the modernists. At the time, the classicists won. I remember myself hearing the Headmaster, Cyril Williams, declare that he was 'against all change, even change for the better.' This seemed to me then a ridiculous remark. Later, I was to read profound philosophers who have argued that every technical progress involves a cultural regress. So perhaps Mr Williams had a point. At least I have been fascinated to learn more about the debate that raged above my childish head.

My son went to Summer Fields, and this gave me the opportunity to renew acquaintance with it. Much had changed, and for the better. The accommodation was less austere and, in spite of bad habits inculcated by the war, the diet seemed to have vastly improved. Since then the school population has increased greatly; indeed, it is now almost as difficult to get into Summer Fields as it is to get from Summer Fields to Eton.

Looking back, I reckon I was lucky. Not many small boys had a future Poet Laureate like Cecil Day Lewis and an outstanding novelist like L. A. G. Strong to teach them. I don't suppose either of them enjoyed the job very much, but we boys were the beneficiaries.

This book tells an interesting and honourable story. It is also a valuable commentary on the social evolution of our country over the last century or so. It should give pleasure to those who have been connected with Summer Fields, and encouragement to those who may think of sending their children there.

JULIAN AMERY

House of Commons,
October 1988.

2. Julian Amery, with Robin Reade at the hay-feast, c. 1930.

CONTENTS

LIST OF ILLUSTRATIONS

ILLUSTRATIONS IN COLOUR

(Between pages 42 and 43)

(Between pages 202 and 203)

ACKNOWLEDGEMENTS

THE cover and title-page of this book are something of a fraud. There could not possibly be only one author of such a history, and I am immensely grateful to my (often anonymous) co-authors, both living and dead, chief among whom are: A. F. Alington, Geoffrey Bolton, C. Day Lewis, David Kidd-May, Peter Nathan, R. A. L. Ogston, Patrick Savage, Sir Christopher Slade, Brian Straton-Ferrier, L. A. G. Strong and H. W. Stubbs.

Many of the illustrations appear through the expertise of three photographers in particular: Michael Dudley, Lord Cranworth and Charles Churchill. Major-General Cosmo Nevill painted the picture of the school which forms the dust-wrapper; few histories surely can boast so excellent an original work of art for so utilitarian a purpose. The book as a whole has been designed by Jeffrey Borer of Oxprint, without whose flair it would have been a poor thing indeed.

Its godparents have been the Headmaster of Summer Fields, Nigel Talbot Rice; two in particular of the school's governors, Richard Butler and Sir David Lane; and Christopher Sinclair-Stevenson of Hamish Hamilton Ltd, whose kind advice and practical help have greatly eased the novice author's task. In addition, Perdita Marston, the great-granddaughter of the Maclarens, and Jimmy Bell have been ever-accessible founts of reminiscence and moral support.

I am also indebted for various sorts of help and information, and supplying me with illustrations, to: Helen Air, Jane Alington, Julian Alington, Rt Hon. Julian Amery MP, Hilary Barber, the Rt Rev. Cuthbert Bardsley, Mrs A. C. Blackburne, Barbara Brinton, Elizabeth Burt, John T. Capron, Nigel Chapman, Mrs C. Day Lewis, Adrian Enthoven, Graham Evans, John and Marion Fuller-Sessions, Edward Guinness CVO, Haro Hodson, Diana Holman Hunt, Roger Jacques, the Hon. Martin Janson, Marie Jaqueline Lancaster, Caroline Larken, Anthony Lewis, Jeremy Maas, Christopher Miles, Professor T. R. Miles, Dr David Newsome, Bethia Ogden, Lady Orr-Ewing, David Pitman, Frank Ricketts, Robert Rudd of Sotheby's, Richard Sorrell, Brigadier Sir A. Stanier, Dr Patrick Strong, Ian Tamworth, Mrs Terry-Bevan, Capt. John Wells RN, and, last because very far from least, Richard Usborne, who produced a far better book than this in 1964.

In addition, permission to use extracts is acknowledged from: Methuen & Co for *A Century of Summer Fields*, edited by Richard Usborne, and *Green Memory* by L. A. G. Strong; Collins for *Pack Clouds Away* by Bernard Darwin; A. D. Peters & Co. Ltd for *Chaytor's* by Adrian Alington, and *The Buried Day* by C. Day Lewis, both originally published by Chatto & Windus, and for *The Last Enemy* by L. A. G. Strong, originally published by Gollancz; Macmillan Publishers Ltd for *A Teacher's Story* by Guy Boas; Century Hutchinson for *Approach March* by Julian Amery; and John Murray (Publishers) Ltd for *A History of Wellington College* by David Newsome. I am grateful, too, for permission to use copyright illustrations from: the Ashmolean Museum and the Bodleian Library, Oxford, Cotswold Portraits, Jeremy's (the Oxford Stamp Centre), the Royal Institute of British Architects, St Michael's Publications and the Victoria and Albert Museum, London.

I have received particular help from the staffs of the Oxford City Library, the County Hall and the Bodleian Library, who never showed any surprise or impatience at my ignorance, and whose courteous efficiency and apparent enthusiasm made research an unmitigated delight.

It has not always been easy to trace the sources of illustrations, so I apologize for any omissions or errors in this list. I am most grateful to the following for providing these illustrations:

Mrs Helen Air: 104.
Ashmolean Museum, Oxford: 20.
C. H. Barber: 27, 76, 117.
The Right Revd Cuthbert Bardsley: 83.
Mrs A. C. B. Blackburne: 8.
Bodleian Library, Oxford: 10, 16, 44.
Mrs Elizabeth Burt: 36.
John T. Capron: 7, 29.
N. J. Chapman: 184, 195, 196.
C.ff. Churchill: 115, 134, 158, 165, 170, 171, 172, 173, 174, 175, 178, 179, 181, 182, 183, 185, 186, 187, 189, 199, 200, 201, 202, 203, 204, 207, 208, 209, 210, 211, 212, and 213.
Cotswold Portraits: Colour photograph of Summer Fields Staff.
Lord Cranworth: 67, 68, 69, 205, 206 and colour illustrations of Dr Williams, Ethel Maclaren and the Chapel East Window.
G. P. Evans: 49, 50, 52, 53, 142, 143, 145.
C. E. Guinness CVO: 95, 112.
Haro Hodson: 127, 128.
The Hon. Martin Janson: 64.
Jeremy Maas: 66.
Mrs J. P. Marston: 43, 71.
Christopher Miles: 130.
P. G. Nathan: 125.
Oxford and County Newspapers: 191.
Oxford Stamp Centre (Jeremy's): 25.
F. Ricketts: 149.
The Royal Institute of British Architects: 37.
St Michael's Publications: 19.
P. M. B. Savage: 82, 126, 135, 136, 137, 138, 139, 148, 151.
Brig. Sir A. Stanier: 118, 119, 120, 121, 122.
Brian Straton-Ferrier: 110.
Victoria and Albert Museum, London: 21.

Finally, my colleagues and pupils have been models of patience and kindness in putting up with what must often have been tiresome monomania. Innumerable boys have helped at various times and in various ways; mention must be made of Andrew Hudson, Jamie Hunter, Jeremy Sugden and Louis Waymouth. I am especially grateful to G. W. Hannah for historical research and to the Rev. W. L. A. Pryor, R. H. C Phillips and M. J. B. Riches, as well as my mother and my brother and particularly Jenny Overton, for their constructive and thorough proof-reading. But any errors and omissions must be laid at my doorstep.

N. E. A

INTRODUCTION

> Only one person could write the proper history of Summer Fields – Geoffrey Bolton. He won't. He says there's not a book in it.
>
> RICHARD USBORNE, *A Century of Summer Fields* (1964)

BOYS learn history; young men make history; old men write history.

There is probably no such thing as an objective history; and, even if there were, this book could not claim to be one. I have tried to make fair assessments of people and events, but inevitably what follows is more often eulogistic than critical. Over the years, Summer Fields has been remarkably successful in what it has striven to do, and the large majority of its Old Boys look back on their prep school with affection and gratitude. I myself am a former pupil, and the fact that I have taught there (off and on) for nearly twenty years suggests that I believe in it. Besides, this is a history both *of* Summer Fields and *for* Summer Fields.

That in itself raises a problem – one familiar to readers of Bertie Wooster stories: how much one needs to explain. In the end, I have tried to explain all esoteric terms, for the benefit of the 'general' reader; and I have included two small sections on 'Language' to help do so. A related problem is that of nomenclature. For example, once J. P. Marston has made his first appearance, it would be possible to refer to him subsequently in any of the following ways: Marston, JPM, Pat, Ogre, or even Melon. Here I have to confess to being wildly inconsistent, but I have tried to be clear. The use of initials to denote staff is prevalent in prep schools and their magazines, but, understandably, many people find it tiresome; so I have tried to keep them to a minimum, only using them when it is obvious who is meant. The use of nicknames could have been avoided entirely, but it seemed to me that, say, 'Bam' is actually how most people who knew G. W. Evans thought of him; and it is most emphatically as Bam that he has passed into SF lore. So, possibly perversely, I have tended to refer to the more legendary characters by their nicknames. It does have advantages. Not a few Alingtons have been connected with the school, but 'Bear' identifies EHA immediately and memorably.

It is not certain if history was on the original timetable at Summer Fields (or Summerfield, as it was called until summer 1891), but the school has not lacked for historians during its 125 years, of both the internal and the external sort. The History Pictures, drawn by L. A. G. Strong in the 1920s as *aides-mémoire* for Lysaght's lessons, dependent upon visual mnemonics and terrible puns, took root

3. A History Picture, devised by Rev. J. A. C. Lysaght and drawn by L. A. G. Strong. This represents part of the reign of Henry VIII, the events being arranged roughly in decades, proceeding clockwise round the circus ring from 9 o'clock. *A rag on* the stand denotes Catherine of Aragon; the *hemp* rope and *dud* shell are Empson and Dudley; the three horses stand for the Holy league formed by Pope Julius II – the shaggy horse is Fer(*fur*)dinand, the spotted horse Maximilian, because six noughts *makes a million*, the horse with a v-shaped tail is Venice; the cushion stuffed with wool is Wolsey etc.

in the minds of several generations. The post-war pupils for thirty years received a thorough grounding in essential dates and facts from Harold Hartley, who also contributed a useful essay upon the history of our buildings to the centenary book, *A Century of Summer Fields*. Any historian of Summer Fields must rely heavily upon that book, and also upon the school magazines, which have given a faithful, if sometimes unbalanced, record of our doings since 1897.

Change and continuity are the counterpoised ingredients of a school's historical framework. It is not merely consoling to know that some things go on from decade to decade; it is essential to the identity of the place. One of the first things that John Evans said to my parents in 1948 was, 'We believe in the Three C's: Chapel, Classics and Cricket.' Cynics of that and previous generations might have been forgiven for adding a fourth C: Cold Baths, which were not abolished until the 1960s, when various (possibly overdue) winds of change began to be felt in the school's corridors. It is remarkable that so much did not change during the first hundred years – or, to be precise, during the first sixty years of this century; for between 1864 and 1904 there was much development and expansion, particularly in the decade after the death of Mrs Maclaren in 1896; the spate of building then is matched only by that of the most recent era.

So many people have contributed to the ethos of Summer Fields that it might seem invidious to select two who appear to me to bestride the history, of our first hundred years at any rate, like twin colossi. But nobody who was here with either Edward Hugh Alingon ('Bear') or Geoffrey Bolton could leave the place without having felt extremes of devotion or terror, and frequently both at once! They had much in common, and most particularly total loyalty to the place in which they led the whole of their working lives. Both were the Platonic ideal of the Assistant Headmaster, immersing themselves in all areas of school life while someone else did the 'front line' work. Bear was nominally headmaster for a

4. Rev. E.H. Alington ('Bear'), master 1884–1927, Headmaster 1918–27.

5. Geoffrey Bolton ('GB'), master 1919–60, partner 1930–1956, Headmaster 1956–1960.

decade, but during that time Dr Williams still held most of the financial (and possibly other) control. GB was a partner for twenty-six years and second-in-command to John Evans for seventeen of them, but his own 'reign' as headmaster lasted for only four years before his doctors ordered him, protesting vehemently to the last, to retire to the South Coast.

GB did much to preserve some of the early history; for, as editor of the Magazine in the 1930s, he induced a number of elderly Old Boys to write articles upon the school in their time. Also, some years later he produced a delightful essay, 'Five Wise Men', about notable masters in the generation previous to his own. His 94-page 'Recollections of Summer Fields', an exercise book filled with his familiar spidery handwriting, annotated by Hugh Stubbs and preserved by Patrick Savage, throws much interesting light upon the school between 1920 and 1960, as well as upon the man himself. All of these I have raided shamelessly, and I am equally in debt to GB for bringing out the first School Register in 1929, which was subsequently updated and improved by Harold Clayton in 1960.

Among the anomalies in the history of Summer Fields is the fact that our first headmaster was a woman and some of our first pupils were girls. Since then, we have had no female headmasters or pupils, despite some understandable pressure for the latter in recent years, when having, say, one son at Eton, another here and a daughter at Wycombe Abbey has enormously increased parental travel and exhaustion. But we remain a boys' school and a boarding-school, though we have taken a regular handful of day-boys since 1976.

There is much that a school history cannot encompass: the bleak, oppressive horror of homesickness; the sudden, triumphant realization of an intellectual or sporting skill; the mixed fondness and embarrassment of parental visits; the fleeting perfection of a new friendship. Such things have gone on, day in and day out, for a century and a quarter, and they must be taken as read into every page of this book; but they will not appear in black and white, because an attempt to encapsulate them would be tedious, even if possible.

To go back mentally to the time when Mrs Maclaren started her school requires quite an imaginative leap from the schoolboy of today, surrounded as he is by comfort, even luxury, and living in a much less stratified society than that of the mid-Victorians. For the microcosm of school reflected the macrocosm of the country. Many children saw little of their parents. Schoolmasters were remote and often unpredictable giants. Big boys seldom deigned to notice little boys, except to cuff them, and were in turn feared or worshipped by the little boys, who behaved in the same way themselves when their turn came to be cocks of the roost. No wonder the fagging system died hard at many public schools: nobody wanted to be the generation which lost at both ends.

So much that is now taken for granted was not conceivable to the Victorian

6. Football during morning break at Summer Fields, St Leonards, c. 1912. showing the boys playing unchanged apart from the removal of jackets.

schoolboy, and so much that he took as the natural law of things now strikes us as cumbersome, unnecessary, or even intolerable. In the matter of costume alone, rituals abounded, many of which were still in evidence as recently as 1950: you must always wear a vest; you must change your shoes to go out; you must wear a dreadful felt sun-hat if the sun is shining in summer. Yet, despite all this palaver, changing clothes completely for games is quite a modern idea: for football one simply flung off one's jacket and sometimes one's waistcoat and then weighed in, braces, boots, trousers and all.

And the notion that one should be seen and not heard inevitably created inhibitions, though one may argue that there was also a good side to it. In the presence of grown-ups, most boys stammered, blushed, looked fixedly at their feet and replied in inarticulate monosyllables. Deportment on the games field differed noticeably from the semi-professional hysteria of today. Those who scored goals or held catches looked faintly embarrassed and would shrug off their success, suggesting that it was a 'fluke'. Such a public exhibition of modesty was of course hypocritical, but not unbecoming.

The differences in costume provide one of the good reasons for copious illustration in this history. Yes, they really dressed like that: see for yourself. In addition, however much one may or may not believe that in the face the character is writ, it is fascinating to match a physiognomy with a name that one has come

7. John and Gerard Capron, c. 1910, while they were at Summer Fields. Their father and their uncle, who were also at Summer Fields, can be seen on page 28 in Chapter 2.
8. William Jones (SF 1891–94), son of Rev. William West Jones, Vicar of Summertown 1864–74 and subsequently Archbishop of Capetown.

across or a character that one has studied. The adages about the length of Cleopatra's nose or the launching capacity of Helen's face contain at least a poetic truth which surely ends up as an important historical one.

Another delight in pictures is the discovery of how greatly a place has changed or remained surprisingly the same. Trees are planted, grow, fall and disappear; buildings rise to block the familiar scene, become creeper-covered, are adapted or added to and in turn partly obscured by some newer edifice. The school records contain a number of views which are simply not possible now. They will appear as you turn the pages; but first, and most suitably, to enter into the mid-Victorian era when the history of Summer Fields began, let us look at the face and character of the pioneer gymnast, Archibald Maclaren.

This being my first foray into researching and writing history, I was surprised to find how inaccurate most written history is. In the light of this discovery, however, I am under no illusions about the chapters that follow. I am sure that they will be bristling with the most obvious mistakes, and I look forward to being corrected by boys, staff, Old Boys and friends of the school on many matters. I hope that they *will* write to point out my errors, for that will perhaps help my successor in 2014 to produce something a little less inaccurate. In the knowledge that much of it may be wrong, then, I cannot call this THE History, but merely

A HISTORY OF SUMMER FIELDS.

Oxford, 1988 NEA

9. A View that is no more: looking from the corner of Summerfield and Mayfield Roads, through the gate that was the main entrance to the school, towards the Lobby, in the late 1930s. In 1978 the Macmillan Gallery and Music Block were built across this entrance.

1

THE GYMNAST, THE PUBLISHER AND THE PRE-RAPHAELITES
c. 1790–1863

BOTH Archibald Maclaren (as I shall spell his surname) and Gertrude Isobel Frances Talboys, who became his second wife and the school's foundress, were remarkable people in their different ways. Maclaren, who was born in 1819, developed from being a simple fencing instructor into a pioneer of gymnastics, particularly as it came to be used in the army. He was widely looked up to, and consulted about the building of gymnasia throughout the country and the then flourishing British Empire. He published a number of books and pamphlets on his twin special subjects, such as *A Military System of Gymnastics for the Use of Instructors* (1862), *A System of Fencing for the Use of Instructors in the Army* (1864) and *Training, in theory and practice* (1866).

He was in fact the founder of modern physical training, and one of the major contributors to the health and fitness of the nation today. But he was no mere narrow-minded muscle-builder; the foreword to his first book preaches the gospel of *Mens Sana in Corpore Sano*, showing that he had equal respect for brain and physique, and believed the two to be mutually dependent.

Our first record of physical training, that is to say, of any system adopted and practised with the single view of improving and cultivating the physical resources, is to be found in the competitive exercises of the early Greeks and Romans; and it has been said that we have lost as much by the discontinuance of the system of bodily exercise of these nations, as we have gained by our knowledge of physiological science. This is one of the aphorisms which men are fond of repeating, but which will not stand criticism. No price can be set upon our knowledge of physiological science ...

There is no profession, there is no calling or occupation in which men can be engaged, there is no position in life, no state in which a man can be placed, in which a fairly developed frame will not be valuable to him; there are many of these, even the most purely and highly intellectual, in which it is essential to success; essential, simply as a means, material but none the less imperative, to enable the mind to do its work. Year by year, almost day by day, we see men falter and fail in the midst of their labours – men to whom labour is life and idleness is death ... and all for want of a little bodily stamina.

10. Archibald Maclaren's Oxford Gymnasium, from the *Illustrated London News,* 1859. [Bodleran Library, G. A. Oxon. a. 65. p. 48]

11. The exterior of what was once Maclaren's Gymnasium as it is today.

Here Mr. Verdant Green, properly equipped for the purpose, was accustomed to swing his clubs after the presumed Indian manner, to lift himself off his feet and hang suspended between the parallel bars, to leap the string on to the mattress, to be rapped and thumped with single-sticks and boxing-gloves by any one else than Mr. Blades (who had developed his muscles in a most formidable manner), and to go through his parades of *quarte* and *tierce* with the flannel-clothed assistant. Occasionally he had a fencing bout with the good-humoured Mr. MacLaren, who

—professionally protected by his padded leathern *plastron*—politely and obligingly did his best to assure him, both by precept and example, of the truth of the wise old saw, "mens sana in corpore sano."

12. Excerpt from *The Adventures of Mr Verdant Green.*

Maclaren's Gymnasium was in Alfred Street in Oxford, just south of the High: it is used today by the Holywell Press, the building largely retaining its exterior form, but being hard to see clearly and whole, as it is cluttered by other buildings. It was built, probably in the late 1850s, to replace an earlier gymnasium on the same site or in Oriel Lane, mentioned in the third part of *The Adventures of Mr Verdant Green* (1857). This highly amusing novel about the adventures of an ingenuous young freshman was written by Edward Bradley, under the pseudonym of 'Cuthbert Bede'. It not only gives us an account of Verdant Green's fencing lessons, but also kindly supplies a sketch portrait of Archie Maclaren himself.

Maclaren's two books on the subject were reissued after his death in a compendium version under the title *Physical Education* (1895), edited and prefaced by his son Wallace, who gives the historical perspective of his father's achievement, together with one or two pertinent comments of his own.

It is now more than thirty years since the demand for systematized Physical Education began to make itself heard in this country; but the sense of its importance, radiating from the centres of Oxford and Aldershot, has since spread throughout civil and military

13. The 'Twelve Apostles' with Archibald Maclaren. James Wheeler Talboys (misspelt) is also in the picture.

England, till to-day there is scarcely a town or a depôt which does not possess its properly equipped gymnasium. The arrival of the first detachment of non-commissioned officers who, under Major (now General) Hammersley, went through a half-year's course at the Oxford University Gymnasium in 1861, proved the beginning of a system which, under that officer and subsequent inspectors of military gymnasia, has been the means not merely of materially benefiting the physique of the army, but of giving an impetus to physical education generally, for which as a nation we cannot be sufficiently grateful.

In fact, the course of training which the dozen NCOs underwent was so successful that they had to have new uniforms, their muscular development having made their original ones at first a tight fit, and then no fit at all! Wallace goes on in his preface to make a point which is of particular relevance to Summer Fields.

The glaring fault in the old days was that gymnastics were left (such as they were) to grown-up men; there was not a single college, for instance, civil or military, which boasted such a thing as a gymnasium, and Mr Archibald Maclaren had to labour to show, what to-day is recognized, that it is while the body is *growing* that gymnastics exercise their greatest benefits, and that the time for mental and bodily education is one and the same.

14. (*opposite*) The first and last pages of the first edition of *The Fairy Family*, from the copy presented to the school by Roger Lancelyn Green, who used one of Maclaren's poems in his *Book of Verse for Children*.

Nor did our pioneer gymnast's character lack the third element. He was evidently a man of great charm, emotional like many Victorians under the imposed façade of stiff-upper-lippery, and highly appreciative of art. When the young and somewhat anaemic Edward Burne-Jones came to the gymnasium to improve his physique, a friendship quickly sprang up between the two men. 'I continue my fencing lessons &c. and feel almost unutterable benefit from them,' he wrote to his father in April 1853; 'my strength grows perceptibly, and Maclaren promises to send me forth a very different object to what I was when I entered.' Soon Burne-Jones and his friend William Morris were regular and welcome guests at the Maclarens' home in Summertown.

We owe to Lady Burne-Jones the description of Summerfield in the 1850s which has been included in both the Register and *A Century of Summer Fields.* According to her memoir of her husband, Maclaren was 'one of the truest friends he ever had, and one whose eyes discerned his pupil's genius from the first ... It was when Edward began to make studies of the landscape and foliage round Oxford, that Maclaren recognized his power, and the unfailing belief and encouragement that he gave in these early days were never forgotten.' In 1854 they began the collaboration that was to result in the publication of *The Fairy Family* in 1857, the illustrations by Burne-Jones and the text by Maclaren – about as far a cry from military training manuals as one could imagine.

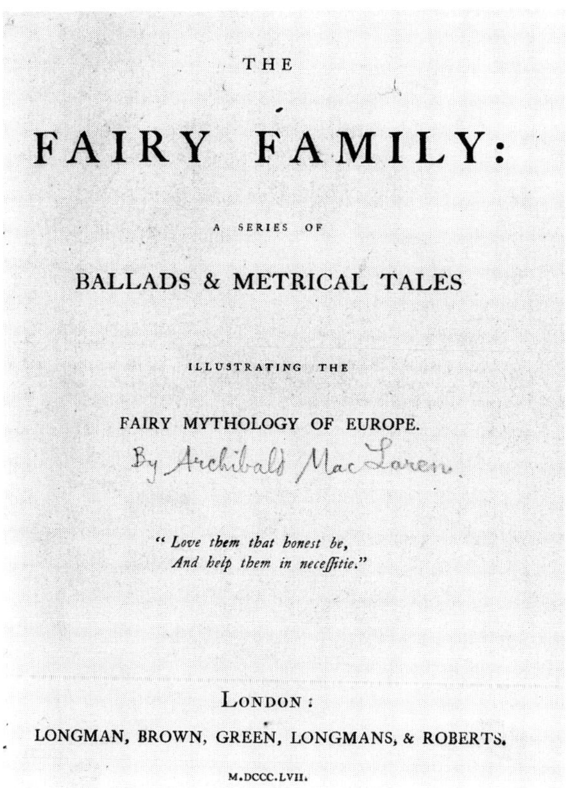
THE

FAIRY FAMILY:

A SERIES OF

BALLADS & METRICAL TALES

ILLUSTRATING THE

FAIRY MYTHOLOGY OF EUROPE.

By Archibald MacLaren.

"Love them that honest be,
And help them in neceſſitie."

LONDON:

LONGMAN, BROWN, GREEN, LONGMANS, & ROBERTS.

M.DCCC.LVII.

The Neck. 279

Then galloping, galloping, up the way
All riderleſs came the dappled grey,
With quivering limb and ſtaring eye,
With bridle broken and girth awry,
All dabbled with froth and river foam
The terrified ſteed came galloping home——
But Sir Eric came back no more.

The girl that he married on 27 August 1851 had qualities which complemented Archie Maclaren's to perfection. To get to know her, we must first look at her father; for, if Archie and Gertrude were unusual, David Alphonso Talboys was equally so. Many of the circumstances of his early life are now lost, probably beyond recall. He was born *c.* 1790, and his second name, together with that of his sister (Cordelia), suggests that his parents were literary and individualistic. These qualities David inherited in abundance. Starting as a bookseller in Bedford, he moved to Oxford, where he rapidly branched out into publishing and translation. Some of his catalogues published between 1820 and 1839 survive: the classics predominate, but he achieved fame for his translations of the Germans Heeren and Adelung, producing works with such impressive titles as *Researches into the Politics, Intercourse and Trade of the Carthaginians, Ethiopians and Egyptians* and *Historical Sketch of Sanscrit Literature*. He must have had a working knowledge of several languages, including Sanskrit, and his Latin and Greek were passed on to his daughter. From 1825 onwards he produced a noteworthy series in conjunction with the London publisher William Pickering, called *The Oxford English Classics*: popular reprints of Hume, Smollett, Johnson, Boswell, Defoe (in twenty volumes!) and others. He was a rival to the Oxford University Press, which owes him a debt in one respect. For at the time of his death he was negotiating an English version of Franz Passow's *Greek Lexicon*; but he died before the project was completed. It was taken over by the O.U.P. and in due course appeared as the famous Liddell and Scott.

Now, attractive though the picture may be of little Gertrude learning her Greek and Latin at her father's knee, it must be borne in mind that he died when she was barely seven. So her erudition

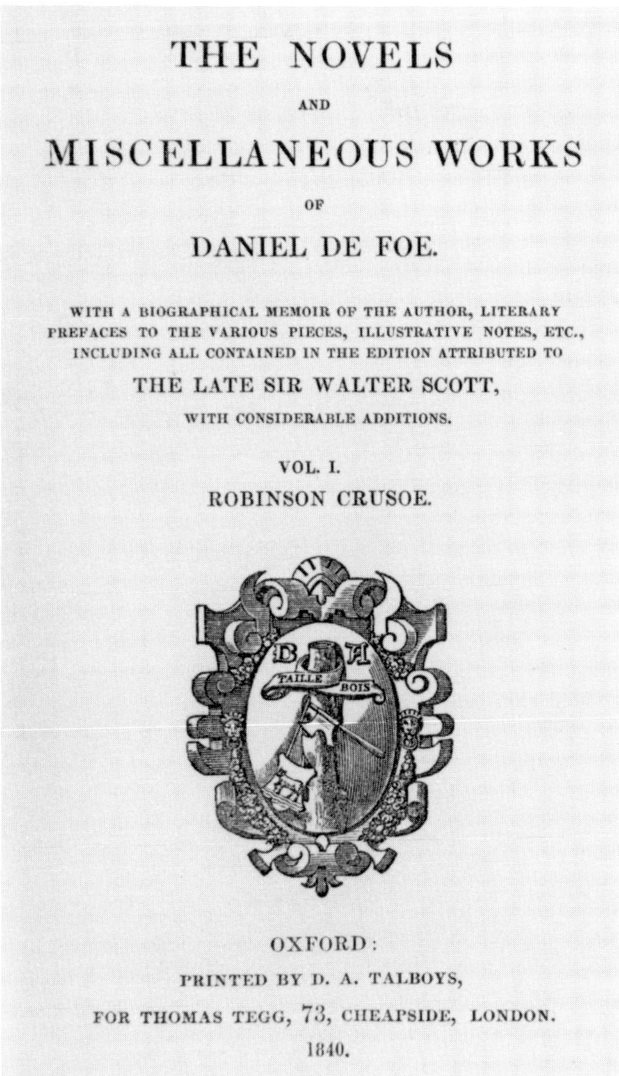
THE NOVELS

AND

MISCELLANEOUS WORKS

OF

DANIEL DE FOE.

WITH A BIOGRAPHICAL MEMOIR OF THE AUTHOR, LITERARY PREFACES TO THE VARIOUS PIECES, ILLUSTRATIVE NOTES, ETC., INCLUDING ALL CONTAINED IN THE EDITION ATTRIBUTED TO

THE LATE SIR WALTER SCOTT,

WITH CONSIDERABLE ADDITIONS.

VOL. I.

ROBINSON CRUSOE.

OXFORD:

PRINTED BY D. A. TALBOYS,

FOR THOMAS TEGG, 73, CHEAPSIDE, LONDON.

1840.

15. Title page of Talboys' edition of Defoe in twenty volumes.

will have been more the result of osmosis, growing up in a household where books and learning, especially of the classics, were respected; the actual teaching probably came from her mother, or older brothers or sisters.

Talboys' own erudition was recognized by Oxford, which in 1827 admitted him to the privileges of a member of the university. In the same year, he moved premises from St Clement's to the south side of the High Street opposite the Queen's College, where he bought Number 86/87, next to what is now Frank Cooper's Oxford Marmalade. The family worshipped at St Peter's-in-the-East, which still stands, but is used as the library of St Edmund Hall rather than as a church. When he died in 1840, he received obituary notices in the *Oxford Chronicle* and the *Gentleman's Magazine*, which referred to his industry, talents and acquirements: 'To great energy and decision of character was added a competent knowledge of the value and merits of books. He was a Councillor of the East Ward of Oxford, and had served the office of Sheriff with credit, but in politics he was an extreme Radical.'

His energy and radicalism were not confined to literature and politics. He made at least three marriages and fathered at least thirteen children, several of

16. High St, Oxford, opposite the Queen's College, at the turn of the century. Talboys' shop, Nos 86–87 is the rather lower building with the seven columns, beyond the lamp-post [Bodleian Library, MS. Top. Oxon. d. 972, fol. 8.].

17. St Peter's-in-the-East, where Gertrude Talboys was christened on 9th May 1833.

whom died in infancy, a common event in those days when cholera and other epidemics raged. His first wife, Jemima Millar, was seventeen when he married her in 1811; his second, Eliza Hurdis, whom he married 1818, was the same age as the century; and his third, Mary Wheeler, was also eighteen. But she was made of more durable stuff than her predecessors, for she bore five sons and four daughters (including Gertrude), outlived David and retired after his death to Summertown, where her son-in-law was soon to buy the house that later became Summerfield.

Archie Maclaren married Charlotte Wheeler Talboys in 1844. One imagines that in commuting from Headington, where he lived, to Alfred Street, he would regularly pass, and increasingly often call in at, the bookseller's shop in the High. But their marriage lasted for less than three years, for she died childless, some time before 1847; within a few years Archie married her younger sister Gertrude, and settled with her in the Summertown house that he had bought in 1847 from the widow Ann Peake.

DAVID ALPHONSO TALBOYS

HIS FAMILY, MARRIAGES AND DESCENDANTS

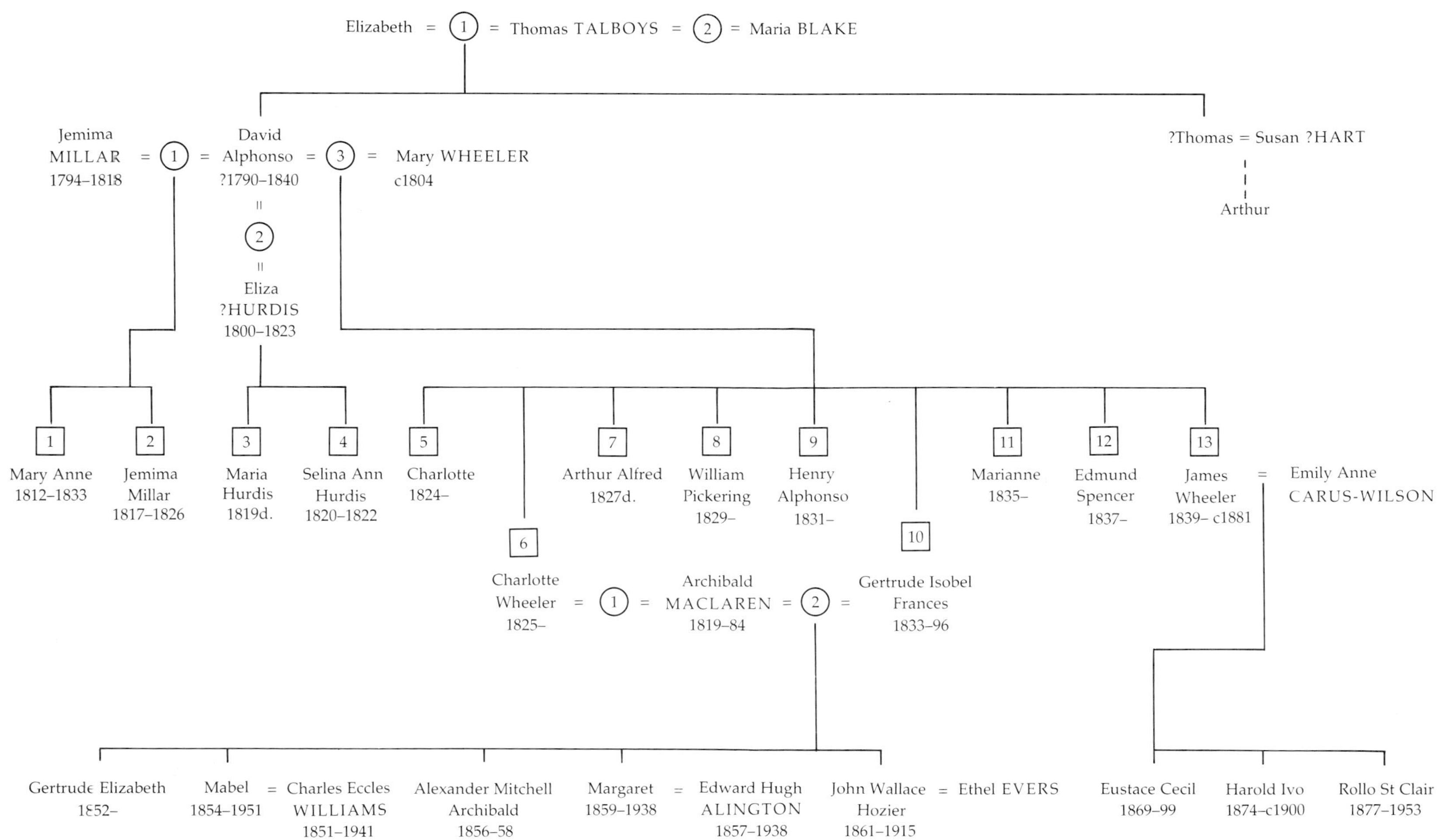

Marriage with one's deceased wife's sister was a problem which vexed the English (and Scottish) church and conscience for most of the nineteenth century. Theoretically illegal and clearly considered by many to border on incest or adultery, it none the less occurred with some frequency, as is borne out by its mention in *Iolanthe*:

> He shall prick that *annual* blister,
> Marriage with deceased wife's sister.

In the mid 1870s Holman Hunt committed this social solecism and deemed it wise to spend some time abroad; this may have been an advantage of the Summertown house, which is variously described as 'withdrawn' and 'remote'. But Archie does not seem to have borne a social stigma for long, if at all; he continued his fencing and gymnastic instruction in Oxford, and, by the time that the school started at Summerfield, the Maclarens were in very good odour.

In July 1852, the first of their five children was christened Gertrude Elizabeth at the church of St John Baptist, Summertown. This church was to play a large part in the story of Summer Fields, and the historian can only lament its sad end. All five Maclaren children were baptized there, and Alexander, who did not live beyond the age of two, was buried there. For thirty-two years, until the building of our Chapel upon the death of Mrs Maclaren, it was the school's parish church, and every Sunday the boys would troop in crocodile round the corner, across the Banbury Road and down Church Street (now Rogers Street), their collection money firmly grasped in their hands.

Both Archie, who died in 1884, and Gertrude (1896) were buried there, as well as Mary Anne Branscombe, Gertrude's cousin and the school's housekeeper for thirty years. But the church began to be considered too small for the expanding and increasingly prosperous parish of Summertown and so, after much argument and frantic appeals for money, the new church of St Michael and All Angels was built in 1909. 'Half-built' would be more accurate, because, like College Chapel at Eton, the building seen today is only the eastern part of an ambitious plan; but the money ran out, and brick replaced stone, to build a west wall at what should have been only the crossing. Meanwhile, St John Baptist's fell gradually into disuse, and then decay. The church was knocked down, and the gravestones arranged (sensibly) along the walls of what had once been the churchyard. But in 1960 the site was sold and, incredible as it may seem, the first action of the developers was to smash the gravestones and use them as rubble for the foundations of their new building. Nobody comes well out of this sad chronicle, and it is regrettable that no one at Summer Fields was sufficiently aware of what was afoot to beg for the gravestones, which could easily have been re-sited in some quiet and suitable spot in the school grounds.

19. St John Baptist's Church, Summertown, the Maclarens' parish church for fifty years.

Lady Burne-Jones affirms that Archibald Maclaren was 'a cultivated man of the highest character and with warmth and tenderness underlying reserve of manner. His home at Summertown, then a small village separated by a stretch of country road from Oxford, was a sanctuary seldom opened to the outer world. A low white house with its rose-covered veranda and a garden like a small Paradise shut in with white walls contained all that was dearest to him, being shared by a gifted young wife, then scarcely more than a girl.' She would have been twenty in 1853, when Burne-Jones started his visits, which he describes in the following note: 'Maclaren interested us greatly, and we him, I suppose, for he did an almost unheard-of thing, inviting us to his home at Summertown, where we went three or four times in the term to dine with him, and his talk was admirable and his tastes inclining greatly to poetry. I think our enthusiasm was always a pleasure to him, and he aided and abetted us in all the inclinations of our hearts.'

Clearly the young painters were not only made welcome, but to a great extent given the run of the place. A party including Holman Hunt arrived on a visit in June 1857 to find 'Morris painting a tree in Maclaren's beautiful garden with such energy that it was long before the grass grew again on the spot where

20. (*left*) Edward Burne-Jones, by Simeon Solomon, September 1859. [Ashmolean Museum, Oxford]

21. (*right*) William Morris: self-portrait, July 1857(?). [Victoria and Albert Museum, London]

his chair had stood'. And it was to the Maclarens' house next year that Burne-Jones went to convalesce after one of his not infrequent bouts of illness. His future wife came to see him there, and on one of these occasions we get an insight into the more superstitious side of Archie Maclaren, cultivated gentleman though he was.

An evening comes back to my mind when after a very hot day we had a terrific storm, and it was revealed to us for the first time that our host was afraid of thunder and lightning. He went upstairs and, taking his little Mabel [then aged three] out of her bed, wrapped her in a blanket and brought her down to the drawing-room, where, as he sat with her in his arms, his anxious face put an end to all talk ... Mr Price good-naturedly took upon himself the task of reviving conversation ... and thought to cheer the company by announcing in a pleasant voice that it was a well-established fact that one ill-kept pig-sty did more harm than twenty thunderstorms; but, as a cannonade of thunder saluted the statement, Maclaren angrily exclaimed: 'Price, you should be ashamed of yourself to speak so!' and the well-meant effort failed.

Mrs Maclaren is not mentioned in this extract: possibly she was attending the sick-bed of her son Alexander, who died that year. It also appears that Gertrude, the first-born in 1852, did not live long, as no mention is made of her on this or subsequent occasions. The three other children, Mabel (1854), Margaret

(1859) and John Wallace Hozier (1861), all survived childhood and later played significant parts in the life of the school. Indeed, it was probably Mabel's starting to learn Greek in 1863 that gave Mrs Maclaren the impetus to offer her teaching talents upon a wider market – a brave and unorthodox step for a woman in those days.

In the spring of 1863, Mr Shirley Brooks, the editor of *Punch*, came to consult Mr Maclaren about the physical upbringing of his two sons, and was so won over by the charm of the place and its owners that he asked the Maclarens if they would take entire charge of the two boys, while they had a course of systematic treatment at Maclaren's Oxford Gymnasium. From this point the story may be told by Dr Williams, the Maclarens' future son-in-law, as he includes it in his preface to the 1929 Register.

Mr Maclaren at first demurred to this proposal; he liked the boys, and he liked their parents, but he resented the idea of any intrusion on his family life. Mrs Maclaren, however, was of quite another opinion: she was a sound classical scholar with an unusual, though hitherto unexercised, gift for teaching and, being at that time a young woman of boundless energy that was running to waste in her peaceful and beautiful house and garden, she was enchanted at the idea of having two boys to educate with her own little girl, and persuaded her husband to agree to the plan. The arrangement was duly made, and that summer saw Reginald and Cecil Brooks, aged about seven and nine respectively, starting their education under Mrs Maclaren's guidance.

The opening words of Dr Williams's preface are of interest: 'In the year 1863 – the year which saw the birth of the School,' and this evidently was the year in which our first pupils were received. Why then has 1864 traditionally been looked upon as our foundation date? This may have come about because the authorities were slow in deciding how best to celebrate the Golden Jubilee, and it was 1914 before they got round to doing anything about it. In another place the Doctor writes that the school really started to be a school in 1864, because it was not until then that it had seven pupils; but one may ask what makes seven a quorum.

SUMMERTOWN

It is comparatively easy for a boarding-school, composed mainly of pupils who come from other parts of the country, to be divorced from the community in which it is set. The school's record of involvement with Summertown is a mixed story: at some periods, a boy might spend all his five years in it with only the haziest notion of what lay beyond the school boundaries; at others, boys and staff might take an active, if sporadic, part in the life of the community.

For a long time Summertown had a definite sense of community, first as a Regency village and later as a suburb. In 1977, a delightful book tracing its history since 1820 and written by the late Ruth Fasnacht, was published by St Michael's Publications. Its frontispiece is a map of the area, which shows that, at its period of greatest expansion, Summer Fields occupied about a third of the total area of Summertown. The school grounds in fact bestraddle a very ancient footpath, probably the old road from Water Eaton to Oxford, along which countrymen could have walked to see Latimer, Ridley and Cranmer being burned in Broad Street.

First Archibald Maclaren, and later his son-in-law Dr Williams, rapidly acquired the houses and fields that go to make up the school (see *'Wills and Property'*, pp. 45–9). So, from 1880 until the outbreak of the

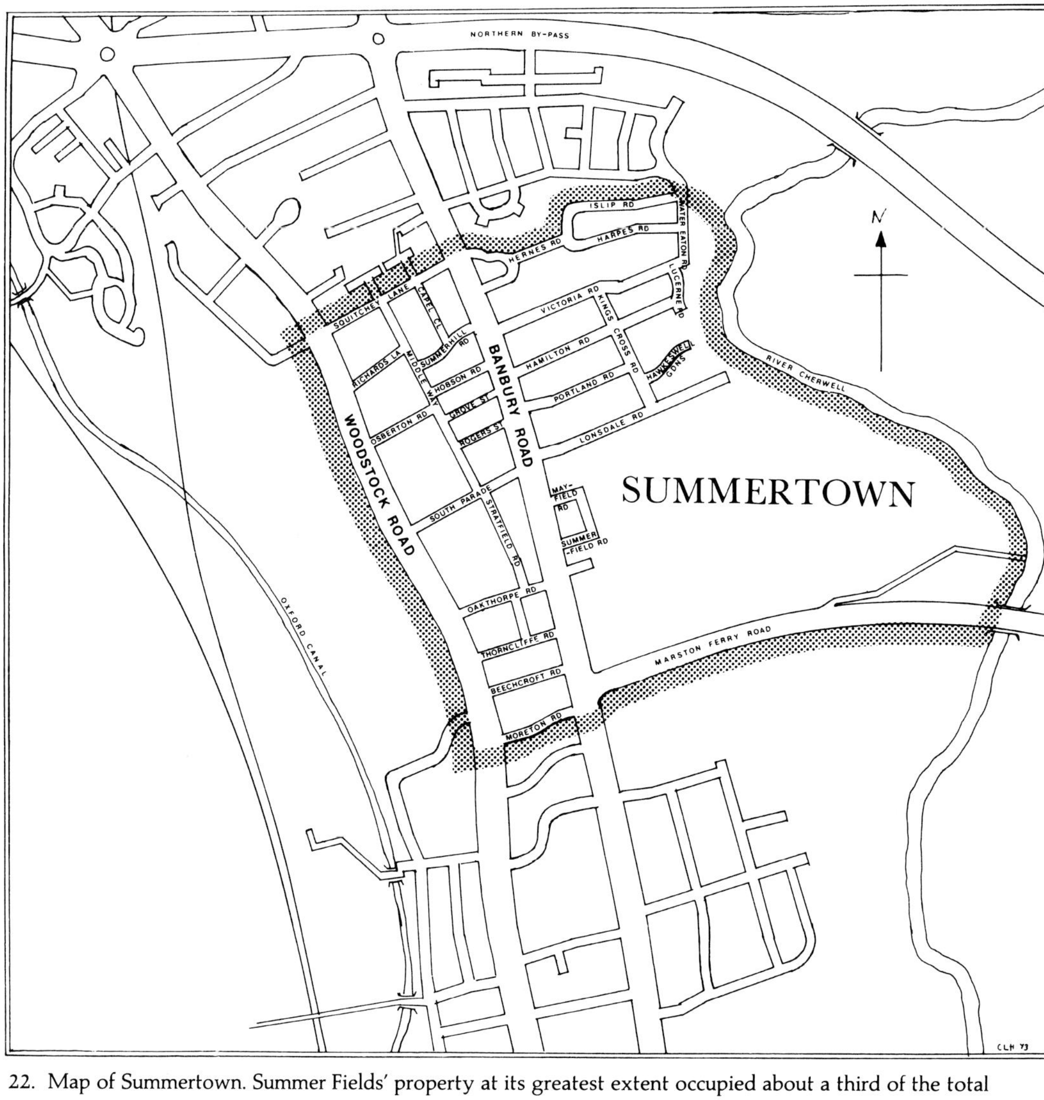

22. Map of Summertown. Summer Fields' property at its greatest extent occupied about a third of the total area, i.e. nearly all that is south of Lonsdale Road and east of the Banbury Road.

23. Ivy Lodge, at the corner of Mayfield and Banbury Roads. The gate towards the right of the picture is the garden gate of Cottage.

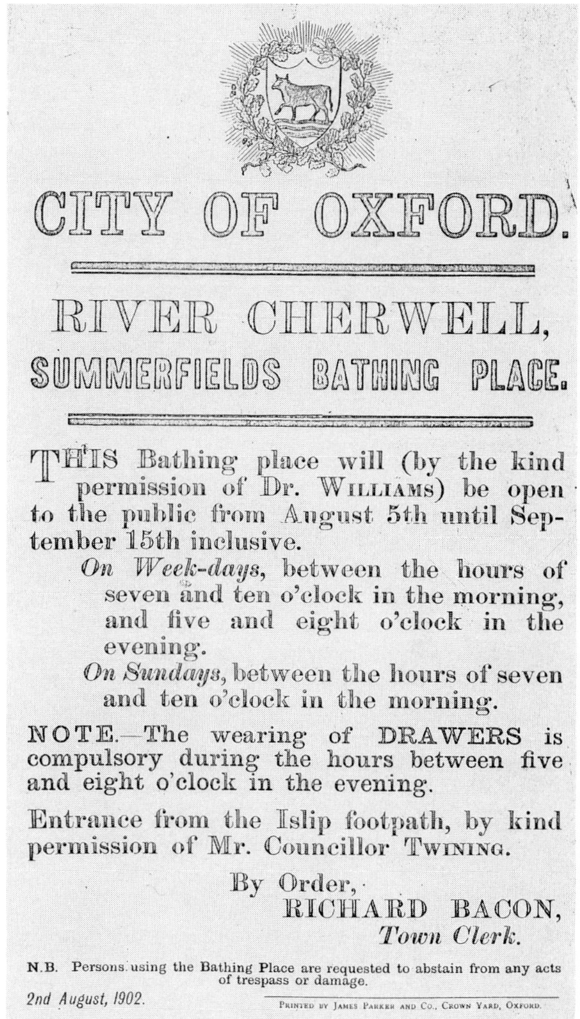

CITY OF OXFORD.

RIVER CHERWELL,

SUMMERFIELDS BATHING PLACE.

THIS Bathing place will (by the kind permission of Dr. WILLIAMS) be open to the public from August 5th until September 15th inclusive.

On Week-days, between the hours of seven and ten o'clock in the morning, and five and eight o'clock in the evening.

On Sundays, between the hours of seven and ten o'clock in the morning.

NOTE.—The wearing of **DRAWERS** is compulsory during the hours between five and eight o'clock in the evening.

Entrance from the Islip footpath, by kind permission of Mr. Councillor TWINING.

By Order,
RICHARD BACON,
Town Clerk.

N.B. Persons using the Bathing Place are requested to abstain from any acts of trespass or damage.

2nd August, 1902.

PRINTED BY JAMES PARKER AND CO., CROWN YARD, OXFORD.

24. Town Clerk's Notice, 1902.

Second World War, there was something of the 'Lordship of the Manor' about the ruling family of Summer Fields. The Maclarens took an interest in the parish church, which the school used until 1896. By the early years of this century, the school owned nearly all of the block east of the Banbury Road and bordered by Mayfield Road, Diamond Street and Summerfield Road: this included Ivy Lodge, the attractive house in its own garden at the north-west corner, but not the Dewdrop Inn and the area to the north-east of it. In addition, the school briefly owned South Lawn, a little further north on the far side of the Banbury Road, but it was somewhat remote for a boys' boarding-house.

Dr Williams enjoyed the role of squire, and he allowed the school's bathing-place to be used by the locals during the summer holidays, as well as opening the school grounds for the Summertown Flower Show. This started in 1903 with the Doctor as president, and took place in the field south of the Farm Drive (the present rugger field) on the third Thursday in August. It represented a special link with the locality, for many local people helped from time to time on the school's farm-fields or had an allotment beside the western fringe of our property or south of the Northern Meadow Farm. A large marquee was erected in the playing-field, and in this flowers, vegetables and handicrafts were exhibited. There were also other stalls and side-shows, such as bowling for a pig. It was open to all comers, and whole families used to attend, as it was enjoyable for children and a real day out for the family. Mrs Soden, who has spent nearly all her life in Summertown, recalls, 'I hated going to fairs, but I remember loving that.' Mr Hewlett, who in the family tradition won prizes in the flower section for many years, looks back on the shows as occasions when all of the community contributed something. The last one was held in 1956.

After the school passed out of the Williams–Alington ownership, it became less a part of Summertown. By now the village had become a suburb, the tram-lines from the Randolph to South Parade were soon to be removed, and the trams replaced by buses, as the small private residences were being replaced by shops. Originally the horse-drawn trams in the early nineteenth century had only gone as far as St Margaret's Road, but many Summerfieldians recall the journeys in the days before everyone had a car or could afford a taxi.

The destruction of Summertown began in 1959, and

25. Postcard showing the horse-drawn tram on the Banbury Road at the turn of the century.

it must be admitted that the school contributed to it by selling off sites, where square and soulless office blocks immediately replaced the little houses. Organ's garage became J. D. Barclay's Rolls Royce sale-rooms, Budgen's supermarket boded the beginning of the end for many local grocers and dairymen, Oxfam House covered the bottom of Cottage garden, and the final piece in the line of horizontal characterlessness came with a building somewhat perversely named Mayfield House. These cut the school off more than ever before from the Banbury Road, but the 1970s and 1980s have to some extent seen a reflowering of involvement in our locality.

In the 1960s, the Cherwell School was built beyond our south-eastern corner, and many of its pupils pass up and down the public footpath, now the North Oxford Cycle Track, twice a day. Relations have not always been easy in this area, and attempts to play soccer matches against them did not take root: perhaps another attempt should be made. A sporting fixture that was prized in its time was the Staff v North Oxford, first played in 1902 when Dr Williams was president of North Oxford. Sadly, this lapsed in the early 1980s, and the Masters now play only against other schools: but 'Splinters' matches between St Michael's and St Andrew's and St Giles's have occurred on our fields since 1979. These, and a visit in alternate years between the school and St Michael's to each other's place of worship, have helped to keep alive our connection with the parish.

Since 1976, Summer Fields has taken day-boys, and, though they tend to come from Oxford or Oxfordshire rather than Summertown, this represents a more open-gated attitude. For many years, David Langdon served as the choirmaster and conductor of the Summertown Choral Society, and since 1976 the Rev. William Pryor has been a member of the auxiliary ministry at St Michael's Church as well as being highly involved with local charitable work, as is his wife Elizabeth. Several afternoons a month, Summer Fields cleans up Summertown, as Willie and his Wombles descend like locusts upon the litter which so easily accumulates in unbiodegradable heaps: an entirely suitable democratic service for ex-lords of the manor!

26. The Summertown Wombles in the 1980s, under the leadership of 'Great Uncle Bulgaria', Rev. William Pryor.

2

EVE SHARES THE FRUIT
1864–96

THE Brooks boys were joined by two brothers called Hoets; two Hughes boys, one the son of the author of *Tom Brown's Schooldays*; and two Macmillan cousins, George the son of the rapidly rising publisher, who did much to recommend Summerfield to his friends, and Maurice the father of the future Prime Minister. Five new boys came in the following year and five more in the year after that, one of whom wrote home as follows:

SUMMERTOWN,
May 3rd [1866]

My dear Mamma,

I am writing this in school-time, as Mrs Mac-Laren has not yet got me a Gk. History, and they are being questioned in that this afternoon. I cannot tell you how much I like this place. Indeed it cannot be called a school, it is more like a home.

The boys are of course most of them too young for me to make friends with, though some of them are much higher than I in the classics – the boy who sleeps in my room is doing *Alcestis*, one of Euripides' plays. All the boys, and especially the Macmillans, are very kind to me, and, as for Mrs Mac-Laren, I never saw so nice a lady. We spend nearly all our playtime in the garden. Several of the boys are very fond of croquet – I haven't played yet.

I was delighted with my little bedroom; there are seven pictures in it besides other ornaments. When I got up at $7\frac{1}{2}$, we all went down to the bath room, and had a nice cold bath; for breakfast we had eggs and toast and coffee or tea. At morning school Mrs Mac-Laren examined me in Ovid, instead of which I am to do Horace; and instead of Xenophon I am to do some pieces at the end of Adam's Gk. Delectus. For dinner we had two enormous helpings of dough pudding and roast beef. Then, as the rain had given over, we went in the garden and amused ourselves in the garden till afternoon school, when I began to write this letter. The girls' guinea pigs, rabbits, cocks and hens are all very nice; indeed there is only one animal I behold with aversion, and it is a vicious looking beast of a donkey which seems very fond of squeezing itself through the railings, and browsing on the apricot trees and which Arthur informed me with great glee they sometimes go out rides upon. But I must end this letter as Mrs MacLaren wants me to show her my French Books.

So with love to all I remain

your aff. Son
Edward

27. Mrs Maclaren with her children, c. 1864. Margaret is leaning against her mother, Wallace (known as 'Tot') is on her knee, and Mabel standing.

Mrs Maclaren was soon known simply as 'Mrs'. George Macmillan tells us that she was 'a most inspiring teacher: she really knew and loved the Latin and Greek authors and did her best to impart that love to her pupils. Moreover, she was very keenly alive to the minutiae of grammar, syntax and idiom, and it was our thorough grounding in that side of classical study which helped to establish the reputation of the school ... Indeed, under Mrs Maclaren's guidance we boys ourselves became keen about unusual words and forms and special idioms, and even out of school used to set each other problems, so that it became a kind of game. Mrs was really the mainspring of all the learning and scholarship at Summerfield.'

Granted that the academic regime was mainly classical, it might shock present-day parents, pupils and staff to learn what was required of the top form at Summerfield in their July examination 1868. They were expected to compose both Latin and Greek prose and verse, and to be able to construe from the following formidable list: St Mark's Gospel and part of the Acts in the Greek

Testament; the *Ajax* of Sophocles; three books of the *Odyssey*; one book of Xenophon and one of Herodotus; one book of Livy, two of the *Aeneid*, two of Ovid and four of Horace. One feels that this cannot have left very much for them to do when they reached their public school, let alone university!

Numbers rose rapidly, and soon the low white house surrounded by an orchard was inadequate to house the boys as well as the family. Dr. Williams tells us that 'Building now became a necessity, and part of the orchard was sacrificed to make way for schoolrooms and bedrooms. Later on, as the little school became more and more widely known and more and more boys flocked in, other portions of the garden had to be used for the same purpose, till at last it became clear that the greater part of the original house must be pulled down and an entire new frontage added. So, to the loudly expressed regret of those who had known the place as it was before the intrusion of the boy element or, as they put it, "before the serpent beguiled Eve to pass on the fruit of the tree of knowledge," this scheme was carried out, and the old house vanished, leaving only the wall that on the fireplace side runs from the drawing-room and Headmaster's study on the ground floor, and from Little Dor and the Matron's room above, to tell of the original building.' (The abbreviation 'Dor' for 'Dormitory' seems to have been peculiar to SF, and has only recently gone out of use.)

It would be interesting to know the dates of the two phases of this building operation, and it appears that at that time money was no object. Doctor seems to be describing the event from personal observation, which would make it post-1874, when he arrived from Brasenose. A print from the early 1880s depicts a largely recognizable building, but the front part of House has only two storeys;

28. The earliest picture of Summerfield, in the early 1880s.

New Room and the further expansion to the north have not yet happened. Within five years, numbers were in the thirties, and within ten years nearer sixty. The earliest photograph that we have is from 1876, and the number of boys in it is fifty-eight. No staff appear in this picture, but it is noticeable that the average age of the boys is much higher than of recent years, most not arriving until they were ten, and in many cases leaving well after their fourteenth birthday.

29. Two of the first generation of pupils: Hugh and Athol Capron, c. 1866, shortly before Hugh started at Summerfield.

As numbers steadily increased, so staff, at first temporary and then by degrees more permanent, came to assist. William West Jones, Vicar of Summertown from 1864 to 1874, later to become Archbishop of Capetown, and his two curates, C.H. Grundy and William Donne, were among the earliest. Donne helped with the games and used to give chocolates to any boy who could say that he had touched the ball forty times during a game of football. This would no doubt have tended to lead to the 'flies round a honeypot' syndrome that can still sometimes be seen on junior games today, but at least it would encourage the young players to take exercise. Grundy was a gifted story-teller and enlivened many a long walk (a feature of SF life even as late as the 1950s) with tales of pirates and smugglers. He also composed light occasional verse, and is reputed to have been the author of the mnemonic for Greek contracted verbs:

Little A wins the day,
Except when O gets in the way.

Mr Sedding, the organist of the parish church, taught music, and a Mr Tollit taught maths and drawing. Miss Sarah ('Sally') Williams arrived in 1867, and taught the youngest form until 1904; and Mary Anne Branscombe ('Polly' or 'Branny'), a cousin of Mrs, was housekeeper and probably matron, too, in the early years. Mr Maclaren was variously assisted with the physical education by his nephew, also called Archie, and by another young relative with the resonant name of Tremenheere Passingham.

It is believed that Mrs' youngest brother, the Rev. James Wheeler Talboys, taught briefly at the school; certainly two of his sons, Eustace Cecil and Harold

Ivo, were educated there, before winning scholarships respectively to Marlborough and Rugby. But their youngest brother, Rollo StClair Talboys, has a question-mark over him. There is no record of his name in either the Register or the (incomplete) school rolls; yet the Magazine from 1919 onwards refers to him as 'our O.S. master' at Wellington, where he taught from 1904 to 1938, with a gap when he served with distinction as an airman in the Great War. He became something of a legendary figure, being an unorthodox schoolmaster as well as a brilliant historian and a connoisseur of art and furniture. After retiring from Wellington, he was snapped up by J. C. Masterman to lecture at Christ Church as a 'Tutor not on the Foundation'. He wrote a history of Wellington, entitled *A Victorian School* (Blackwell, 1943), and himself plays a large part in the official centenary history written by David Newsome for 1959. Evidently a man of culture and originality in the tradition of his grandfather.

His teaching was a revelation, perhaps because he did not teach in the accepted sense. There was no blackboard. The only visual aid he ever used was an occasional reference to one of the series of reproductions of old masters arrayed against the white panelling behind his desk. His lessons were enlivened by private readings from all kinds of unheard-of books, and essays were woven round every sort of unlikely subject, such as: 'Write a few lines on wind, wit and Winston Churchill'. Now and then he would read in his most wonderfully expressive voice, which was a sheer delight to listen to ...

During its first years, as George Macmillan relates, Summerfield was more like a family than a school, and the Maclaren daughters, Mabel and Maggie, shared in the boys' lessons and, to some extent, their games. Nor were they the only girls: H. C. Hayter (1871–75) says that, when he arrived, he had three cousins at the school: 'Walter, Tom and Ella, who was being educated with Miss Maclaren (now the wife of Dr Williams). The present Mrs E. H. Alington was then quite a child and was, I think, in a boys' class; I have an idea that she was at one time in the 2nd Cricket XI.' Evidently this upringing must have agreed with the Maclaren girls, as they greatly outlived the males of the clan, though Margaret was extremely deaf from quite an early age. The menfolk, despite their immersion in gymnastic training, tended to become invalids: Mr Maclaren died at the age of sixty-five, having been lame for some time, and his son Wallace at fifty-three, after a period of protracted illness.

Maurice Macmillan was the first boy to win a scholarship from Summerfield, to Uppingham in 1866, and George was the school's first Eton scholar, two years later. 'In the summer of 1868 two boys, Walter Rawnsley and myself, were sent in for the Eton Scholarship under the personal charge of Mr Maclaren. I do not know what hopes of success Mrs Maclaren had cherished in this first attack on the Eton citadel ... but to my dying day I shall remember the July morning when the bow window at the end of the long schoolroom was thrown open from outside, and Mr Maclaren triumphantly shouted, "George is in for Eton!" Since then I suppose that scarcely a year has passed without boys from Summerfield appearing in that roll of honour. I naturally feel some satisfaction at my good fortune at being the first to earn the distinction.'

The pupils at this time had more freedom than was later the case when the school grew. They could play about in the garden and orchards, where the apples and pears were at their disposal, and roamed freely about the fields at the back of the house, the first of which was soon converted into a games field. They ran across the country, went birds-nesting, and fished and bathed in the Cherwell: daily in the summer they used to go down to the river before breakfast with Mr Maclaren. Even in winter he would be seen going off with his towel, though it is not recorded whether he really went in when he got to the bank. No doubt this image of Spartan toughness helped to institute the custom of morning cold baths, which was to endure for many generations.

Within a few years, organized cricket and football were taking place, as well as regular athletic sports and swimming competitions. Rugger did not appear until after the Great War. For gymnastics until the turn of the century, the boys walked in crocodile to the Oxford Gymnasium, all wearing bowler hats adorned with the yellow and black Brasenose ribbon, according to Bernard Darwin; but Hayter remembers that 'we wore blue and white ribbons (arranged like the Trinity colours) round the bowlers or wideawake hats which some parents seemed to prefer to caps.' The former is more likely, as Dr Williams was a Brasenose man, and proud of it; Archie Maclaren was not at an Oxford college, and no Trinity connection has come to light. In the early years every boy had a red cap with yellow piping, but this changed to plain red during the 1870s, and remained so until the abolition of school caps in the early 1960s. It may be that the photograph of the school in 1876 records the change from 'piped' to plain caps: look at the boy fifth from the left in the middle (seated) row.

Despite the liberty allowed to the pupils, Mrs could show herself a stern disciplinarian: Hayter recalls that she was near-sighted, and wore two pairs of spectacles, one over the other, when she meant business!

I was only once caned, and that was when some boys were playing horses with string harness, and running around the only field we had in those days. A band of robbers (I was one) were assembled and waiting in a ditch, armed with hurdle pikes in order to attack and break up the harmless players. While in the ditch, I knelt in a cow-pat and had to go in to change my trousers. On coming out again, I found a fight going on between one member of our band and one of those playing horses. Mr came out, very lame and full of righteous wrath, and asked for the names of all the robbers. Of course, as there is honour among thieves, everybody gave himself up. I really had had nothing

30. The earliest surviving 'School Photograph' (1876). It originally belonged to H. J. Elphinstone, whose penned-in initials identify him in the back row. There are no staff in the picture, which is also remarkable for its variety of costume, and for the fact that few boys appear to be under ten, while several are clearly over fourteen.

to do with what Mr called Bullying, but he did not know that, and I was caned with six others. We were all told to 'kneel doon' – Mr was a wee bit Scottish – and no doubt we all deserved it.

When my cousin Walter left to go to Uppingham, my brother and I were sent to sleep in what was then known as 'the kids' dormitory'. There were six or seven beds in this room, and Mr or Mrs would come round at bed-time to see that everything was in order. On one of these occasions we heard Mrs coming along and, as we were not in bed but in our nightshirts (pyjamas were unknown then), we all thought that there might be trouble and knelt down by our beds so as to be found in the attitude of prayer. It happened that a boys' maid named Jane was there, and Mrs said to her, 'I hope no boy in this room uses bad words.' To which the reply was, 'Only Master Willie 'Ayter.' Mrs looked at him and saw that he was kneeling in such a way as to sit on his heels, this being less trouble than 'kneeling up'. Said Mrs, hauling him into the orthodox position, 'No wonder a boy who kneels like that uses bad words.' The word in question was 'Beastly'.

An equally interesting story, and one with more far-reaching consequences, is told by Macmillan.

One fine afternoon, some of us were in the back garden and, finding a barrel of tar, amused ourselves by playing with it, sprinkling each others' hands and the like. On this happy scene emerged a small boy, his golden curls gleaming in the sunshine, and the temptation to anoint them with tar proved irresistible. The little victim did not much appreciate the attention and, when he ran back to the house, the fat was in the fire. The child was at once put into a hot bath to remove the tar, and the perpetrators were confined to their rooms for a season. But it was felt that after such a misdemeanour stricter methods of punishment must be instituted ... Accordingly, the so-called Black Book was established, in which a pupil's faults of whatever kind were duly recorded, and after three entries he became liable to bodily chastisement.

The spiritual side of life was well cared for, it being usual for schoolmasters to be in holy orders. In 1874 arrived Charles Williams, a dapper Welshman from Swansea via B.N.C., aged twenty-three and 'sporting possibly the loudest check suit anybody could wear'. In the following year he was ordained deacon and became curate at Summertown, and in 1876 he was ordained priest. In 1879 he married Mabel Maclaren, and returned to the permanent staff, becoming a partner with Mrs Maclaren and taking over the Fifth (scholarship) Form. The same year saw the arrival of Edward Hugh Alington ('Bear'), from Westminster and Hertford College. Born in 1857, one of seven children of the Rev. John Alington, the

31 and 32. The 'dapper Welshman' and his wife. Dr Charles Williams, aged 28, in the year of his marriage; and Mabel, elder surviving daughter of the Maclarens, with the infant Cyril, five years later.

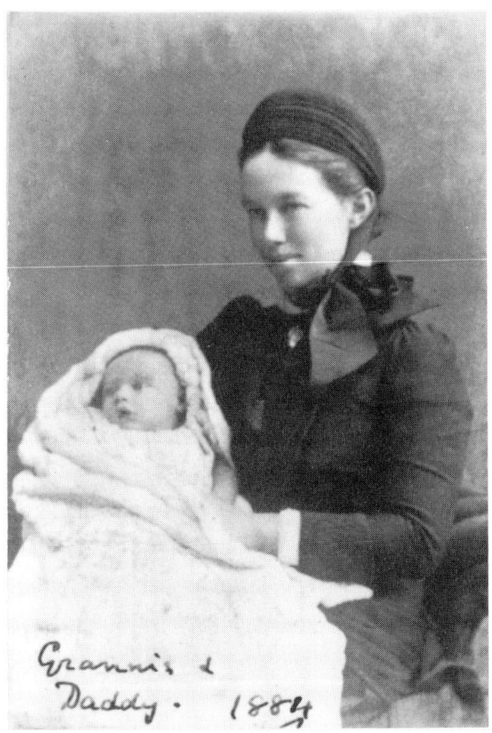

33. E. H. Alington (seated left) in the 1878 Oxford University Football Team.

Rector of Candlesbury in Lincolnshire, he too left to take holy orders, serving as a curate at St Mark's, Leicester, and returning finally in 1887. At Oxford he had got a blue for football, playing against Cambridge in 1877 and 1878, and he took charge of the games at Summerfield. He married Margaret Maclaren in 1885; thus, by the middle of the 1880s, the twin family was established, which was to rule the school through four 'Heads' until 1939.

During the 1880s others appeared on the scene who were to play a large part in the life of the school for several generations. J. F. Crofts ('Crab') taught from 1883 until 1920, and G. W. Evans ('Bam') from 1884 until 1924. F. P. Penny, who also put in more than thirty years, did not arrive until 1893. Dr J. C. R. Freeborn became the school doctor in 1884, and continued as such until 1927. Apart from his medical care, he contributed a window in the Chapel, which perpetuates his name as well as commemorating the foundress, in whose memory the Chapel was built. Mr Paine senior was established as school carpenter and factotum, and, reputedly in the 1880s, Charlie Fathers began as a lad the job of groundsman which he retained until 1951. If he really did start that early, his service was of nearly seventy years, spanning the Boer War and both world wars. Certain it is that he both excavated and, sixty years later, filled in the 'ha-ha' which divided the Masters' Lawn from the playing-fields – a record which gave him great satisfaction.

34. The school in the early 1890s. The major differences between this and the 1880s print are the addition of New Room (in its shorter version with as yet only one roof-lantern), and the kitchen/dining-room/domestic quarters block behind it. The wall dividing the front garden from the Masters' Lawn has gone, and the Vinery is clearly visible at the right, beyond New Room. The recently dug ha-ha separates the Masters' Lawn and tennis court from fifth game cricket, at which the players are all wearing their 'small coats', though the boy on the extreme left seems to favour a sailor-suit. The poplar-tree behind the main building lasted into the 1950s.

There were other masters at this time who made their mark, even if they did not stay for so long: T. J. F. Haskoll (1885–96), who was afterwards Headmaster of Brendon House for nearly twenty years; C. Gathorne-Orr (1886–9); Sir Samuel Servington Savery (1886–8), who subsequently founded Bramcote School, Scarborough; W. Salter (1887–96); the Rev. P. C. Joy (1889–96) and T. S. Morton (1890–7), who, after preparing the young Harold Macmillan for Summer Fields, set up a full-time pre-prep school in London, which exists to this day as Eaton House. These masters are visible in the excellent and plentiful staff photographs of the period, but, regrettably, women were not deemed worthy to appear in them.

As the fame of Mrs and her school was noised abroad, many eminent Victorians sent their sons there. Generals, judges and churchmen were numbered

35. The Masters in 1890, showing 'Bear' still young and slimmish, and the Doctor, as so often, giving the camera his half-profile.

among the parents, though the school roll also has both a literary and an aristocratic ring to it: Wordsworth, Tennyson, Arthur Hugh Clough (namesake and so presumably a relation of 'Say not the struggle''s author); several members of the Redesdale family (Freeman-Mitford), including the prototype for the delicious Uncle Matthew; Richard D'Oyly Carte sent his son Rupert, who went on to Winchester in 1889 and then succeeded his father in the running of both Savoys, the hotel and the opera company. Holman Hunt, perhaps on the advice of Burne-Jones, sent his son Cyril Benone: this unusual name is Hebrew for 'Child of Sorrows', and such indeed he was, to start with at any rate. Born on 26 October 1866, *not* 1867 as stated in the Register, he nearly died at birth in Florence; but he survived, although his mother, Hunt's first wife, died six weeks later. He was then nearly starved to death by a negligent nurse while being returned to England, after which he saw little of his father, who was abroad for the next five years. In 1876 Hunt, now back in England, finally married his deceased wife's sister (shades of Archie Maclaren!), and in the next year Cyril was sent to Summer Fields. Considering all that he had been through, he looks a remarkably healthy and mature nine-year-old in this charming sketch done by his father the year before he came here: one wonders whether his long locks survived his prep school. He had a successful and varied scientific career and, upon his death in 1934, he left a legacy to the school to provide an annual prize for a natural history essay. This is still presented, but its scope has been widened to include all branches of science.

A majority of Victorian Summerfieldians went into the Church, the army or the navy: the Register at this period bristles with admirals and generals. A less conventional soldier was Charles Noel Lyall (SF 1870–6 and visible in the first school photograph). After Wellington and the RMA, he joined the Royal Artillery and was at the Battle of Abuklea (1884) as a junior subaltern in the last British square. The opposite side gave way, and he was 'run through the back by the spear of a Fuzzy Wuzzy', left for dead but rescued by a brother officer. He was put on to a boat and shipped down the Nile but the craft sank; a fellow-officer rescued him. Eventually reaching home, he was given a pension for injuries equal to the loss of a limb; he retired to hunt, shoot and play cricket, and in 1908 he married a girl of nineteen; they had four children. He returned to the army as an instructor for the Great War and retired with the rank of major; he died in 1942. Although his father had been Governor of the Bank of England, Lyall's opinion was that 'work is for the working-classes'.

Luckily, not all Summerfieldians shared this view, and many achieved eminence in a multitude of spheres. The Barons Strachie and Colebrook, who were both here in the early 1870s, became, among much else, respectively Paymaster-General and Master of the Robes. W. F. Cave, as well as playing cricket for Gloucestershire, was vice-president of the RIBA and designed the Aeolian Hall off Bond Street, now occupied by Sotheby's. Arthur Clutton-Brock was a critic and journalist of distinction;

36. Cyril Benone Holman-Hunt, the 'Child of Sorrows', drawn by his father in 1876, the year before he came to Summerfield as a pupil.

37. Walter Frederick Cave, F.R.I.B.A. (1863–1939), who was more successful as an architect than as a county cricketer. [Royal Institute of British Architects]

38. Bernard Richard Meirion Darwin (1876–1962), international golfer and man of letters.

General Sir F. B. Maurice was a war correspondent and historian, as was later M. H. H. Macartney; and Bernard Darwin was a fine blend of literary and sporting ability. Cecil Arthur Hunt became a notable water-colour painter, having pictures in permanent collections throughout the world. J. F. Crace was one of the more celebrated masters at Eton, while C. W. Hannah, after an educational career much disrupted by ill-health, took a temporary teaching post at Michaelhouse in Natal and stayed there for thirty-five years, during which the school expanded from 30 to 300 boys. The closing years of the century saw through the school Geoffrey Mander, Evelyn Wrench and Archie Wavell, among other famous names.

In a delightful essay called 'Mr Bultitude Looks Back', Bernard Darwin recalls the school as it was in his day.

I was only there for two years from 1887 to 1889, but I remember it with extraordinary clearness. If I were now set down in the lobby with its floor of coloured tiles and its rows of squash rackets (we called that game 'Fives') in a rack, and its pigeon holes for slippers, I think I could walk straight to the particular pigeon-hole wherein my own slippers lived. I can repeat the two Latin graces which those in the top forms had to say, one before lunch, one after. I can feel the ghastly sensation of someone getting mixed between the two, and of hearing a clear cold voice from the dais, as it were a voice out of heaven, 'Say grace again, please.'

The famous Mrs Maclaren, who had created the school, was still there in my time and we always called her 'Missis' as Mr Maclaren had been called 'Mister'. I have a fairly clear picture of her, rather an alarming figure in a black dress with a good deal of white cuff and collar, but my only distinct recollection of any personal contact is of her pouncing suddenly on me and reproving me for a crime of which I was entirely innocent. She had to a considerable extent retired, and the real driving force of the school was Dr Williams. He had a genius for teaching in the sense that he made learning seem the best and most exciting fun in the world, and I cannot believe that anybody ever came to much harm by being happy and interested, even passionately interested, in his work.

Oddly enough, though I did get a scholarship at Eton, I did it with comparatively little teaching from Dr Williams, for I was not in the top form and my first attempt was supposed to be little more than a trial run. However, Mr Wallace Maclaren took a fancy to me, coached me a good deal by myself, and I think rather enjoyed the chance of bringing his young and unknown horse in ahead of well-backed and reliable animals in his brother-in-law's stable. This is not to say that I did not get some final polishing from the Doctor. I remember in particular half-hours of Latin grammar before breakfast at his house, Borva, sometimes in the garden, when doubtless we paid attention to the outrageously irregular behaviour of *jecur* and *supellex*. It does not sound appetising but it was, in fact, a thrilling experience; it was romance, it was excitement, it was in short a treat, and we got up early and went to it joyously. I say that the man who can produce that effect on small boys is a genius in his own way, and nothing will shake me.

This is the first mention both of Borva and of the famous, and sometimes dreaded, *Borva Notes*. Borva was a house built by the Williamses in 1881–2 on the site of the old King's Arms pub, which had been pulled down; its garden stretched from the Banbury Road along the north side of Summerfield Road to the playground, from which it was divided by a low redbrick wall. Its name was that of a place in the Hebrides which seems to have caught Mabel's fancy, though whether it is the Harris or Barra Borve, or the Uist or Benbecula one, is not recorded. An alternative theory is that it was named after a character in a novel by William Black called *A Princess of Thule*, in which a Mr Mackenzie is the 'King of Borva'; but this book did not appear until 1892. The house was later inhabited by the Alingtons, and various others succeeded as the hierarchy changed. Its final occupants were Patrick and Perdita Marston and their family of six, who lived in it from the Second World War until its demolition in 1963.

Its name, however, was preserved in the new Colt House, built first for the Marstons and later used as a sanatorium and then a junior Lodge, on the Front

39 and 40. 'Borva', the house built by Dr Williams in the early 1880s, which was used over the next eighty years by his relatives and descendants. The western, or Banbury Road, side seen c. 1914; the eastern, or Playground, side c. 1960.

41. A page from Dr Williams' 'Borva Notes'; the first two words would be very modern inventions when these notes were compiled; some of the others would defeat a modern Fifth-former. The logical spelling of *kaleidoscope* is interesting.

GRAMMAR NOTES 8

8. English Derivations.

Derive :—

Telegraph — Telephone — Rhododendron
Chrysanthemum — Heliotrope — Trivial
Complement — Gymnasium — Athletics
Monopoly — Cosmopolitan — Metropolis
Asylum — Symmetry — Cemetery
Orthography — Etymology — Conchology
Diphthong — Vowel — Hippodrome
Disastrous — Cenotaph — Enthusiast
Preposition — Phthisis — Parotitis
Measles — Tragedy — Comedy — Hygiene
Physiology — Psychology — Caitiff — Benison
Enormous — Parable — Devil — Mesmerism
Meander — Electricity — Pagan — Heathen
Stethoscope — Venison — Petroleum — Simony
Caleidoscope — Hypnotism — Nepotism
Cataclysm — Mausoleum — Protoplast
Thermometer — Barometer — Entomology
Proletariat — Catechism — Prejudice
Solecism — Empiric — Anchorite — Hermit
Monk — Acolyte — Priest — Deacon
Bursar

Drive in the Old Lodge orchard. Originally called 'New Borva', this house became simply 'Borva' as memories of its predecessor faded. The *Borva Notes*, used by generations of fifth-formers, were *aides-mémoire* over the finer points of Latin and Greek grammar, as well as English terms that might be confused. Certain variations were introduced by Bear Alington and later GB, but the central idea persisted for nearly a century.

Darwin has happy memories of games and sports at Summerfield: the early golf-course created during his last year, Bear Alington playing football, and Bam Evans bowling lobs at him in the nets to teach him to play forward. He also gives a detailed description of the 'Torpids', called after the Oxford boat races of that name, and consisting of hurdle races on the bumping principle.

There was a number of flights of hurdles leaning over at an angle, so that they were extremely low and it was possible to skim over them in the proper hurdling stride and at a good pace. To add verisimilitude, each competitor took to himself the name of a college boat club either at Oxford or Cambridge, and a popular college had a large number of boats on the river. Most people naturally chose Oxford colleges, but I was faithful to my father's club at Cambridge, First Trinity. I could run reasonably fast and was full of hopes of distinguishing myself, but I did First Trinity very little credit, for I had not mastered the elements of hurdling and jumped far too high in the air. I can still recollect the feeling of my pursuer's hand on my shoulder signifying that I had been bumped, a severe and salutary shock to my vanity.

We were certainly well off for games as, apart from cricket and football, we had five 'Fives Courts' in the playground. There, by the way, on a rather stony surface, we used to play a kind of football that must have been as the Eton Wall Game was in its early days. Our ground was bounded on three sides by a wall on which goals were marked out. 'Fives' was, as I said, squash in a court with side walls but no back wall. How good a game it would be for grown-ups I do not exactly know, but for small boys it was admirable. You got a court periodically (there was a list put up in the lobby), and to ask someone to play fives with you in your court was amongst equals to confer an honour and a mark of friendship, while to ask some superior being was in the nature of 'side' and might be courting a snub.

The academic structure of the school in 1888 (the earliest extant school roll) had assumed the shape that was to be familiar for many years to come. In fact, in the Michaelmas Term, there was no Fifth Form, but it came into being in January. The other forms were:

Upper and Lower Remove;
Upper, Middle and Lower Fourth;
Shell;
Upper, Middle and Lower Third;
Second Form;
Upper and Lower First.

Of these twelve forms, three contained only five boys, five contained six boys and the largest had ten boys: the parents were certainly getting value for money. Down to Upper Third, the boys were examined in Greek, Latin (presumably, i.e. translation), composition and grammar. The school was set in divisions, numbered, I–IX, for the other examinable subjects: mathematics, French, divinity, history and geography. The Upper School was divided into classes I–IV for dictation, and the Lower School into classes I–IV for dictionary and writing. Holiday task prizes were also awarded for sets of maps, and for reading one of *Ivanhoe, David Copperfield*, or *Tales of a Grandfather*.

The School Magazine was not started until the year following Mrs Maclaren's

42. (*opposite*) The first edition of *The Summer Fields Magazine*, July 1897, edited by E. D. Compton, who became the first Headmaster of Summer Fields St Leonard's six years later.

THE

Summer Fields Magazine.

Mens Sana in Corpore Sano.

JULY, 1897.

Contents.

EDITORIAL.

THE chief object of the *Summer Fields Magazine* is to serve as a record of all School events, and of news so connected with all, who have been, or are being educated here, as to interest parents and friends as well as the boys themselves. The editor will therefore be only too grateful to anyone at Public Schools, Universities, or elsewhere, who will send any items of news concerning old boys and their doings. It is proposed to issue one number at the end of each term, containing as far as possible, accounts of all the chief events which have happened during that term, such as Football Matches, Concerts, Scholarships, etc., with Letters from Eton, Winchester and other public schools. At the same time we shall be very pleased to print original articles, poetry or correspondence from the pens of boys, past or present, and their friends, subject of course to the approval of those in authority. We have already secured correspondents at Eton and Winchester whose articles in this number will no doubt be read with great interest and who will, we hope, continue to supply us with plenty more of the same sort. It is rather a pity that the idea of starting this *Magazine* had not taken definite shape when the Winchester old Summer Fields boys came here to play their annual match against a combined team of boys and masters; this would have been an excellent opportunity of hearing their views on the subject and of securing their help; however we trust that the former are favourable, and that the latter will be forthcoming whenever we ask for it. Quite a large number of old boys turned up in addition to those taking part in the match.

We hope too that boys in the School at the present time, will not be shy of sending contributions of one sort or another. Out of 120 boys there must be several embryonic poets or prose writers—indeed the Editor knows of one or two—and though their effusions might not be accepted, there is no reason why they should not be sent in. Letters containing suggestions, or even airing grievances, if any such can be found, about games or other matters will be welcomed unless they are frivolous or in any way objectionable, and as a *nom de plume* may be used, the authors' names need not necessarily appear in print, though it will be necessary for the Editor to know them; all such communications will be regarded as strictly confidential.

As regards this first number, there is no lack of "copy" provided by the events of this and last death; so we do not have its valuable record during her headship. We do, however, have photographs, letters and one or two other oddments. Like many Victorians, Mrs was a great letter-writer, as subsequently were her daughters and sons-in-law. One cannot fail to be impressed by the quantity and length of letters that they wrote to parents in those days before the typewriter and the telephone; and, even with the introduction of these inventions, old habits died hard. The Doctor was still writing closely packed, four-sided letters in his ninetieth year, as can be seen in what survives of a fascinating correspondence from him to Austin Anderson (SF 1879–83), which spans nearly sixty years.

These letters meant a lot to both parties: Doctor was extremely proud of his pupil, who fought with bravery in the Great War, became a general and was then appointed secretary to the Governor-General of New South Wales, where he remained until the outbreak of the next war. Anderson for his part worshipped his old mentor. As a boy he had been entered for Eton; but, while he was at Summerfield, his father died, and his mother, faced with the prospect of maintaining a family of six and three houses on a depleted income, took fright and felt that she could not afford Eton. But Dr Williams's view of the situation was 'Very well: we must get him a scholarship.' So that was what they did. Anderson adored Eton and felt immense gratitude towards the Doctor, writing to him regularly until the old man died in 1941. The pair also 'set' each other a nursery rhyme every year, to be rendered into Greek verse during the year and then returned to the sender.

This letter comes from 1882, just after Anderson's father had died; the boy had been whisked off home, presumably leaving a note for Doctor.

Dear Old Boy,

I have just come back & read your letter, though I had heard the sad news from Mrs before. We are indeed grieved to hear of your double misfortune & loss, & trust that your mother will not be prostrated by the blow. I don't think, as perhaps you may know, that we ought to be sorry for a good man when he goes to his rest, because he has then left all trouble behind him, but it is those he leaves behind him that deserve our sympathy and condolence. Mrs sends her love and we think that if you can come on Monday it will do very nicely. Stay longer, you know, if you feel you ought to, or your mother wishes you to, but myself I think it will be quite the best thing for you to plunge into work, as soon as ever you can. There is no Comfort like trust – and time – and an honest fulfilment of duty.

Give my love to your brothers, one & all.
Yours affectionately,
C. Eccles Williams.

Doctor Williams, Headmaster of Summer Fields, 1896–1918.

Ethel Maclaren, an unfinished portrait by Charles Wellington Furse.

East Window of the Chapel, 1896, dedicated in memory of Mrs Maclaren and depicting William of Wykeham, St Monica, St Catherine and Erasmus.

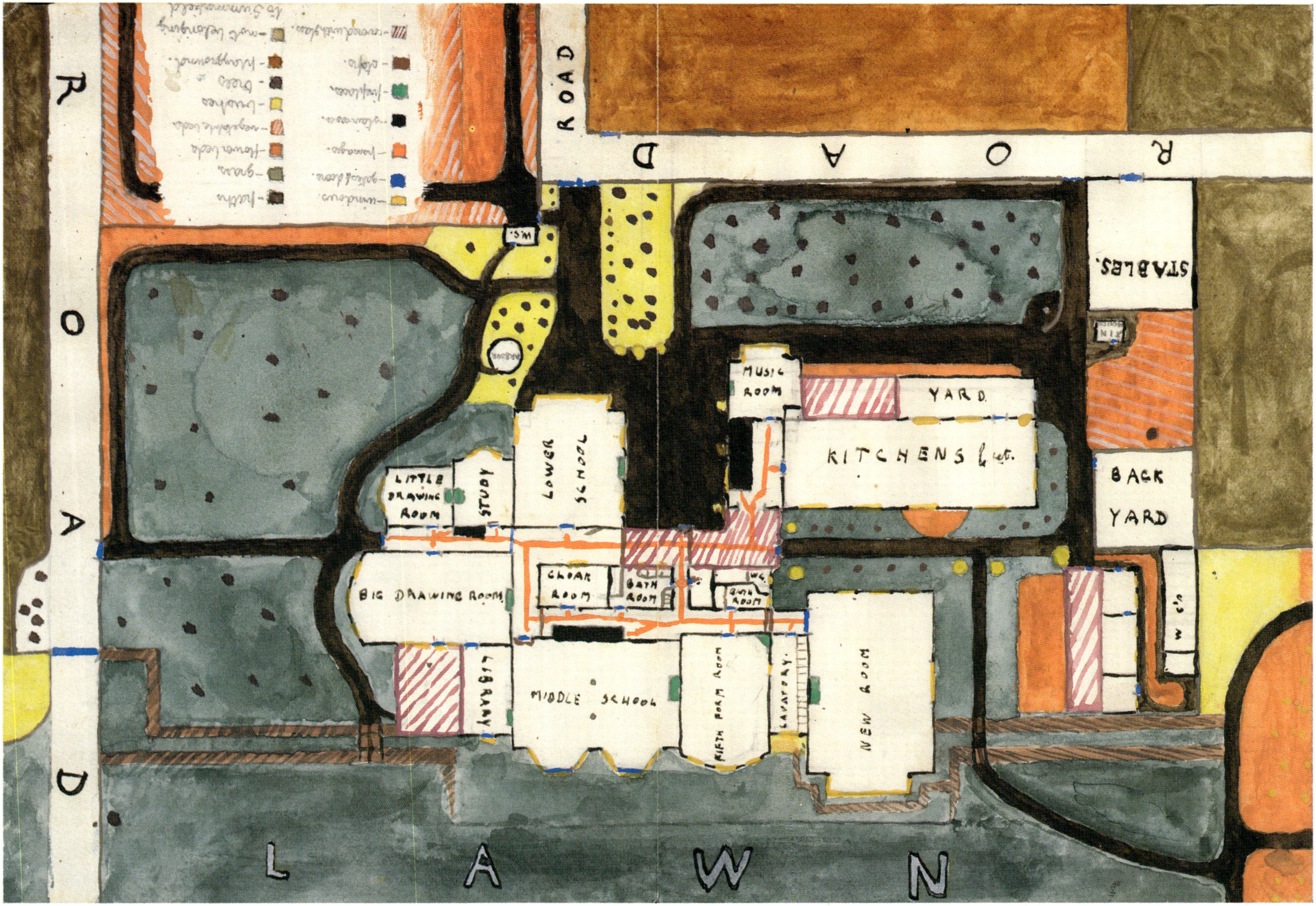

Map drawn by T.R. Bridson of the school c. 1890 as he remembers it.

Turning out a drawer recently, Perdita Marston came upon a letter from Mrs (her great-grandmother) to Cyril Williams (her father) written, she believes, about 1892. Evidently Mrs had been ill and was now recuperating at Bournemouth and avid for news of the school term. The 'Torpids' hurdle races had just happened, and now the Sports proper were about to take place.

We also have from T. R. Bridson a number of school rolls of his period (1888–91), a Summerfield cheque-book, cricket fixtures for 1890 and 1891, and a most instructive plan of the school, done from memory when he was over eighty in the 1960s.

43. Letter from Mrs Maclaren to her grandson Cyril, c. 1892.

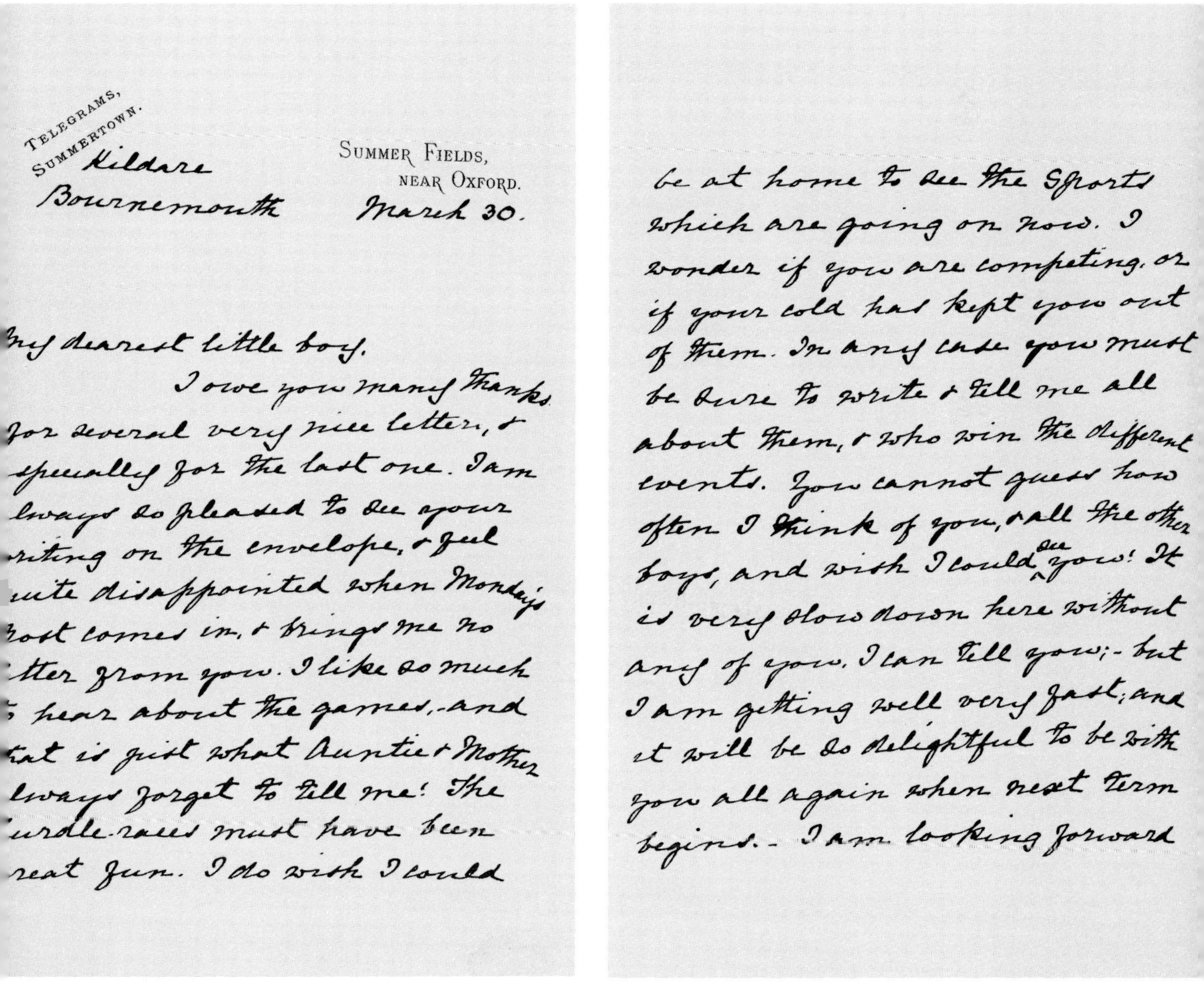
TELEGRAMS, SUMMERTOWN.

SUMMER FIELDS, NEAR OXFORD.

Kildare
Bournemouth

March 30.

ny dearest little boy.
I owe you many thanks
for several very nice letters, &
specially for the last one. I am
lways so pleased to see your
riting on the envelope, & feel
uite disappointed when Monday's
post comes in, & brings me no
tter from you. I like so much
hear about the games,- and
hat is just what Auntie & Mother
lways forget to tell me! The
urdle-races must have been
reat fun. I do wish I could

be at home to see the Sports
which are going on now. I
wonder if you are competing, or
if your cold has kept you out
of them. In any case you must
be sure to write & tell me all
about them, & who win the different
events. You cannot guess how
often I think of you, & all the other
boys, and wish I could see you! It
is very slow down here without
any of you, I can tell you;- but
I am getting well very fast; and
it will be so delightful to be with
you all again when next Term
begins.- I am looking forward

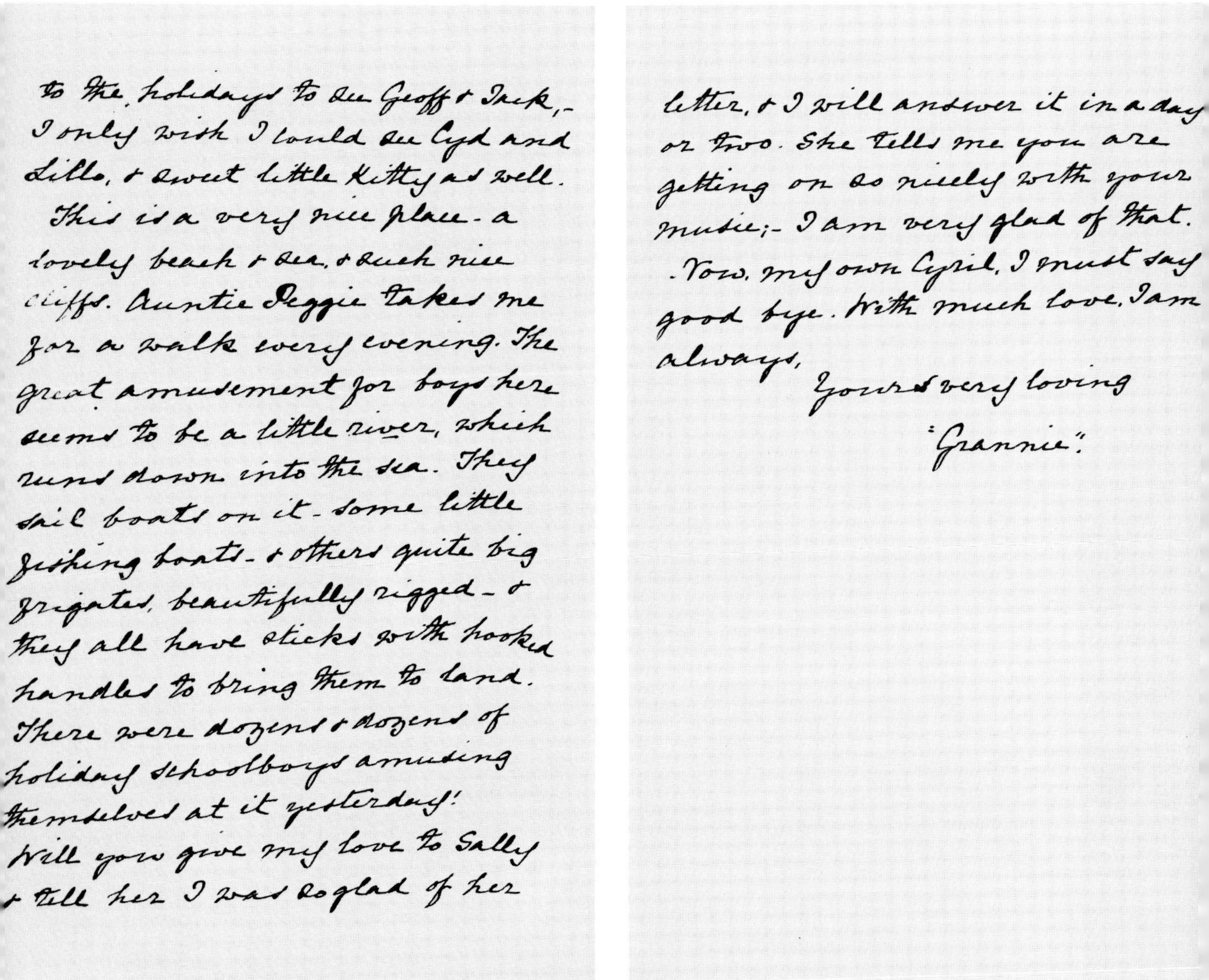
to the holidays to see Geoff & Jack, –
I only wish I could see Cyd and
Lillo, & sweet little Kitty as well.
This is a very nice place – a
lovely beach & sea, & such nice
cliffs. Auntie Peggie takes me
for a walk every evening. The
great amusement for boys here
seems to be a little river, which
runs down into the sea. They
sail boats on it – some little
fishing boats – & others quite big
frigates, beautifully rigged – &
they all have sticks with hooked
handles to bring them to land.
There were dozens & dozens of
holiday schoolboys amusing
themselves at it yesterday!
Will you give my love to Sally
& tell her I was so glad of her
letter, & I will answer it in a day
or two. She tells me you are
getting on so nicely with your
music; – I am very glad of that.
Now, my own Cyril, I must say
good bye. With much love, I am
always,
Your very loving
"Grannie".

Mr Maclaren had died in 1884, and Mrs died on 1 March 1896, only a fortnight after her kinswoman Mary Anne Branscombe. The three names appeared on the same tombstone in St John Baptist churchyard, though her heirs were vague about Mrs's age, giving it as sixty-one, when she was in fact very nearly sixty-three.

WILLS AND PROPERTY

The Bridson map (opposite p. 43) poses a number of problems, the accuracy of an old man's memory not being infallible. The basic structure of the school rooms – Lower School, Middle School, New Room and Fifth Form Room – is as it was for over a century. But was the Study really what became French Room, and was the Library where now the Study is? What precisely do the partitions by the bathroom opposite Fifth Form Room all betoken? His scale has failed in the 'Little Drawing Room' area, for all pictures show that the bows either side of the front door were always the same size. But, despite its inaccuracies, it is a fascinating document.

It is easy to think of Summer Fields as a unit, although it embraces rather more than sixty acres; but it was bought piecemeal over quite a long period, and bits have been added and sold off continuously. The first piece was an area of half an acre containing a 'Messuage, Coach-house, Stable and Outhouses with garden on the South and West' which Archibald Maclaren, gentleman (a widower) bought on 10 December 1847 from Ann Peake, widow of Thomas Peake, who had died in 1845. That parenthetical 'a widower' shows that the first Mrs Maclaren (Charlotte Talboys) lived for less than three years after her marriage. An 'Abstract of Title' from the same year declaring the right of Ann Peake to the property goes into more detail describing it as a 'Messuage or Cottage then lately consisting of the Ground floor only but then having one story above & a Coachhouse 2 stalled Stable Scullery and other the buildings then lately erected upon the said lands.' This is presumably the 'low white house' that Burne-Jones was to enjoy visiting, and the two stalls bore hand-painted wooden labels, 'Tom Brown' and 'Puggins', which over a century later were resurrected by Jack Edmonds and given as names to two form-rooms by the then headmaster, Patrick Savage. Sadly, Puggins was lost in the 1978 modernization, but Tom Brown survives and now, repainted by Michael Dale, graces the door of the Black Hole.

The next year Maclaren bought the area immediately north of this, 'a piece of garden ground in occupation of Anne Thornton situate on the East side of a road running parallel with the Turnpike Road from Oxford to Banbury' (which is now called Mayfield Road). On 28 February 1855 he paid £300 to 'Samuel Quartermaine late of the City of Oxford but now of No. 100 Piccadilly in the City of Westminster Livery Stable Keeper' for an acre of land which seems from the description to be the western end of the present rugger field. On 29 September 1860 the area which is now the garden of Old Lodge and the Front Drive in the vicinity of Front Lodge was bought from James and William Brain, yeomen of Eynsham, and Mark Horn, a pork butcher of Summertown. This had in fact been three of the seven parallel allotments, eighteen feet wide, which Mr Horn leased out; two more of these were acquired in May 1871, and the last two in the following month, thus making up what are now the Rose Garden and the gardens of Borva and New Lodge; finally, in June 1873 Maclaren bought the remaining ground between this and the Banbury Road, where what was previously Front Lodge and the Radio Oxford/Allied Carpets block now stand.

Meanwhile, continuing to play his game of Monopoly, as it were, on 25 March 1868 Maclaren had bought for £1,000 from John Thompson 'All that Close or Parcel of Meadow Ground Situate in the Parish of St Giles near the City of Oxford containing by Statute Measure Four acres two roods and thirty nine perches or thereabouts part of an Inclosure formerly called Hawkwell and now part of the Northern Meadows and which said Close abuts on its Western Side the Allotment of St John's College'. Eight months later he bought from Catherine Sarah Parrott and Frederick Joseph Morrell for £1,500 two adjacent closes and a cottage. These three closes comprise roughly what is now the athletics field, Wadham playing-field and the Laundry Cottage.

On 18 May 1870 Maclaren moved in the opposite direction and bought what was to become the eastern half of the playground (now Parmoor Court) for £80. This was a complicated sale because William Cantwell had left the property equally to all his children; so the vendors on this occasion were: Thomas Cantwell, Plumber; Jane Cantwell, Widow; Charles Cantwell, Lime Burner; Josiah Cantwell, Milkman; James Aries, Dairyman, and Sophia his Wife; James Cantwell, Gardener; Thomas Dumbleton, Gardener, and Elizabeth his Wife; and Ann Streaks, Widow. Some of them had difficulty in signing their names, and James Cantwell was content with 'his mark'. From the description it would appear that Maclaren had previously got possession of the area west of this (the rest of the playground) and to the north (Cottage garden), but there are no records of these purchases. In this document the road running parallel to the Banbury Road is called 'Frederick Place'; but on the 1876 Ordnance Survey map that name is applied to Manor, which at the time was apparently divided into two separate dwellings.

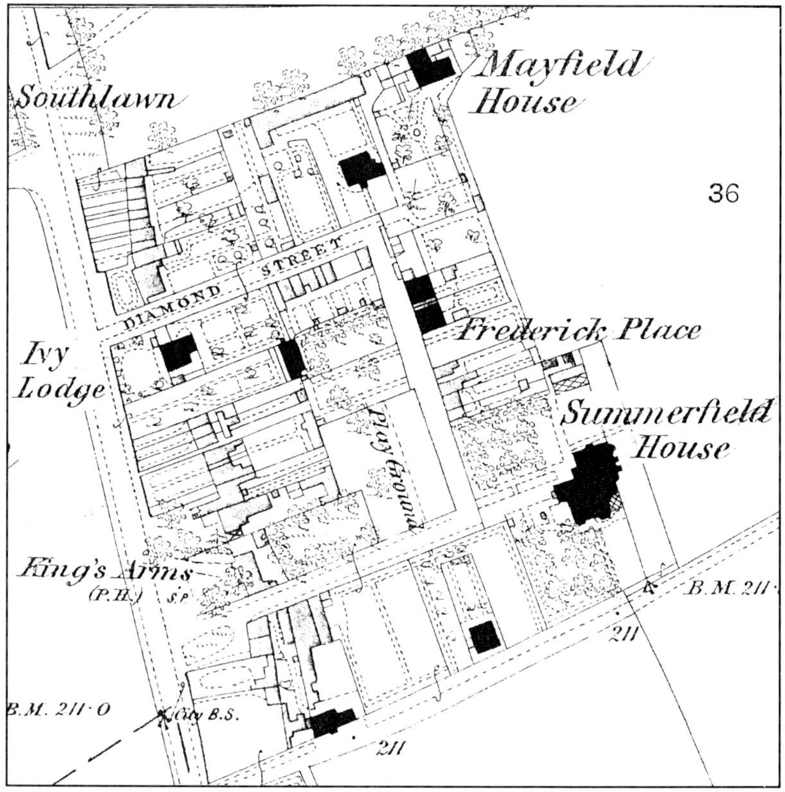

44. Part of an Ordnance Survey map of 1876, showing (blacked in) most of the houses that the school acquired. Newton, Front Lodge (bottom left) and Old Lodge are not named, and Manor is still two separate residences known as Frederick Place. Between them and Ivy Lodge is the original cottage which was demolished when Cottage was built. [Bodleian Library, O/S Oxon XXXIII.II]

Manor itself was bought on 30 November 1880, and its vendors were even more complicated than those of the previous document. The conveyance of 'Two Cottages and Premises at Summertown' is drawn up between Mr J. W. Harris and thirty-seven others on one side and Archibald Maclaren Esq. on the other, the vendors being resident in various parts of the country and embracing the whole social spectrum from gentleman via chemist and bookmaker to labourer. For these two cottages and their gardens (now occupied by the Carpenter's Shop and the squash court) Maclaren paid £249 15*s* 0*d* – presumably to be divided thirty-eight ways!

Archibald Maclaren died on 19 February 1884, leaving an estate of gross value £13,649 4*s* 6*d*. In his will, dated 21 December 1882, he took the bull by the horns and dealt firmly with the matter of his two marriages, as follows:

WHEREAS some years ago I went through the forms attending the solemnization of marriage with Gertrude Isabel [sic] Frances Talboys Spinster one of the Daughters of David Alphonso Talboys late of the City of Oxford Bookseller deceased and we have ever since lived together and do now live together as Man and Wife and we have issue three children AND WHEREAS I am advised that inasmuch as the said Gertrude Isabel Frances Talboys is the Sister of my first Wife (who had died without issue before my aforesaid marriage) my said marriage with her the said Gertrude Isabel Frances Talboys is not legally valid NEVERTHELESS I refer to the said Gertrude Isabel Frances Talboys as my said Wife throughout this my Will . . .

He then proceeded to name as executors his wife, his son Wallace, his son-in-law Dr Williams and his solicitor John Hester. He bequeathed to his wife all his 'household furniture and domestic chattels' and to her cousin Mary Ann Branscombe an annuity of £100 for life to be charged to the school. Then come the more important bequests to his children.

I GIVE DEVISE and BEQUEATH to my only son John Wallace Hozier Maclaren all I possess in land and houses namely The Gymnasium in Alfred Street High Street Oxford The House at Summertown near Oxford aforesaid called Summerfield and all the lands belonging to it the two Houses adjacent to it situated on the above mentioned land my four cottages in Summertown . . .

45. A later map, probably from the turn of the century, showing areas annexed to Mayfield at the northern end of the Shrubbery and where now the kitchen and kitchen yard are.

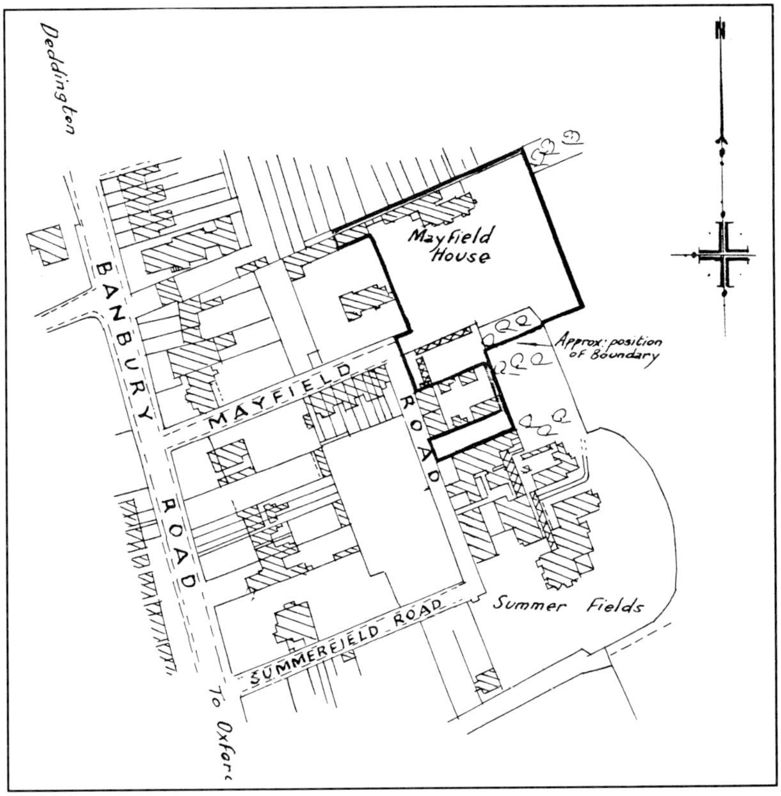

In addition he gave Wallace £1,000, Mabel £3,000 and Margaret £6,000 'part of my money in the Funds', and then:

I GIVE and BEQUEATH my School at Summerfield and the good will thereof (but not including the houses and lands wherein the same is now carried on previously devised to my said son John Wallace Hozier Maclaren) to my said son John Wallace Hozier Maclaren and my son in law Charles Eccles Edmond Williams in order that the same may be carried on by them conjointly the profits accruing from the said School after the payment of all expenses connected therewith ... to be equally divided between the said John Wallace Hozier Maclaren and the said Charles Eccles Edmond Williams.

One might have some misgivings about such an arrangement, but it could have worked if Wallace had been a forceful personality and had remained in good health, if either of his sons had been interested in taking on the school, and if his wife and Dr Williams had been less forceful personalities!

The Doctor was certainly a shrewd businessman: had he not been so, it is unlikely that the school would have flourished or even endured as it has. When the King's Arms public-house at the corner of Summerfield and Banbury Roads was pulled down in 1881, he acquired the site and built Borva on it: this, incidentally, was one of the first houses in Summertown to have mains water. He had clearly acquired some other plots of land, for by an indenture of 1 July 1886 he made over to Wallace Maclaren the central strip of the playground adjoining Borva garden and also an area to the north of it which is rather hard to identify, but is possibly the northern corner site where Mayfield Road now joins the Banbury Road 'in consideration of the natural love and affection which the said Charles Eccles Williams hath for his Brother in law the said John Wallace Hozier Maclaren.' Is there a faint flavour of Mr Pecksniff in this?

In 1895 a scandal rocked Summertown. Charles Titian Hawkins, an accountant and businessman who had lived at Mayfield since buying it in 1851, was declared bankrupt and was discovered to have committed various embezzlements on quite a grand scale. The result of his bankruptcy was that his numerous properties in Summertown came up for sale by auction at the Golden Cross Hotel in Oxford on Wednesday 20 November 1895. These included Mayfield, initially sold to Sir Walter Gray for £1,750; Newton, snapped

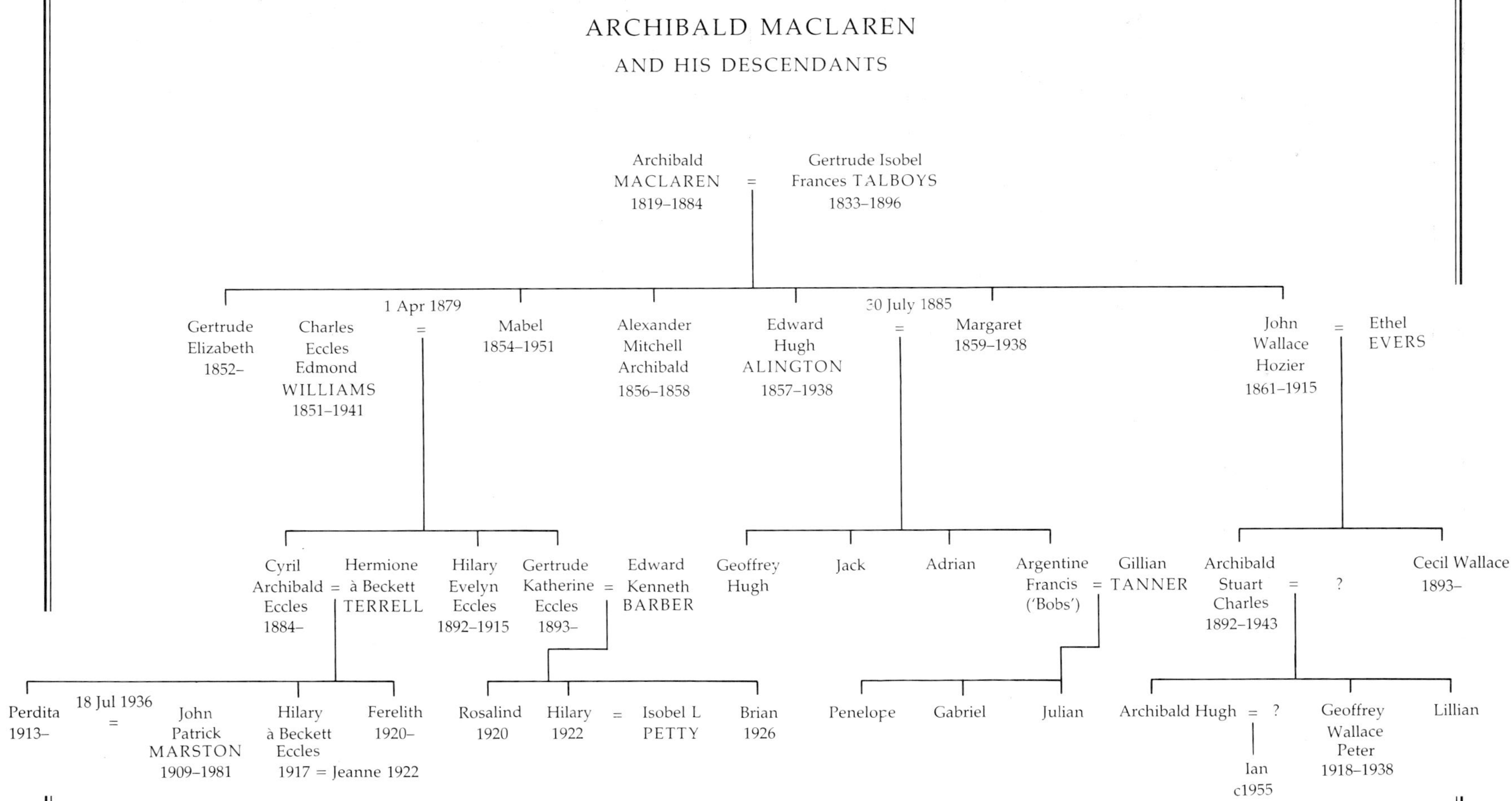

46. Family Tree of Archibald Maclaren and his descendants.

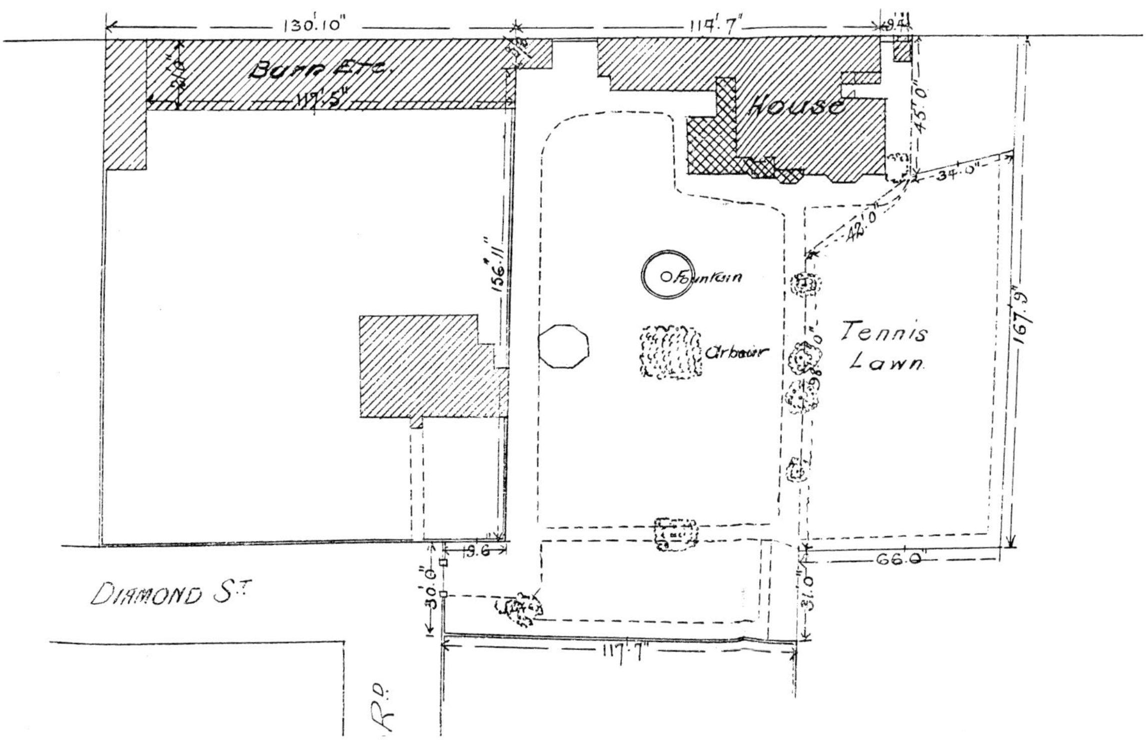

47. Map from the sale particulars of Mayfield, 1895. Though the Tennis Lawn survives, Mayfield can no longer boast a fountain or an arbour.

up by Mr E. E. Pigott at £760; and Ivy Lodge – all of which were quickly acquired by the school. On 25 January 1896, Mayfield was bought by the Rev. E. H. Alington, and soon afterwards he bought half an acre to the east of it from Mabel Williams and Margaret Alington for ten shillings! A conveyance dated 4 August 1896 suggests that the Doctor rented Newton before that date, upon which he bought for £825 'All that Messuage tenement or dwellinghouse garden and premises situate in Diamond Street Summertown in the City of Oxford and known as "Newton Lodge" and now in the occupation of the said Charles Eccles Edmond Williams.'

Mrs Maclaren died in 1896, leaving an estate of gross value £2,501 1*s* 0*d*. In her will, dated 7 February 1894, she made her son and her two sons-in-law her executors. With a great deal of verbiage and legal jargon, she instructed her son and her two daughters to divide her estate between them, and thus she set the stage for future trouble.

3

DOCTOR IN CHARGE
1896–1914

DOCTOR WILLIAMS had effectively been headmaster throughout the 1890s, as Mrs Maclaren took less part in the day-to-day running of the school. When he actually assumed the role after her death, he took charge of a thriving institution with fully subscribed enrolment lists and an outstanding record of scholarships at public schools. This is an extract from a letter which he sent to Anderson in 1897, in fact on the anniversary of the death of Mrs.

> The school is flourishing enormously – 122 boys now – and we have sent away 19 applications since Septr: I think that we could be 200 in very little time, if we cared to be as many, but it would spoil us. So I am going to resist every temptation. We have won nearly every match we have played this year & got 3 Schols at Eton & 4 at Winchester last summer & a very good lot for this, all going well. I do not forget Polycrates of Samos, though …

Physically, the place was in good shape, too, and the central area from New Room southwards was to remain virtually unaltered for the next sixty years. North and west of that, he began to erect buildings with great rapidity. First was the Chapel, which he designed himself as a memorial to his mother-in-law, but in such a hurry that he forgot to make provision for an organ or a vestry: they were built during the next couple of years, as was the Vinery, which was merely a conversion of a real grape-growing conservatory. It consisted of a number of cubicles, each housing a rudimentary water-closet; the system of flushing was much like that which Hercules used in the Augean Stables. At regular intervals a stream of water would sweep down the channel under the compartments, carrying all before it. It was not unknown for mischievous boys to collect some paper, wait for the 'Vinery Rush', then ignite their bundle and send it floating down, to fire the spirits of those in the compartments downstream. Five more remote and august thrones were reserved for the exclusive use of Fifth Form and were named, perhaps suitably, after the rivers of Hades. The Vinery Rush was done away with in 1928, but the basic structure remained for another fifty years. When the Governors decided in 1977 that something more modern and hygienic was needed, one of them recalled with feeling that the Summer Fields Vinery was 'one of the classic horrors of British education – a great deterrent.' Enough said.

48. (*above*) A Garden Party c. 1896, presumably shortly after Mrs' death. *Standing:* T. J. F. Haskoll, T. S. Morton, 'Bear' Alington, J. F. Crofts, Ethel Maclaren and 'Bam' Evans. *Seated:* P. C. Joy, Dr Williams, Mrs Haskoll, Mabel Williams, Margaret Alington and Mrs H. T. G. Alington, (also a Margaret.) *On the ground:* Cyril Williams, Wallace Maclaren and H. T. G. Alington, Bear's nephew who taught at the school 1889–1896.

49. (*below*) The original driveway to the school, leading up to the more recently added glass-roofed Lobby, barely altered between 1900 and 1960.

50. The Gymnasium, built in 1898, the architect being a Mr Quinton, and the fittings by Messrs Heath and George.

Opposite to the Vinery was built what in those days they called the Change Room. Boys' coats and shoes, however, were housed in the central area by the Lobby until 1960; and the rows of wooden lockers with their white-painted numbers and, opposite them, the wooden slots for rackets form a vivid part of many Old Boys' memories of the Lobby as it was before then.

Having built the Chapel and added the vestry and a splendid organ made by Father Willis (who also made that which Mrs had herself presented in memory

51. For some time after the school had its own gymnasium, the medals awarded for gymnastic proficiency still bore the picture of Maclaren's Oxford Gymnasium. This one, which was won by H. G. McMinnies in 1902, is reproduced by kind permission of his daughter, Lady Orr-Ewing, herself the grandmother of three recent Summerfieldians.

52. The school from the south-east, c. 1900, the extended New Room now sporting both its lanterns.

of her late husband to the parish church in the 1880s), the Doctor then turned his attention from the spiritual welfare of his charges to the physical. The Gymnasium was built between April and September 1898, 'in the Orchard, just opposite the gravelled Playground', and was hailed as a 'fine, lofty building, excellently fitted up with every kind of bar, ladder, ring and rope imaginable'. It was opened officially with a concert on 12 November, and ever since then has served the multiple purpose of gym-cum-theatre-cum-concert-hall. This was the end of the two-mile walks into Oxford for the weekly session in the Alfred Street gymnasium. In the same summer the Pavilion was also built, and considered 'a great boon, especially on showery days, of which we had a great many at the beginning of the term.' *Plus ça change*...

A few years later, the Doctor lengthened New Room, which had indeed been New in the previous decade, by some twenty feet, with a second fireplace, side-window and roof-lantern. These lanterns were charming, if Victorian, and New Room has never managed to look so proud of itself since they were removed in the 1960s because they leaked badly. In the same year (1901), the western extension was added to Newton, providing four new dormitories to accommodate the boys who up to then had slept in Ivy Lodge, the attractive house on the corner of the Banbury and Mayfield Roads, where the Oxfam block now stands. Two years later, Ivy Lodge became the sanatorium, when the school gave up South Lawn, another gracious house on the further side of the Banbury Road.

53. The Dining-Hall, built in Spring 1903; no Honours Boards at this stage, but plenty of table decoration!

But the major building project of 1903 was the Dining-Hall, and a Hall indeed it was (and is), modelled on that of an Oxford college: built to cater for 120 boys and a dozen staff, it still copes in the 1980s with 200 boys and two dozen or more adults every day at lunch. We are lucky that the Doctor 'thought big'. The kitchen remained in what is now the Science Laboratory, but the room above it was converted from being a dining-room into a dormitory with cubicles somewhat similar to the Long Chamber at Eton. Domestic servants continued to sleep in the top storey; a butler's pantry and domestic common room were built in the area south of the Change Room, and a small scullery was built at the east end of the Dining-Room. The site of the Dining-Room and Scullery was described in the contemporary magazine as being 'in the garden between the Stables and Manor'. The carpenter's Shop had been built *c.* 1898, but the area surrounding the school was still largely garden and orchard, and was to remain so for half a century.

At the same time as this building and expansion, there were several changes in the staff. Haskoll, Salter, Morton and Joy all left within a year of Mrs' death and, while Bear Alington, Crofts, Evans and Penny remained, other masters came and went, most of whom made an impression upon the school and its life. Gilbert Jenner (1896–1902) of Magdalen went on to be an assistant master at Wellington in the same year as Mrs Maclaren's nephew R. StC. Talboys, and thence to be Headmaster of Hazelwood School. Cecil Willett (1897–1902) came from Malvern and B. N. C., that nursery of SF masters; he died young in 1909. E. D. Compton also arrived in 1897, and stayed for six years, during which he was the first editor of the School Magazine, before departing with his wife to found Summer Fields *mi* at St Leonards-on-Sea in Sussex. The idea was that the South Coast would provide a healthier climate for those boys who were inclined to be frail. Both schools were under the management of Dr Williams, and shared the same magazine until 1930, but otherwise ran largely separate lives. St Leonards started with eleven boys, the Comptons, two dogs and Wallace Maclaren.

John Wallace Hozier Maclaren, the only son of Mr and Mrs to survive childhood, is a somewhat sad and shadowy figure. He was a man of the highest culture, having been educated at Summerfield, Wellington, Magdalen, Heidelberg and Berlin, where he became a PhD, but his health was poor. So he creeps in and out of the history of both schools, appearing in photographs and occasionally mentioned in memoirs. He seems to have been a gentle and scholarly person, all for the quiet life; and, like many such men, he married a domineering beauty, Ethel Evers, by whom he had two sons, Archibald and Cecil.

54. The first school photograph of Summer Field, St Leonard's-on-Sea.

Ethel's picture hangs in the Dining-Hall to this day and is frequently admired by visitors, being a superior work of art to the two other oil-paintings there, portraits of Doctor and Mabel. The painting is by Charles Wellington Furse, who in his time was compared to Sargent with advantage and whose most famous picture, *Diana of the Uplands*, is still celebrated and much reproduced. He died young at thirty-six, a sufferer from tuberculosis. For the last few years of his life he travelled extensively in Europe for his health and wintered in Davos, where he would certainly have met the Maclarens. Ethel was taller than her husband and was a great one for the social whirl. At Davos, where many of the Summer Fields hierarchy went in the season, she was bobsleigh champion, collecting gold and silver medals as well as six broken ribs. She also took her husband, who was no mean photographer, on treks from Cairo to Capetown, and through India to Burma. Her two sons were much in awe of her, and it is said that she had no compunction in horse-whipping them if they displeased her. It was probably she who had the family name changed to Stuart-Maclaren in 1903: it was fashionable to be double-barrelled!

55. Cyril Williams' 21st Birthday Party, 4th August 1905, showing the assembled Maclaren, Williams and Alington families, though two of the ladies have so far eluded identification. *Back Row:* Ethel Maclaren, Cyril Williams, an unknown, Geoffrey Alington and Jack Alington. *Middle Row:* Wallace Maclaren, Mabel Williams, Dr Williams, an unknown (could it be Doctor's mother?), Margaret Alington and Hugh Alington. *Front Row:* Cecil Maclaren, Archibald Maclaren, Hilary Williams, Kitty Williams, 'Bobs' Alington and Adrian Alington.

56. The Masters, 1904. *Standing:* W. D. Nixon, R. D. Slater, R. G. Pidcock and G. D. Barne. *Seated:* F. P. Penny, J. F. Crofts, Rev. C. E. Williams, Rev. E. H. Alington and G. W. Evans. *On the Ground:* C. E. Smyth and Rev. C. H. S. Gmelin.

Though theoretically a partner in the St Leonards school, Wallace became increasingly less involved in its running as ill-health forced him to winter abroad. He bought a villa at La Oratava in the Canary Isles, and there he died on 16 February 1915, at the age of fifty-three. His obituary spoke of 'his great kindliness of heart and a certain cheery optimism, combined with great personal charm of manner and a ready wit, causing him always to be a desired and much-sought-after companion. The present generation of boys have necessarily known less of him of late years, but ... his death leaves a blank which will not readily be filled.'

George D. Barne (1902–8) of Oriel and a member of the university golf team, had a baptism by fire, for his first act as a master was to discover and help to extinguish one in Old Lodge. He took holy orders while he was here and subsequently rose in the Church hierarchy to become Bishop of Lahore. Throughout his career, the school held a high place in his affections, and he often revisited it and wrote letters to the staff. His name is perpetuated on the Fielding Cup, which he presented.

Richard G. Pidcock OS (1902–9) and R. Douglas Slater (1903–9) both went on to become headmasters of Bramcote after Samuel Servington Savery, who had left Summer Fields in 1888. He started Bramcote in 1893 with three boys; he named the school after the house in the Banbury Road where he had lived with his sister. He (and his sister) ran Bramcote for sixteen years; by the time Pidcock and Slater arrived, the school had sixty-one pupils. Clearly it was successful and expanding, but Savery was unorthodox in his ideas, and the next two years must have been somewhat uncomfortable, with the two young men straining at the leash. In 1911 Savery retired from schoolmastering, and thereafter had a successful career in politics, being an MP for fifteen years and being knighted in 1937, the year before his death.

Pidcock ran the school for the thirty-five years until 1946, and is still remembered with affection and gratitude. Mr Bevan Gamble, who retired recently from teaching at Bramcote, recalled him as a 'most efficient and charming man: a model schoolmaster in his love for the school. He also interested us in History, which he had read at Oxford.' Slater was less easy, having a sharp tongue and a stubborn streak; but he demanded, and got, high standards. He must also have been a more than useful cricketer, as he made a century for the Summer Fields staff against North Oxford. He married in 1924 and retired from teaching in the following year. Today, Bramcote is still flourishing and has many Summerfieldian touches, including the same school colours (red) and cricket caps (red-and-white) and the same Grace. On this last, there is a rather charming comment in the Bramcote archives: 'In the Grace before meals our pronunciation of "sumpturi" to rhyme with "bumped your eye" would not find favour today.'

Pidcock, Barne and E. D. Compton put on a performance of *Cox and Box* in 1903, the first known 'staff play'; this was shortly before EDC left to take on the newly created daughter-school. After his departure, Barne took over the editorship of the Magazine. *Cox and Box* was staged again in 1908, this time with a cast of Slater, who was the music master, Pidcock and J. H. E. Besant (1905–11), another product of B. N. C., who proceeded to the headmastership of a prep school at Pietermaritzburg in Natal. All these were fine schoolmasters, immersing themselves thoroughly in every area of school life: Summer Fields at this time, as at some subsequent periods, was a veritable breeding-ground for headmasters!

In an appreciation of Dr Williams written some years later, RGP gives a picture of what it was like to be a member of his staff in the early 1900s.

The Doctor got the best out of everyone. He was a very hard worker himself and he expected his staff to work hard, and they did so willingly, for he was always ready with a word of praise or encouragement. But no-one was more ready than he to let you have a day off to play Football or Cricket or to go to the National (two of us went four years running) and, when you came back, he was full of interest to know how you had fared. He was himself keenly interested in every kind of sport. He used to play Golf and Lawn Tennis in term time on the Summer Fields ground, and was a pretty keen opponent. He

57. Bramcote School, Scarborough, today: the school founded by S. S. Savery, and subsequently run by R. D. Slater and R. G. Pidcock.

always went up to the Varsity Sports and returned full of gloom and righteous indignation when the day had gone against Oxford. About once a term he used to dine at B. N. C. on a Sunday night, known as 'Tram Lines Night': the staff's small jest that, to find his way home, he needed the guidance of the tram-lines which in those days carried the horse-trams between Oxford and Summertown.

More permanent arrivals on the staff were Miss Lilwall Peirce, who ruled the matronal roost and much else with a rod of iron and a ready supply of the notorious 'fizzy doses' from 1896 till 1923; the Rev. C. H. S. Gmelin (1896–1914), the first housemaster of Cottage, which was built in the early years of the century; C. E. Smyth OS (1897–1924), a brilliant classical teacher and football coach; and the two Miss Hills (Rhoda 1903–46 and Mildred 1905–46), who together took charge of the lowest forms and so were responsible for launching many distinguished careers over nearly half a century.

The academic record over the twenty years 1897–1916 was in fact quite staggering: during that period Summer Fields *averaged* more than eleven scholarships per year, and more than five at Eton. In eleven of those years we had first at Eton, and in most of the others second and/or third; in 1909 and 1916 we had eight on the Eton Election Roll. At this time one boy in every three in College was a Summerfieldian, and it is worth recording that we also had a good percentage of the 'Beaks'. But though predominantly Etonian, we were not exclusively so: we also gained twenty-six scholarships at Winchester, thirty-six at Radley and

58. The Scholars of 1900: in the centre, R. A. Knox, 1st Scholar at Eton.

forty-nine at a good spread of other public schools. It is hardly surprising that the accusation of 'cramming' was frequently hurled at Summer Fields in general and at Doctor in particular. Though the term is of course a relative one, at this distance in time one may see some substance in it: if the boys were not force-fed, they were certainly stuffed. But then Doctor merely saw this as the natural and sensible course: the public schools required a certain product, and he did his best – which happened to be a very good best – to provide it, as Mrs had done before him and 'Bear' Alington was to do subsequently. The education was too predominantly classical, but most other areas were not neglected (maths arguably being the exception, and it was to remain so for many years to come).

Had we merely crammed our boys, it is unlikely that they would have gone on to such successful and frequently glorious careers. Among the scholars from those two decades, distinguished names catch the eye. Archibald Wavell won an award at Winchester the term after Mrs died, while Christopher Stone was winning the First at Eton, from which he went on to become a notable writer and musicologist. Ronald Knox launched the new century with a first at Eton, which his elder brother Arthur had also achieved three years earlier. The 1901 list

59. An interesting photograph of the Summerfieldian King's Scholars at Eton in 1909, 21 boys and 4 masters. *Back Row:* G.S. Madan, P. Malcolm, P.E. Hobhouse mi, M.A.P. Graham, G. Parker-Jervis, F.T.K. Caroë, unidentified, C.C. Maud[?]; *Middle Row:* J.R. Hobhouse ma, A.H. Armstrong mi, C.J. Rowlatt, J.F. Thompson, H.E.E. Williams, H.F.C. Crookshank, H.R. Walker, E.W. Hamilton, D.J. Darley; *Front Row:* R.P.C. Whitcombe, J.R.C. Rawnsley, The Rev. J.C. Chute, an unidentified master, R.C. Gelderd-Somervell, The Rev. G.J. Chitty, J.F. Crace (Master-in-College), E.W. Armstrong ma, Conspicuous by their absence are: M.H. Macmillan, V.J.C. Edgehill, H.A.M. Napier and C.W. Stuart-Maclaren.

included H.G.J. Moseley, the eminent scientist and discoverer of Moseley's law for X-rays, as well as Hugh (later Lord) Dalton, who held a number of ministerial offices during and after the Second World War, including President of the Board of Trade and Chancellor of the Exchequer. Harold Macmillan, so far our only *British* Prime Minister, followed five years later, and after him came Geoffrey Madan, whose anthology of *bon mots* has recently been republished in paperback, Guy Boas, Christopher Hollis, Steven Runciman, Roger Mynors, distinguished Professor of Latin first at Cambridge and then at Oxford and uncle of five subsequent SF scholars, and Anthony Asquith, who directed many of the best films in the middle decades of this century.

And those were only the scholars. We also produced a spate of military and naval commanders, many of whom did not survive the Great War. Among these

60. 'A Regular Fix', the play of Michaelmas 1900. *Back Row:* H. C. Cowie as First Postman; C. B. Moss as Mrs Carter; H. G. J. Moseley as Abel Quick; G. L. P. Henderson as Matilda Jane; K. Mackay as Second Postman; and C. L. Hargreaves as Smiler. *Front Row:* A. L. R. Parsons as Mr Surplus; A. McD. Eddis as Emily; H. D. Simonds as Hugh de Brass; E. W. Horner as Mrs Surplus; and A. E. J. Nicholls as Charles Surplus.

was the poet Julian Grenfell, eldest of the three sons of Lord and Lady Desborough, all Summerfieldians; and two VCs, Billy Congreve and Thomas Colyer-Fergusson. Nor did we neglect the 'Junior Service', for A. C. Stuart-Maclaren, the grandson of Mrs, was one of the earliest flying 'aces' to win the MC with Bar; he continued his aviatorial exploits after the war, flying from England to India and attempting to fly round the world.

The School Magazine first appeared in 1897 and contains records of much that may already have been established before the turn of the century, but had not previously been noted. Cricket and soccer matches had probably started as early as the 1870s; and we know, for instance, that in 1890 we played cricket against Cothill, Cordwalles (which later became St Pirans) and Dragons (already known by this name, although officially called the Oxford Preparatory School) as well as junior teams from Pangbourne and Radley, Eton and Winchester OSS and a Fathers' scratch XI. Was the Broomstick Match in existence by then, too? This is a game played at the end of term between the First XI and the Staff, who have to use bats shaved to a perilous narrowness. Perhaps originally real broomsticks were used; perhaps one day a photograph of the original match will come to light.

61. A rather glum picture of the triumphant 1901 1st XI. Though this photograph is unnamed, Julian Grenfell, opening bat and future war poet, is identifiable standing on the right, gloved and padded for action.

By 1897 we had added to these fixtures Magdalen College School, St Edwards Under-15, Woodcote House, Osberton House and Haseley Manor, and we were playing football against a similar group, incuding Park House, Kidlington School, the famous Horris Hill and Bedford House. Equally established were the Athletic Sports and the Torpids, as described by Bernard Darwin in Chapter 2. The golf-course was created in the 1880s, and swimming and fives were also indulged in – though it is not certain at what date the original fives courts were built, or exactly what sort of fives was played in them (see below, Chapter 4).

The summer of 1901 was a fine one; indeed, the Magazine suggests that the only reason we did not get top scholarship at Eton for the sixth consecutive year was that one of our best candidates was overcome by the heat in an important paper. Still, seven on the Eton list, as well as three at Charterhouse and a couple of others, was no mean performance. In a splendid cricket season, with Julian Grenfell opening the First XI batting, there was no match in which at least one side made less than a three-figure total. We made 155–6 and 166–3 against the Dragon, who could only reply with 32–8 and 42 all out. An unusual feature of the season was the Fifth Game Match, of which the score-card and Magazine's comments appear overleaf. The river picnic and hay picnic were both enjoyed. This is only the second mention of the Hay Feast, the first being in the previous year, which talks of 'All the other usual events which make the Summer term so

—o—

FIFTH GAME MATCH.

XI. of 5th Game *v.* Miss Owen's XI.

It is six years or more since a fifth game had a real match all to themselves, so the excitement was intense when it was announced that a team was being raised among the small boys of Oxford to oppose them on their own ground—or rather on 3rd game pitch which was borrowed for the occasion. After two postponements, the match took place on Wednesday, July 17th, and ended in a great victory for 5th game by an innings and 89 runs. Our boys won the toss and soon coll(i)ered the bowling, which they said was juicy or Spic(er)y; eventually Collier and Spicer bowled most of them out, but not before the total had reached 150. The other side had two innings and only made 61 altogether; they were most of them a bit smaller than our chaps, and we heard one of the numerous ladies, who came to watch the play, describe them as "little ducks"; that description was fairly accurate, for there were no less than 14 ducks all together, five in the first innings and nine in the second. They had one Driver amongst their clique, who made 4 not out in the 1st innings and was driving the bowling about freely in the 2nd, when his wickets were bowled Down. The only other scorer in their second innings was Cumberlege, who, with Driver, scored 28 out of the total of 32. Scores:—

5th Game XI.

Down, l-b-w, b Spicer	40
Arbuthnot, b Collier	3
Clauson, b Spicer	14
Gregory, b Collier	26
Maxwell mi., b Spicer	14
Baynes, b Spicer	25
Maclaren, b Spicer	0
Williams, run out	10
North, b Hodge	1
Simpkinson, b Collier	2
Douglas, not out	1
Extras	14
Total	150

Miss Owen's XI.

First Innings.		Second Innings.	
Hornsby, b Down	3	b Clauson	0
Collier, b Gregory	0	b Arbuthnot	0
Cumberlege, c and b Arbuthnot	1	c Clauson, b Down	14
Moberly, b Gregory	2	b Clauson	0
Spicer, st Down, b Arbuthnot	0	b Down	0
Hodge, b Down	17	b Down	0
Campbell, b Clauson	0	not out	0
Morris, c Maxwell, b Williams	0	b Arbuthnot	0
Macdonell, b Gregory	1	b Arbuthnot	0
Driver, not out	4	b Down	14
Hudson, b Gregory	0	c Arbuthnot, b Clauson	0
Extras	1	Extras	4
Total	29	Total	32

62. A Fifth Game Match, 1901.

pleasant – bathing, hay picnic, river picnic...' Darwin makes no mention of it, but Mark Young (1894–9) recalls 'the fields in which we enjoyed occasional treats ... with nests of hay and feasts of fruit'; so probably it came into being during the 1890s.

A great feature of the school year was the Concert, usually in November; and plays became increasingly popular in the early years of the century. The concerts were mainly, but not entirely, musical; performers were boys and staff in about equal proportions, but friends of the school and OSS might also appear. Doctor, Bear, Compton, Penny, Pidcock, Slater and Besant all performed regularly – as did C. Edgington, whose solo items were evidently high spots and who returned faithfully for the occasion each year after he had moved on from here in 1901. Slater directed the musical side from 1902 to 1908; he was succeeded by B. M. Barker, and both were assisted by Miss Hill *ma*. The music of the school was much enhanced by the arrival in late 1909 or early 1910 of William Sterndale Case, who not only sang but composed: in 1912 the choir performed a set of songs from his 'Titania'.

At first the plays were staged in December, but later they supplanted the concerts at half-term. The earliest plays were of the pantomime type with songs and general direction by Penny, and often preceded or followed by a short staff play: *Ali Baba, The Tinder Box, Ching Chang Fou, Brown Among the Brahmins* and *Rumpelstiltzkin* covered the years 1901–5. In the last-named, M.H. Macmillan

63. The 1911 play, 'Queen Bridget and the Dragon', by Geoffrey Alington. This picture shows the stage as it was before the Paine-Strong proscenium was made. 'Among the gems of the performance were Colquhoun's song and dance.' W. R. Colquhoun, seated bottom right, won a scholarship to Eton, where he was subsequently a distinguished master for thirty-five years, but he did not send his sons to Summer Fields. His favourite Greek tag was 'ὦ παι, γενοιο πατρος εὐτυχεστερος'. Perhaps there was a connection?

'as the Prime Minister was very obsequious and did his part excellently.' When Geoffrey Alington arrived on the scene, he wrote plays specially for the school to perform, such as *Queen Bridget and the Dragon* and *Alexander the Great*. Three of his plays were published in 1913.

Some letters from the future Duke of Sutherland written at the turn of the century give us glimpses of the school's 'sub-culture' as well as social insights into the period. One wonders whether 'gut' was received SF slang for 'tuck' or whether it was part of Geordie's family language. His mixture of assured sophistication with schoolboy orthography and phraseology is appealing ('Boys are all practicing for Sports now like the *juice* . . .').

Darling Mummy,

I hope you are quite well.

I had a letter from Duncan MacRae the other day and he told me that the jarboa which I gave [?] Dominic MacRae was very well. I think I have never told you before that a new kid came this term called Leveson-Gower he says he is a cousin of mine. He came from Holland. He is pretty good at work and is in lower remove.

When you get to London will you send me some Queensborough relief nibs or ordinary relief nibs. Will you please have Pussey down to London to meet me when I go home. Also I should like my roller skates down in London as I am going to practice roller skating next hols.

I should like to have a time machine to go and see the end of the world when 'the heavens would roll together like a burning parchment' and then come back again.

* * * * *

Will you send me a book called Micah Clarke. Could you send me a Mexican repeater pea-shooter they are awfully good things for ragging with. I and Grenfell could have splendid fun with them, you must pack it safely so that Doctor will not scent a rat. Could you get me some long brown field boots, as well as a new pair of ordinary ones. Will you ask them to order a refill for my electric torch at Vickery's mine is No 2.

* * * * *

Remember to get my new tweed trouser suit. I also want a new cover coat and pair of pumps and brown boots. I am seriously contemplating writing another story which I have called 'A Modern Joseph' all about a father and mother who beat their son, who ran away and eventually became a millionaire then he forgave his mother and father and treated them nicely and gave them money. Will you send some autographs of the Russian nobility, of you and of the Marlboroughs to me for a boy who collects [them]. It is true we don't come back until the Thursday after Easter and Alistair comes back long before Easter so you must take me back early.

* * * * *

What fun we will have at the exeat, especially if we go to Blenheim, I suppose we shall have tea and dinner in Neil's rooms after we come back from Blenheim. What a pity you could not have come down on [*sic*] Daddy's motor car. I suppose the Duke and Duchess of Marlborough will be at Blenheim. Mind you bring down plenty of gut with you as you will not be able to get it on Sunday in Oxford. I will give you a rough sketch of my favourite things: Newgar, chocolate caramels, caramels, marquis chocolate, barley sugar, walnuts, roast chestnuts, assorted sweats. Thanks for the autographs.

* * * * *

Doctor told me that you had to go off to some place to drink waters, so that you won't be back for my exeat till about a week later, all right. Next holidays will you get me some of those collars, which are like Eaton collars but stick up much more. Like most of the masters wear, they are so nice and smart. Also will you get me some white *buckskin*

64. (*opposite*) Geordie's mother taking the waters.

Summer Fields
Oxford.

Darling Mummy.

I hope you are quite well Doctor told me that you had to go off to some place to drink waters, so that you wont be back for my exeat till about a week later, all right. Next holidays will you get me some of those collars, which are like Eton collars but stick up much more. Like most of the masters wear, they are so nice and smart. also will you get me some white buckskin, (not canvas) shoes or boots with india-rubber soles - really smart. also a coat & waistcoat of white flannel to match my white flannel trousers. Also some new & smartly coloured & variegated neck ties. At my exeat I'll have tea in Mr Mayhew's rooms in New College. Please have Nanny up to Dunrobin or Lilleshall next holidays She said she wanted to come awfuly.

I am sending to Jamie to have Rosemary's bike up at Lilleshall next holidays for me to teach her to ride. I should like from you I think as a birthday present a really smart tie pin. I am going to ask Daddy to give me a small shot-gun.

Goodbye
from your
Loving. Geordie

You drinking the waters and then spitting them out again because they taste so nasty.

(not canvas) shoes or boots with india-rubber soles – really smart. Also a coat and waistcoat of white flannel to match my white flannel trousers. Also some new and smartly coloured and variegated neckties. At my exeat let's have tea in Mr Mayhew's rooms in New College. *Please* have Nanny up to Dunrobin or Lilleshall next holidays she said she wanted to come awfully. I am sending to Jamie to have Rosemary's bike up at Lilleshall next holidays for me to teach her to ride. I should like from you *I think* as a birthday present a really smart tie-pin. I am going to ask Daddy to give me a small shot gun.

Goodbye

from Your Loving
Geordie

The informal side to school life should not give a false impression. Discipline was strict, genuinely spare time was almost unknown, and most boys lived in fairly constant fear of corporal punishment. None the less, by the lights of those times, it was probably a happy community and one with a sense of achievement. Though some boys have written in later life of too academic a grind and too unbending a regime, several clearly have the happiest memories of their time here. A. D. Finney (1903–6) recalls the teas on the lawn, from where one could watch the cricket, and crawling down a hay-tunnel at the Hay Feast, which was called in the ingenuous punning of the day 'Sampling the Simplon'. He also calls Dr Williams 'the best of teachers' and remembers his wife's reading to the little boys, and the particular thrill of being saluted by Bear, who would come up to one without a word and touch his hat in a significant manner, which meant that one had been awarded one's First XI colours.

In the summer of 1914 the school celebrated its Golden Jubilee. A special service in Chapel, still awaiting its final three stained-glass windows from the studio of Henry Holiday, was held in the morning; Mabel Williams, whose muse was never silent for long, wrote a hymn for the occasion; the chancel was decked out with masses of scarlet and white geraniums; and a host of parents and OSS flocked to the school to help celebrate the day. Telegrams of congratulation were sent by those who could not be present, including the Captain of the Boats and twenty-three Collegers at Eton. Both before and after lunch, under a now glorious June sky, the Fathers and Sons cricket match proceeded, accompanied at intervals by the strains of a brass band. As the evening shadows lengthened, a short Evensong in Chapel concluded a happy and successful day.

But at the same time, other shadows were lengthening over Europe ...

65. Plaque showing the dedication of the Chapel in memory of Mrs Maclaren, 1896.

(a) The windows, 1896–1916

The stained-glass windows in the Chapel are all the work of one artist, Henry Holiday (1839–1927), a disciple of Burne-Jones, famous in his time for his paintings of Dante and Beatrice and various Old Testament subjects. The East Window is contemporaneous with the building of the Chapel and, like it, is dedicated to the foundress. Its four main lights depict William of Wykeham, St Monica, St Catherine with her wheel, and Erasmus. These were presumably chosen by Dr Williams, the suitability of the outer two being more immediately obvious than that of the ladies. Patrick Savage has observed a nice mnemonic for their order in that each name follows on from the last letters of its predecessor: WILLIAMONICATHERINERASMUS. The upper and lower sections of each light contain swathes of indeterminate vegetation, which have been criticized as looking like cauliflowers. The central upper light is occupied by Eunice and Timothy, and on either side are angels proclaiming 'Hear the words of the wise: apply thine heart unto my knowledge.' The inscription along the foot of the window contains a visible correction in the Latin, where *'In piam memorium'* has had its *u* amended to *a*.

66. Henry Holiday; photograph reproduced by kind permission from the collection of Mr Jeremy Maas.

Two single-light windows were removed from the Choir, when the vestry and the organ were shifted from its northern to its southern side in 1984 to make way for the Changing-Rooms. It is perhaps sad that this pair (HOPE and LOVE) is least seen now, for they are particularly characteristic of the genre. They now adorn a small side-chapel, and a nice touch upon their removal was the creation of a kneeler embroidered with FAITH, thus completing the trinity. HOPE was presented by Dr Freeborn in memory of Mrs Maclaren, whose Christian names are here transposed for no obvious reason; and LOVE is a memorial to Mary Anne Branscombe, Mrs' cousin who died two weeks before her and was buried in the same grave as her and her husband.

The windows in the body of the Chapel span the years 1900–15. The earliest is a memorial to Edward Horace Percival, who died aged fourteen in March 1900. It depicts a boy giving alms to a beggar, and the boy is reputed to be modelled on Percival. Next to him on the south wall is a soldier in armour (decorative rather than practical) with angels protecting him in the thick of the fray, presented by his loving mother in grateful thanks for the safe return of her son G. H. B[arnett] from two African campaigns. The warm, dark colours in this and the fourth window contrast with the pale, cold whites and greens of the third, which shows the same soldier being armed ('Put on the whole armour of God'), this being erected in memory of the dead at home and at war by staff, comrades and friends in 1908. The last window on the south side is a thank-offering from Doctor to God for benefits bestowed. It shows three figures in long draperies, with flames licking round them; its superscription is 'O All Ye Works of the Lord, Bless Ye the Lord', the Song of the Three Holy Children in the Burning Fiery Furnace.

67. Love, by Henry Holiday, in memory of Mary Anne Branscombe, 1896.

68. The Percival Window, by Henry Holiday, 1900.

On the north side, the first two windows both commemorate the early deaths of Summer Fields pupils. Holiday obviously had the plan for the whole wall in his mind because, though the windows were inserted from east to west, the events that they depict in the life of Christ go, more naturally and comprehensibly, from west to east, i.e. left to right. These events are: 1. the stable scene, with Joseph, Virgin and Child; 2. the Presentation in the Temple, with the *Nunc Dimittis*; 3. the Flight into Egypt; 4. 'The Child grew and waxed strong' in the house at Nazareth with Joseph carpentering in the background; and 5. Christ in the Temple ('Wist ye not that I must be about my Father's business?'). This window commemorates Theodore Meyer, who died in 1910 aged twelve under strange circumstances. He was sitting on the lockers in a crowded New Room and somehow got the cord for opening a window round his neck and was asphyxiated by it. Next to him is the window to Tom Coventon (1903–13) who died when he developed pneumonia on top of measles. The remaining three windows are those described in Chapter 4 (page 80), the Flight into Egypt being the long-unpaid Etonian offering, the Presentation the Wykehamist one, and the Nativity presented by pupils and parents to the greater glory of God and in memory of the foundress. So the wheel went full circle in a sense.

The large, clear west window exists no more, as the Gallery and Common Room were added to the west end in 1980.

(b) The Organ

The organ was installed in the summer of 1900, after the vestry had been extended to make room for it. It was made by 'Father' Willis, the leading organ-maker of the last century. He was chosen to build the great organ for the West End Gallery at the Great Exhibition (1851), which was later transplanted to Winchester Cathedral. Directly concerned during a career of more than half a century with the building or rebuilding of over 1,000 organs, he made those of several cathedrals, including Oxford. In 1878 he took his two sons, Vincent and Henry, into partnership; so he came to be known as Father Willis, as opposed to his sons, who continued the business after his death in 1901.

He was busily involved in his work until the end. He was always a scientific builder, and his organs are distinguished for their excellent engineering, clever contrivances and first-rate workmanship, as much as for their brilliance, force of tone and orchestral character. The SF magazine of August 1900 pays a backhanded compliment: 'The New Organ comes up to our highest expectations. We hear that Mr Willis, the builder, was so pleased with its tone, when it was finished and put together in his studio, that he could scarcely bear to part with it. This may partly account for its late arrival.'

69 and 70. The Organ. Pumping the organ was a much-remembered feature in the life of many boys.

The 1984 rearrangement of the Chapel involved the dismantling and rebuilding of the organ on the south side of the chancel. Its new site in fact does it more justice, giving the organist a better view of the proceedings in Chapel, and making the sound both louder and clearer. Visiting musicians exclaim with delight upon discovering so fine an organ in a school chapel; it is evidently a pleasure to play as well as to hear.

4

WAR AND ITS AFTERMATH
1914–20

THE war came with appalling suddenness. It was to affect every school in ways that left their mark in feelings and attitudes for years to come, and to produce a quantity of literature unparalleled by any other such event. In works like *Goodbye to All That* and *Journey's End* the step from the school parade-ground to the front-line trenches is a small and swift one, and so it was in fact. By December, more than 200 Summerfieldians were on active service, ten had already been killed, and fifteen wounded or taken prisoner. For the next five years every edition of the Magazine began with 'Our Roll of Honour', and several numbers after those were largely concerned with 'The War Memorial'. Very few were to go through the Great War without the loss of at least one close friend or relation. Both Doctor and Bear lost sons: Hilary Williams was killed at Loos in autumn 1915, and Geoffrey Alington a year later. He had, as we know, been involved with school plays before the war, and even during it he set and corrected Latin translations for Upper Shell from the trenches.

71. Hilary Williams, the Doctor's son who was killed in the War.

After the war, his brother Adrian wrote a novel, *Chaytor's*, which is substantially based on Summer Fields. The setting by the sea is more St Leonards than Oxford, but there are recognizable portraits of Mrs Maclaren, Crofts and Penny, and the central character, William Chaytor, is a composite of the Doctor and the Bear, though made physically different from either of them. The moment when he hears of his son's death at the front is based upon their experiences.

It was just before chapel ... that the second telegram was brought to William Chaytor. He sat for a long time, staring at the envelope in a stupid, frozen sort of way. He knew well enough whence this telegram came, for it was addressed with unnecessary completeness:

'Rev. E. W. Chaytor, M.A., Rambling Hall, St. Anthony's Bay.'

Only wounded perhaps. Maybe just a slight wound, serious enough to bring him home out of that hell of France, to make him safe. Oh, God, let him only be wounded. Even if he were to lose an arm, or a leg – that he could bear, that would be reasonable. But not – not John.

The words 'Killed in Action' seemed to leap at him out of the pencilled message. There were other words, too, filling out the formula. Deeply regret. Capt. J. Chaytor. That meant John, didn't it? John, who was never going to walk cheerily into his study any more, John who would never rule now over Rambling Hall. Deeply regret.

He sat there with the telegram in his hand, and presently his lips moved, and he began to mumble like an old man.

'John, John.'

The bell rang for chapel, but he did not move. The sound increased his anger. To go into the chapel, which he had built, to offer praises to the God who had done this to him. That was a bit too much to expect.

It was Tomlinson who presently came in to call him.

'The chapel bell has gone, Chief. Hope I – ?'

He left the question unfinished, for he caught sight suddenly of William Chaytor's face. And then his gaze travelled to the orange envelope lying on the writing-table.

'Chapel?' said William Chaytor. 'Don't go, Tomlinson. It's a trick. It's – '

And after that, it seemed, he could say no more.

Some strange and very terrible moments followed. William Chaytor got to his feet, erect to all his great height, and it seemed to Tomlinson that he strove to speak. But no words came, only a thick, incoherent gurgling in his throat very dreadful to hear. Tomlinson, looking at his face, saw that it was distorted so that it was almost unrecognizable. The mumbling mouth sagged horribly. In the eyes which looked into his was an expression Tomlinson had never seen before, a look of wild fear and appeal.

And then all at once, as though he had wrestled with and fought off an invisible enemy, William Chaytor was himself again. With a deliberate movement he squared his shoulders.

'Chapel,' he said, his voice almost normal, 'I will come.'

'No, let me read prayers,' Tomlinson protested. 'I'm afraid you've had bad news.'

'John is killed.'

'God. Chief, I'm sorry.'

William Chaytor seemed not to hear.

'The school must go on,' he said. 'John didn't give way. Chapel.'

With Tomlinson following, he walked out into the passage.

William Chaytor read the service that night in an unfaltering voice. And while, at its end, the assembled school sang 'God save the King' he stood in his place straight as an iron rod.

Upon the following morning it was seen that the Chief had inscribed John's name with his own hand upon the Roll of Honour in the hall.

That may seem a melodramatic passage to include in a history, but they were melodramatic times. Nor does Adrian Alington exaggerate. Here is a description of his father, Bear, written by another son, Bobs, who joined the staff in 1922:

72. Bear, 1917.

He was the most conventional of men. He lived by the values and standards of the mid-Victorian middle classes. He was also the simplest of men. His religion was that of a child. He had an acute sense of sin, and was convinced, I think, that he was bound for the everlasting flames. In old age he used to go to a special Communion service for the aged, when he would repeat aloud very slowly the whole service at the same time as the priest (who always waited for him to catch up). During the Confession his voice was blurred with sobs.

His values, too, were straightforward and unsophisticated. He believed unreservedly in the ten commandments, the British Empire, the Conservative Party, the importance of the Classics and all forms of outdoor sport, and in anything traditionally venerated, such as Beethoven, Shakespeare and the Parthenon. He abominated Cambridge, Roman Catholics, Socialists, the Germans (after 1914) and all aspects of modernity. He was frightened of the telephone, poverty, overdrafts, contemporary literature, social functions and foreigners. For him the Wogs began well before Calais.

He was painfully inarticulate and shy. In the early days of his marriage he was reluctantly taken out 'calling' in North Oxford. Moving uncertainly among the drawing-room clutter and knick-knackery, he knocked over a small table laden with plates of bread and butter and cakes. 'Awfully sorry,' he growled, stepped back in horror and knocked over another table of tea-cups which had just been poured out. He never went calling again. He had a terror of any demonstration of emotion and, like so many who bottle up their feelings, he was intensely emotional. Just occasionally, as in 1916 when he received the telegram from the War Office with the news that his eldest son had been killed, emotion burst its barriers with results that were agonizing for him and everyone else.

Inevitably, the younger men were 'called to the colours' and the staff that was left soon consisted of the elderly or 'crocks'. Apart from Doctor and Bear, there were Crofts, Evans, Penny, Smyth and the Miss Hills. Case provided a slightly more youthful element, together with some birds of passage: G. W. S. Alington stayed for four terms before joining up in July 1917. He was killed just over a year later, two days before the Armistice was signed. L. A. G. Strong came while still up at Wadham in 1917; after the war, he finished his course and then returned to the permanent staff, remaining on it until he left for a full-time literary career in 1930. His autobiography, *Green Memory*, includes a number of brilliant pen-portraits of the major characters at that time at Summer Fields, which make it worth quoting from at length. As an undergraduate, Strong had put his name down on a list of those willing to take on the civilian work of men who had been called up.

News of a vacancy came quite soon. A preparatory school in North Oxford, Summer Fields, had lost a member of its staff, and wanted to replace him. My name was next on the list, and I was invited to tea by the headmaster and his wife. Dr Williams, venerable and benign in appearance, had a trick of looking past one as he spoke. I felt no contact with him, but his wife, who blinked rapidly through thick lenses, seemed more accessible. Halfway through the meal, I saw him direct a glance of enquiry at her. She nodded, whereupon he suggested that I should come into residence in September. Both sped me on my way with friendly assurances, the Doctor becoming paternal and patting my arm.

Two interesting footnotes to Strong's comments upon Doctor. In the numerous photographs which we have of him, hardly ever does he look directly at the camera. His daughter Kitty believed that his judgement of grown-ups' characters was not as sound as her mother's, whom he used to consult about everything.

When Strong joined the staff in September, he felt very much on his own, but was soon befriended by Case, Cyril Williams and Lysaght.

Another member of the staff had turned up early, in order to discuss with the headmaster's son the score of an operetta they planned to produce before Christmas [*Ever Afterwards*].

Cyril Williams, then just over thirty, had written the libretto, and his colleague had composed the music. Taking pity on my loneliness, and finding that I was interested in such things, they asked me to come to the composer's room while he played over his settings for various songs. Thus I met W. S. Case, who was for a few years one of my closest friends.

Then, at dinner, my next-door neighbour engaged me in conversation and won from me a regard which never wavered. J. A. C. Lysaght was revealed as a clergyman by his collar, though he wore it only on official occasions. He realized how forlorn a boy of twenty-one would be feeling, and set himself to put me at my ease. This was typical. In all the years I knew him, I never had from him anything but kindness, never once saw him out of temper, never heard him complain.

Certainly, as I looked round the table, I needed reassurance. Dr Williams, smooth, suave, of benign and slightly foxy appearance, was well on in his sixties. His second in command, the Rev. E. H. Alington, could not have been much younger. A white moustache and a fuzz of white hair sat rather oddly, as if the wind had blown them there, on the indeterminate features with the round, protuberant eyes. Extreme shyness made him gruff, and, as I soon found out, extreme nervous irritability caused him to fly into rages which contradicted the basic gentleness of his nature, and earned him the nickname of Bear from generations of terrified schoolboys.

The senior assistant master, J. F. Crofts, lean, with a grizzled beard and rheumy eyes, must also have been well in his sixties. Next came one Evans, an Irishman who taught French in a broad Dublin accent, and whose little moustache and beard called for a beret on top of his round bald head to set him on the banks of the Seine. Affable, and learned in an odd, haphazard way, he played obsequious second fiddle to Crofts, thrust his face forward for conversation until it was a few inches from one's own, coughed with his tongue out, and was known to the boys as Bam, a monosyllable of obscure derivation which, like most school nicknames, perfectly suited his appearance and personality.

74. William Sterndale Case.

There was another Irishman on the staff, Cecil Smyth. Aged round about fifty, he was of insignificant but slightly horsy appearance, had a smoker's cough, and made no secret of his contempt for those above him. He lived in the furthest outhouse, by the very gates of the entrance drive, and dissociated himself as far as possible from the social life of the school. I received from him, once his preliminary shyness and mine had thawed, a great deal of shrewd advice on teaching, and much brusque kindness.

Of all these the strongest personality was that of Case. Trained for the profession of music in England and Germany, Case worked first on the staff of *Literature*, a periodical which died in the early nineteen hundreds, and then as assistant music critic on *The Times*. He reviewed, he wrote verse, he composed, and then, finding the late hours of musical journalism bad for his digestion, he took up schoolmastering. He was also a fine cricketer, playing for the Authentics and I Zingari. In all he did, he was handicapped by heart trouble. It was not so bad as to debar him from leading a reasonably active life, but he needed to take care; and the objectivity with which he followed his régimes, never considering for an instant what anybody would say or think, added to the aura of oddity which hung about him. He had no self-consciousness, and would gambol with the smaller boys in a way that sometimes excited the derision of the older; but no one took liberties with him, for, if provoked, he could command sarcasm of a kind no boy can stand up to.

73. (*opposite*) F. P. Penny (standing) and J. F. Crofts, both archetypal schoolmasters in their different ways and both to some extent models for characters in Adrian Alington's novel, *Chaytor's*.

During my first two years at Summer Fields, while I got to know him fairly well, I never reached the intimacy which came after the war when other young men joined the staff, the reign of the greybeards was broken, and Case came out triumphantly on the side of youth. But my respect for him grew steadily. Secure in his position, or never for a moment fearing that any danger could threaten it, he said things to the Doctor which not even Crofts or Bam dared say. Mrs Williams was fond of him, and he could always make her laugh; and the Doctor, who possessed the shrewdest of business brains, knew perfectly well that he could not get anybody else to do the work Case did, and play the organ, and train the choir, for anything like the salary he was paying this man-of-all-work. As a result, he put up with things from Case which would have got anyone else the sack.

One morning at breakfast the Doctor gave out in his best Mount Sinai manner that we were no longer to help boys with their prep. It was not fair, he said, that, when two boys were puzzling how to do something, one should ask the master on duty, and so have an unfair advantage of the other. Case leaned forward in protest.

'Oh, my dear Doctor! Surely prep is inhuman enough already, without depriving it of one of its few amenities, a conversation between a master and a boy.'

The Doctor's jowl became crimson, and he gobbled like a turkey.

'Whatever improvement anybody puts forward, there is always some silly ass to oppose it.'

White with rage, Case took a helping of marmalade.

'Bloody old fool!'

There was a horrified silence. The Doctor heard the comment, but even in this extremity he had the sense not to precipitate a scene which could only end to his disadvantage.

It was otherwise with the rest of the staff. When, at a masters' meeting, he suggested something which traversed Bam's domain, the Irishman began to demur.

'Well, Evans,' the Doctor told him icily, 'if you don't like it, you have your own remedy.' And Bam subsided.

This incident used to be related afterwards with great joy by another of the senior staff. Frederick Prescott Penny, Ping-Pong to his pupils, was a little, active, dry, spare man with a moustache which jutted out whenever he was indignant or incommoded. 'Make an effort, boy! Make an effort!' He sang tenor in the choir, voted Tory, and could be relied on to take the conventional view of any topic. Agreeable, kind-hearted, a small martinet, he taught in a series of clichés which boys quickly learned and afterwards remembered with affection. When I first arrived, he was overshadowed, both by Crofts, whom he deferred to, and by Bam, whom he disliked. After the war, the vigorous leg-pulling of the younger man relaxed his tension, and he was revealed as a delightful, if limited, person whom an authoritarian régime had hardened.

Most of the staff at Summer Fields had been there a long time, and the discipline was rigid to the point of harshness. Beatings were common, and the high standard of classical scholarship derived almost as much from fear as it did from the system of teaching. The system had been thought out by a mind which, having experienced great difficulty in its own youth, understood all too well the errors into which young minds were likely to fall, and ensured against them. Before attempting to translate any sentence of Latin or Greek, the boys were taught to bracket off all subordinate clauses, to underline all words that went together, and mark the mood and tense of every verb. This method, while it guarded against enthusiasm and carelessness, tended to produce anxious and pedestrian translation. But it paid. Scholarships at Eton and Winchester fell regularly to these well-drilled aspirants. I do not mean that the aspirants were not highly intelligent. It was the combination of intelligence with accuracy that made the Summer Fields attack so deadly.

But, despite the war, the agedness of the staff and the rigid discipline, there were lighter aspects. Pidcock and Slater evacuated Bramcote from Scarborough, where the school had come under dramatic bombardment from German warships, to Bradfield; and so the two schools, normally 200 miles apart, were able to play matches against each other. Even after they had both been called up, these two masters managed to revisit their old school from time to time. The concerts continued in the Michaelmas terms, until replaced by the musicals of Case and Cyril Williams. A less tuneful note was sounded by the lobby bell which, in December 1915, developed a serious crack from overwork – not surprising if, as was believed, it had been ringing for fifty years! It was replaced in the following month, but its passing was marked with a sonnet in the Magazine, possibly not from the ever-ready pen of Mabel Williams, for her offerings were usually initialled, though the style is very similar to hers.

VALE!

Full fifty years thine iron tongue hath swayed
  Our comings and our goings. At thy call
  We flocked to Chapel, schoolroom, dining-hall,
Rose, and retired to rest, ate, worked, and played;
For every pleasure sought thy ready aid.
  And only Time, who all things, great and small,
  Alike devoureth, could have wrought thy fall,
Brave Bell! and claimed thee in thy sixth decade.

A stranger now, with unfamiliar ring,
  Thy place usurpeth. All unmeaningly
  Its echoes smite our ears; we pause, and sigh
To hear no more thy kindly summoning.
  Tout lasse, tout casse, tout passe. Old friend, good-bye!
We better could have spared a better thing.

In 1915 the final three stained-glass windows completed the set by Henry Holiday in the Chapel. 'The middle light, presented by Wykehamists alone, is considered by our art critic as the most admirable of the three. The Eton window (on the right) has nothing like been paid for yet ... We hate begging, yet we think that if every Eton Colleger, past or present, who has not as yet subscribed would send only half a guinea, the matter would be ended.' The Doctor was a shrewd businessman, as Strong pointed out, and the response to his appeal paid not only for the window but for oak choir-stalls which he had set his heart upon and which were in place by January 1917. Later in the year Hilary Evelyn à Beckett Williams, grandson of the Doctor, was christened in Chapel.

And, of course, games continued and matches were played, though sometimes the fixture list was curtailed by war or weather. In the Jubilee summer of 1914 had occurred the notorious Horris Hill match, in which each side contained a future England player, we having G. O. B. Allen and they D. R. Jardine. Summer Fields, fearing a defeat might ruin their record, batted for most of the afternoon under instructions from Bear. Jardine took seven wickets and caught an eighth, but Summer Fields stuck there doggedly, none more so than Christopher Hollis, who made 17 in two hours. Horris Hill were left nothing like enough time to make the 113 needed for victory after our token declaration at 112 for 9. In the event, they made 19 for 2 and Jardine left the field in tears. Not a very glorious business, and not the last time in prep school history that such an unsporting declaration has been made.

Another sporting contretemps took place at the end of the war: not involving Summer Fields directly, but concerning our most distinguished athlete Jim Pitman, who was victor ludorum here in 1914 and 1915 before going on to Eton, where he soon started to win things too. In 1918 he carried all before him, and his house (Brinton's) won the athletics cup for the third consecutive year and by a comfortable margin. Clearly in 1919 they were likely to repeat this achievement and by an even wider margin; but then the Athletic Committee stepped in. They decreed in February 1919 that nobody who had won an event in the past could compete again in that event. There was an immediate and prolonged outcry: letters to the *Chronicle* from Etonians and beaks were soon followed by protests from London:

DEAR SIR – I have read with much interest a letter which appeared in *The Times* to-day, and which I understand is a copy of one which was published in the *Chronicle* with reference to the new regulation – that a boy who had won an athletic event one year may not compete in that event in the following year.

My father presented the 'Victor Ludorum' Cup to the School and I am sure if he were alive today he could have written asking that such a ruling be reconsidered. It was presented with the object of being held by the best athlete ...

75. The Pitman brothers, with an assortment of cups that they won at Eton. This picture has long hung in the Pavilion, which may account for its poor state of preservation.

Below this letter appeared the Editor's 'This correspondence must now cease', and the athletics events were duly held. Brinton's still won with ease, totalling 177 points, nearly a hundred more than the next house; Pitman, ousted from his best events, still managed to be within eight points of the victor ludorum, winning the steeplechase, long jump and hammer. Towards the end of November, a bleak little paragraph appeared in the *Chronicle*:

Athletics: Since the undermentioned rule, passed by the Athletic Committee on Sunday, February 2, 1919, has not achieved the purpose for which it was drawn up, the Athletic Committee have decided that from henceforward it shall be considered null and void...

and then, for the last time, they printed the notorious rule: it had had a life of ten months. And what had been the purpose for which it was drawn up? Merely to prevent Brinton's from winning the cup for the fourth year? Presumably so; and it was unfortunate for Pitman that he was the sufferer from so dubious an aim. Still, both he and his brother C. E. Pitman covered themselves with glory at Eton and subsequently. Jim represented Oxford at athletics, skiing and rugger, in which he also played at international level; he was a director of the bank of England,

and later MP for Bath. He was an ardent campaigner for the Initial Teaching Alphabet, which his family's firm promoted with some success during the 1960s.

At the end of the Great War, 'Gubby' Allen was also making his mark on a wider cricketing scene, and in 1919 he 'stopped the rot in Eton's second innings at Lord's and made the match secure'. In the same month Kitty Williams married E. Kenneth Barber, with Messrs J. F. Evans, A. R. and A. F. Alington as groomsmen, a Summer Fields choir and W. S. Case playing the organ. John Evans had returned before the end of the Summer Term, and others came back in September. As well as EKB, there were the Hon. Bryan Buckley OS, who taught for seven years here before becoming a partner at Rose Hill, Banstead, serving on many educational committees in the House of Lords and editing the IAPS magazine, *Preparatory Schools Review*; and Geoffrey Bolton, who was to be part of Summer Fields for more than forty years as assistant master, partner, assistant headmaster and finally headmaster. While recording these arrivals and some departures, the Magazine

76. The wedding of Ken Barber and Kitty Williams, 1919: the bride and groom driving away from the side of the school towards Front Lodge. This photograph was presumably taken from an upper window of Old Lodge.

permitted itself the pious hope: 'Mr Lysaght will still be staying on as one of the regular staff for some time longer, we trust.' He did – for thirty years.

An arrival not recorded in the Magazine was that of Charlie Simms, who, starting as a houseboy in 1918 at the age of fifteen, worked for a wage of 6*s* (30*p*) seven days a week, with three hours off on Thursdays. He then graduated to assistant groundsman under Charlie Fathers and worked in the gardens and fields until 1966. Both Charlies mowed the playing-fields using the famous 'Potted Meat' horse; only the two nearer fields would be mown, and the rest left for hay. When he began to find outdoor work rather too much for him, he moved to the kitchen, where he worked until 1983. He died in 1986, having had the longest working career in the school's history, and one that spanned more than half the school's own life.

Another notable character behind the scenes at this time was the saintly Oxford figure of 'Codfish' Whiting, sometime masseur to Queen Victoria and vividly remembered by many generations of Summerfieldians. When he first came to massage the boys is not recorded, but he retired in 1933, and died in the

77. The Potted Meat Horse, Charlie Fathers at the helm.

following year. He was popular not only for the physical relief that he gave to the injured, but also for the amazing stories that he told during these sessions, especially ghost stories. A genius as well as a saint, he was unfortunately very deaf, and is reputed on one occasion to have been discovered with Margaret Alington in the Mayfield drawing-room, where they had both been talking for a while without either realizing that the other was unable to hear a word of their conversation!

The question of what should make a fitting war memorial for the school's 139 dead exercised the authorities for some time. Memorial brasses were erected on the west wall of the Chapel and dedicated by the Headmaster of Eton, Dr C. A. Alington, 'in proud and loving memory of those Boys and Masters of Summer Fields who gave their lives for God, their King and Country in the Great War (1914–19)'. But what should be done with the rest of the money subscribed? In 1920 the favoured solution was a swimming-bath 'with dimensions of about 50 feet in length and 36 feet in breadth ... An excellent site is ready in our own grounds, at the top of the Drive, and within 100 yards of the School-house, in a position absolutely ideal for the supplying and emptying of the water. Nothing need hinder us now except the cost ... probably nearer £3,000 than £2,000, and this of course puts it definitely out of court, unless indeed some father, to whom money is of little importance, would present it to the school and have it named after his son.'

Nobody rose to the Doctor's bait, and in 1921 a compromise solution of fives courts was adopted; but the cost of materials and labour again proved a difficulty. In the end, it was decided to convert the existing courts. It was an unsatisfactory arrangement, and made worse by some muddled thinking, as GB records in his *Recollections of Summer Fields*: he and Bryan Buckley, the two masters who were well versed in Eton fives, had their heads bitten off when they demurred at the hybrid designs on which the Doctor seemed intent. Within a few years, the courts became virtually unplayable, and they simply mouldered away for two more decades. More successful was the Second Game Pavilion, upon which some of the residue was spent; the rest went towards two panels for the Chapel representing the Archangels Michael and Raphael as depicted in Perugino's celebrated altar-piece. Regrettably and mysteriously, these disappeared in the 1970s, when new brooms were sweeping the chapel perhaps a little too clean.

During the Great War there were many boys who were to become distinguished in later life. John Maud, as Lord Redcliffe Maud, was Master of University College, Oxford, after an outstanding academic, political and diplomatic career; and Roger Mynors was Professor of Latin at both Oxford and Cambridge. Equally notable was Harold Caccia who, after a career in the Foreign Office culminating as HM Ambassador to the USA, became the Provost of Eton,

78. (*top*) The Fives Courts, which never really worked.

79. (*centre*) Second game Pavilion, part of the War Memorial.

80. (*bottom*) The Perugino Triptych, St Michael on the left, Tobias and the Angel (Raphael) on the right.

81. (*below*) Harold Caccia, at his installation as Provost of Eton.

82. An early Pasmore, done while the artist was at Summer Fields.

where this generation of OSS also provided several masters, such as Richard Martineau and Fred Coleridge, who was later Vice-Provost. The navy was represented by Admirals Sir William Davis (later one of the school's first governors) and Sir Robin Durnford Slater, whose younger brother John had a supreme wartime record as the first commando, operating all over Europe between 1940 and 1945, when he laid down his arms to become a nursery-gardener, beating his bayonet into a pruning-hook. Another general of this vintage earned fame in Normandy and elsewhere, but later took up the peaceful palette: Cosmo Nevill, whose 1987 oil-painting of the school provides the dust-wrapper for this book. We also had professional artists in Victor Pasmore and John Spencer Churchill. Jasper More had a fine legal and economic career, and was for many years MP for Ludlow. Cuthbert Bardsley became a pillar of the Anglican Church as the Bishop of Coventry.

83. A report on Cuthbert Bardsley.

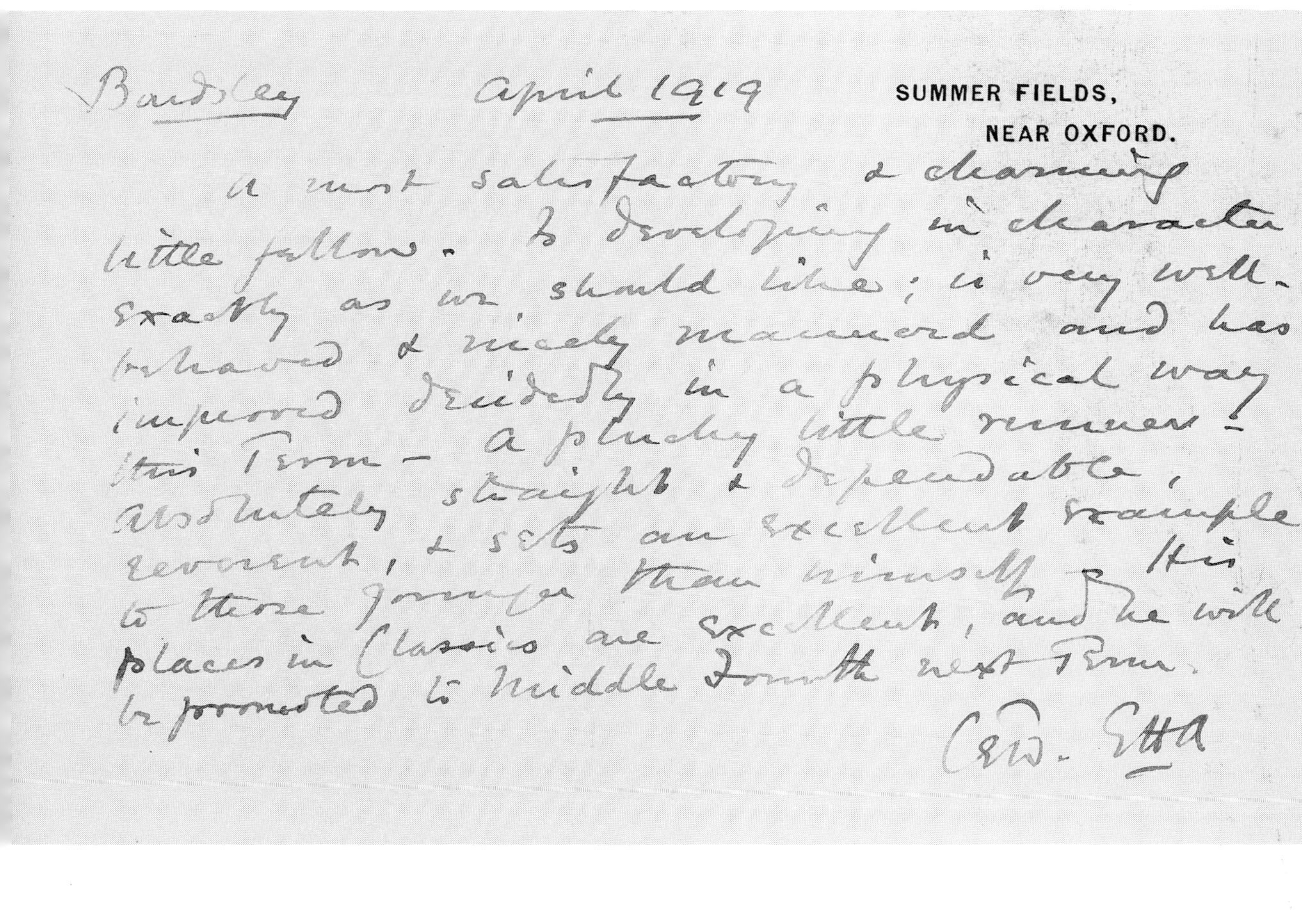

Bardsley April 1919

SUMMER FIELDS,
NEAR OXFORD.

A most satisfactory & charming little fellow. Is developing in character exactly as we should like; is very well-behaved & nicely mannered and has improved decidedly in a physical way this Term – a plucky little runner! Absolutely straight & dependable, reverent, & sets an excellent example to those younger than himself. His places in Classics are excellent, and he will be promoted to Middle Fourth next Term.

[illegible]

TWO VIEWS, 1907–10 AND 1918–22

Naturally, not all memories of Summer Fields are pleasant ones. Here are two contrasting views, separated by just over a decade, but a significant decade in which a cataclysmic war occurred, Dr Williams retired, and the new ideas and attitudes of the post-war young men began to appear. The first is the unhappy experience of Guy Boas, who went on to become a celebrated teacher himself as well as a gifted director of Shakespeare.

The Headmaster was the Rev. Dr. Eccles Williams, a Doctor of Divinity, whose talent for anticipating questions to be asked in Eton Scholarship papers amounted to genius. I liked my fellow pupils, and had I had any capacity for learning Greek irregular verbs or turning arid English sentences into correct Latin I might have enjoyed myself. But as I was totally unable to master Greek or Latin syntax, which seemed to me as dull as they were difficult, I was nothing but a problem: 'a thorn in his side', Dr Williams called me. Having examined my answers to a Latin examination paper, the Doctor announced that I 'made him feel sick' and that I didn't know the difference between right and wrong. I was also unable to spell, and the fact that in my Geometry paper I wrote that 'the size of an angel in no way depends upon the size of its arms' further added to the Doctor's indignation and sickness.

No doubt Summer Fields meant well, but in those days it regarded grammatical competence as the be-all and end-all of education, and if you could not construe Caesar and Xenophon – two of the dullest of the world's authors – you could not hope for salvation. When I wrote a mild poem on cricket which was accepted and printed in a current magazine, Dr Williams was both incredulous and vexed, and even when a peculiar kink which I somehow developed for doing Latin verses brought me to the head of the class, they wrote in my report that 'he came out first through no fault of his own.'

The partner of Dr Williams was the Rev. Hugh Alington, who taught Xenophon and the easier plays of Euripides ferociously with a cane. He also organized cricket and football with almost religious zeal and, though he was apt to treat an XI as pariahs if they lost a match, he inspired a kind of terrified devotion, and at an evening party which he gave shortly before I left I remember writing and reciting a poem in his honour, which he received in a mystified but not unappreciative silence. Mr Alington's younger son, whose experience of the school was no happier than my own, became in later years a gifted novelist, and his account of Summer Fields in *Chaytor's* was a first-rate and subtle psychological exposure of what was wrong as well as right with the place. The book contained a masterly study of the headmaster, which I am told both Dr Williams and Mr Alington read with delight, each thinking it to be a portrait of the other.

The medical supervision of the school as in the hands of a terrifying matron, who if one's draught was unpalatable was wont to hold one's nose while she administered it. She was assisted by a nurse in the infirmary, who, though in many ways kind, was apt to be formidable, and who was reputed to keep discipline when necessary by the application of a hairbrush.

The Summer Fields I knew was a school of its day. It was not unique, for Sir Osbert Sitwell in *The Scarlet Tree* describes just such another rich preparatory purgatory in the north, where he evidently suffered as I did. I feel sure that such schools are different now, and that the perpetual state of fear in which we seemed to live is a thing of the past ... [But] my experience of Summer Fields raises a question distinct from the particular nature of that school at that time. Is it right to send children away from home at all to boarding-schools at so young an age? Some it suits, but others it does not, and in acute cases the procedure amounts, however unintentionally, to cruelty.

That is from *A Teacher's Story*, by Guy Boas (Macmillan, London, 1963). Contrast it with this excerpt from the autobiography of the artist John Spencer Churchill, *Crowded Canvas* (Odhams, London, 1961).

I hate schools, but have quite pleasant memories of Summer Fields; everyone there was most considerate. To my mind, much as I dislike the boarding school system, it is better than any other. It forces boys to develop their characters in a way an ordinary day-school does not and cannot. They are pushed around a lot and taught to be independent, so that they quickly learn to tell everyone to go to hell. There is much to be said for it.

Summer Fields was rather a tough place and one had to stick up for oneself to survive. My nickname was 'Hedgehog' because of my unruly hair. They were trying days for me in that everyone was brilliant except J.S.C. I was stupid and artistic, befriending that now-famous painter, Victor Pasmore. Many of my contemporaries at Summer Fields have distinguished themselves. Name any profession and, as likely as not, one of my former school-friends has made his name in it. My closest friends were Charlie and Johnnie Max-Muller, sons of the British ambassador in Poland, and Michael and David, sons of Sir Reginald McKenna. To me, the McKenna boys were phenomenal. Both were able not only to play but sing Bach cantatas and fugues.

We were all elected to the school chapel choir, and this must have been the time when I started to become a 'lapsed' Catholic. Summer Fields was Protestant, and although I could have gone to a small Catholic chapel some distance away, I did not bother. I had inevitably got caught up with the school choir's 'Magnificat' and 'Nunc Dimittis'.

5

THE NEW YOUNG MEN
1920–27

BEAR ALINGTON took over officially as headmaster in July 1918, though the Doctor was to retain much of the financial control for a dozen years more. Cyril Williams, Doctor's surviving son, who had taught at St Leonards until the war and at Oxford thereafter, became Bear's partner. The average age of the staff dropped dramatically with the arrival, or return, of the young men: J. F. Evans, G. Bolton, the Hon B. B. Buckley O S, E. K. Barber and L. A. G. Strong, who came back after completing his Oxford degree in 1920, when Barber went to St Leonards.

At the end of that year 'Crab' Crofts retired after thirty-six years and presented a brass alms dish, which is still used in Chapel. Born in 1854, he had come as a stop-gap for a fortnight in 1883, a fine, tall figure of a man. But time grizzled his beard and added a stoop to his long thinness: in his latter years he seemed a rather daunting Methusaleh. At heart he was a kindly man, but the necessity (in his view) of keeping the boys on a tight rein had soured his temper. When his retirement had been announced, the boys presented him with a claret jug, and his voice nearly broke with emotion when he tried to express his thanks; but five minutes later, he was in full cry, blaring down the passage after some luckless boy who had left his room without permission. Whoever was on duty, Crab was in charge. He is believed never to have watched a match; what leisure he allowed himself, he spent in tending the garden at Cottage, which he had taken

84. A rare 'Playground' photograph. John Max-Muller is the boy talking to John Evans and Bryan Buckley.

on when the Gmelins departed in 1914, and which he passed on to John Evans.

He was replaced in January 1921 by Ralph W. G. Robinson, who had been educated at Haileybury and University College, Oxford, before serving in the war with great heroism in the Durham Light Infantry. In May 1918 he held a bridgehead on the Aisne for four hours, by his determination and leadership enabling 3,000 troops to cross the bridge in safety. After other battles, he was captured and made a prisoner of war on 27 May. For his valour he received the MC, leaving the army with the rank of captain; he then came to Summer Fields, where he was dubbed 'Rhino', presumably a comment on his rather large nose.

GB has left an account of the daily routine of the school as he found it upon arrival in 1919. The day started with Prayers in New Room before 7.45 Breakfast; at 8.40 one did 'physical jerks' with the form that one was going to take at 8.45. There were two periods of an hour before Break, which was 10.45–11.30, and two more after it. Lunch at 1.30 was followed by Games at about 2.30; afternoon school consisted of two more periods between 4 and 6 p.m. Tea was at 6 (the masters then dining in the Miss Hills' rooms, which were conveniently next to the Kitchen), Chapel at 7.10, and Prep from 7.30 to 8.30. Apart from Break and half-holidays, the only period of free time was that between Tea and Chapel. But to call it *free* time is perhaps a misnomer.

How did the boys employ this time? They jolly well sat at their desks like little gentlemen and read books (or learnt their grammar). Chess, bridge and ping-pong were not discouraged; but any form of ragging or running was, and any noise was punishable by entry in the Black Book. Often, as I sit in the Study [GB was writing in 1960] and listen to the noises off, I feel inclined to say 'O mihi praeteritos . . .!' – but who can unscramble an egg?

Sunday was in truth a day of penance, though the boys liked it because it was different from other days. Consider the programme:

Breakfast,	8.15.
Bible-reading,	9.10.
Letter-writing.	
Choir Practice,	10.20.
Chapel,	11.
Congregational Practice,	12.
Lunch,	1.
Walk,	2–3.
Sit at desks,	3–5.
Tea,	5.
Prep,	5.45.
Chapel,	7.

85. (*left*) It is hard to find a good picture of Rhino Robinson. He is absent from several school summer photographs, and in others tends to disguise himself in hats and dark glasses. This picture, taken by GB in 1922, shows him talking to Peter Findlay.

86. (*right*) Sunday morning costume in the 1920s. Eton collars and suits were still *de rigueur*, though some boys wore shorts with them.

On fine Sundays in the Summer (and for four glorious Sundays in September–October 1921), boys were allowed to sit in the field, the operative word being *sit*. Any breaking into a run was sternly checked by a bellow through the study megaphone; the production of a cricket ball would have involved 'six of the best'.

The cause of this was that Uncle Hugh [as the younger masters called Bear Alington] had been brought up in a really strict Victorian parsonage; what was right for him as a child must *ipso facto* be right for others. Some of us once suggested that Sundays would be made more tolerable if boys were allowed, say, to bowl in the nets. Uncle Hugh was deeply hurt by the suggestion and dismissed it out of hand. Once, on a wet Sunday, I asked if I might play my gramophone to the boys. This was allowed, but 'Don't make it too secular.'

An odd thing which I didn't discover for some time was that there was an unwritten tradition that no master was ever about in the field or in the boys' rooms unless he were on duty or playing in an official game. To us younger ones it seemed only natural to be about with the boys, playing chess or ping-pong with them, bowling to them or just talking to them. The older masters – except Case – looked askance at this innovation, and Crofts missed no opportunity of saying unpleasant things to the air in the hearing of the boys. But Uncle Hugh, though he seldom said much, approved with all his heart. He couldn't have done it himself, but, appearances notwithstanding, he really loved the boys and rejoiced at our interest in them.

G B's Sunday timetable compares interestingly with that of today, when a wide variety of occupation is offered, including sport: 'Grid League' football in winter and pick-up cricket matches in summer are available for those who aren't rehearsing for plays or choral concerts, or representing the school in tennis, squash, swimming or basketball matches. There is usually only one Chapel, either morning or evening, but letter-writing and a sort of prep still take place.

The year 1921 was a vintage one: a bumper crop of scholarships, with nine at Eton including John Lehmann's 1st and F. J. R. Coleridge's 2nd, and a good cricket season in a glorious summer. The war had changed certain things for good, including the received idea of a structured society (but that was going to take another war to underline the point); prep schools were slower to change, but the 1920s and 1930s were not without their minor revolutions. One of the revolutionaries was Bear's son Bobs (A. F. Alington, Marlborough and Magdalen), who joined the staff in 1922, filling the gap caused by the sad and sudden death of Case in the March of that year. His death was felt terribly by the whole school; a few words of G B's must stand for the many tributes paid to him:

It has often been said of schoolmasters that they can see but one point of view – their own – but never could such an accusation have been levelled at Case. Small wonder that he was greatly loved by the boys and that his influence with us young masters was considerable. His manners were exquisite and his conversation polished. Even when he was reducing us to helpless laughter, he would often let fall (perhaps unconsciously)

87. A young golfer (Kennedy Trevaskis) who seems to be aiming *across*, rather than along, the fairway.

words of wisdom whose value to us was inestimable, though we probably didn't realise it at the time.

He died very suddenly in 1922. On a Monday he was with us at coffee, obviously feeling unwell; by the Saturday he was dead from a clot of blood in the heart. As he was taken off to hospital, he said to someone, 'I hope this isn't the end.' In one sense it was, but not, surely, in any sense that matters.

G B, John Evans and L. A. G. Strong had the profoundest admiration for Case, and were desolated by his death. So, a few years later, it seemed natural to choose his name for one of the newly formed Leagues; thus, in the most literal sense, as well as on the simple brass plaque beyond the choir, 'His Name Liveth' and will do so as long as Summer Fields is a school.

The death of Case brought to an end the home-made musicals in which he had provided the music and Cyril Williams the book. There had been three of these: *Ever Afterwards* in 1917, *The Emerald* in 1919, and *Moonshine* in 1921. Much in the Gilbert and Sullivan tradition but having the advantage of being tailor-made for Summer Fields, they were greatly enjoyed by their casts and audiences. The accompanying programme and picture give a good idea of what they were like; the reverse of the programme carries the famous note: 'The Revolver in Act II

88 and 89. Programme and Picture of *The Emerald.*

…mmer Fields. November, 1919.

THE EMERALD,
(A FANTASY)
BY CYRIL ECCLES WILLIAMS.
MUSIC BY W. S. CASE
LYRICS BY M.W. AND W.S.C.

Dramatis Personae.

Iris (*the Princess*) - T. F. TIERNEY
Hepzibah (*her Old Nurse*) - G. A. H. PRATT
The Wicked Fairy - A. A. MARTINEAU
Percival, Reginald (*the Brigands*) - D. LOMAX, P. E. NATHAN
Peregrine (*the Prince*) - N. M. FORD
Aubyn, Garth (*his Knights*) - L. B. ALEXANDER, E. K. H. KARSLAKE
O. S. Toppit (*the Detective*) - H. C. LEWIS
The Sea Breezes:—
A. COBB, W. W. WILLIAMS, K. F. A. JOHNSTON, P. H. BAYNES, A. S. BIRKBECK, C. W. GOTT, J. D. A. LEWIS, C. J. SUMMERFORD, P. WILD, M. A. S. PEMBERTON, P. D. SANDBACH, J. W. G. BIRKBECK, G. D. CHAMIER, E. R. C. INGE, C. R. C. THURSFIELD, M. MCKENNA, C. H. D. WILD, J. S. B. NOBLE, and D. M. GLASBROOK.

SCENES.

INDUCTION, before the Curtain: *Invocation of the Emerald.*
ACT I., Scene 1. *Iris' Library on her Island Home.*
(The curtain falls for one minute to mark the lapse of a day.)
Scene 2. *The same.*
ACT II. *The Sea-Shore of the Mainland* (*some hours later*).

90. King Henry IV Part II, November 1925.

is not actually fired off.' The demise of these musicals marked the beginning of a long succession of Shakespeare productions which were as notable for the length of parts that some boys learned in remarkably short times as for the imagination and skill that went into their décor. The moving spirits behind this were Hermione Williams, Cyril's wife, and Gill Alington, a highly artistic young woman whom Bobs Alington married in 1923; this next generation of Alingtons ran Mayfield in the 20s and 30s.

The year 1923 was the only occasion on record when there was a 'tie' for top scholarship at Eton. 'Never before have two boys been bracketed first at Eton,' says the Magazine, 'and we are rather at a loss to understand why the examiners this time have broken with all precedent. Was it that they found it impossible to separate them and that they wished to do both equal honour and to show that they were appreciably ahead of the next boy on the list? At any rate, we are proud to think that they considered two Summer Fields boys worthy of this other "blue ribbon".' The boys concerned were Bernard Burrows, who went on to a distinguished diplomatic career with a knighthood and the embassy

Poems and Essays written at Summer Fields

THE CHERWELL

NYMPHA (*loquitur*):

Spirit of Youth, Spirit of Youth,
Why do you vanish away?
You stay for a moment,
Then you are gone:
Back to your toils, you say.

But why do you toil, Spirit of Youth?
Why, on a hot summer day,
When you might be free
'Neath the open sky,
Why toil, when you might be at play?

When you might be cooling your face in
my stream,
Cheering my sorrowful soul:
I am old, very old,
Spirit of Youth,
And my waters are heavy to roll.

Youth is beautiful, active, and strong,
Age is both sluggish and slow;
So pity me, Youth,
And love me, Youth,
And love the reeds that grow

Within my stream, and the Willow trees,
And love the forget-me-nots blue,
Those starry flowers,
That cover my banks;
And the Kingfishers, love them too.

These are my joys, Spirit of Youth:
These do I love; but before
All, your smile
And radiant face,
Spirit of Youth, I adore.

. . . . . . M.M.

91 and 92. Michael McKenna and his poem *The Cherwell.*

at Ankara, and Michael McKenna. He showed extreme promise throughout his early years: he was captain of the cricket XI and Head Prefect as well as winning top scholarship; he sang well, and W. B. Yeats commended his youthful poems when shown them by L. A. G. Strong, who said of him, 'Michael was brilliantly gifted in body, mind and spirit. Even as a small boy, he had a radiance which impressed everyone, including his contemporaries.'

But whom the gods love die young. Michael coruscated at Eton and did well at Cambridge, and one summer took a group of part-song singers to Sweden. On his return he seemed strained; at first this was put down to exhaustion after the taxing trip. But a nervous breakdown followed, and Michael went into a steady decline, from which he never recovered. Strong's theory is that he suffered from an inner conflict, originally induced by having a nurse who was one of the Plymouth Brethren, and something happened in Sweden which led to a crisis; this seems as near to a reasonable explanation as one is likely to come. A memorial volume was edited by Strong and Ralph Hodgson, and a copy was presented by Michael's mother, Pamela McKenna, to the school.

In the autumn of 1923, there were two lectures which deserve mention. One was by A. C. McLaren, the Lancashire and England cricketer, which included some 'fast and slow moving motion pictures' of Australian and MCC players in action – the first cinema show at the school, perhaps? There were to be plenty more before the decade was over. The other lecture was arranged by Lady Noble, mother of three Summerfieldians, and was given by Monsieur Coué, whose celebrated maxim, 'Every day in every way I'm getting better and better', was gaining a wide following. Though delayed by fog and so unable to 'give a demonstration of his methods', he outlined the principles of his teaching, speaking in English and avoiding any technical terms, so that even the youngest could understand his arguments. 'This great little man,' cooed the Magazine, 'with his humorously twinkling eyes and genial optimism, who carries his sixty-seven years so lightly, won all our hearts.'

Miss Peirce retired in July 1923, having been matron for more than a quarter of a century. Known by the nickname of 'Cussus' and formidably efficient though not lovable, she believed that boys should be brought up the hard way. If someone were really ill, there was nothing she would not do for him; but she required proof and was apt to regard castor oil as a panacea. At times her iron discipline overreached itself, and the words 'severely punished' were often on her lips.

She enjoyed harrying the young masters as well as the boys. Once she bade the novice GB take the boys for a walk; GB, 'cocking a mental snook', as he put it, replied that he had the Headmaster's orders to keep them indoors. She vanished into the Study and emerged triumphant a minute later with 'Mr Alington wishes you to take the boys for a walk.' Bam Evans would not kowtow to her and allegedly advised young masters to 'look out for that woman!' On one occasion when he was cornered by her and brought to bay, he turned upon her and in his heaviest brogue demolished her with 'Miss Peirce, I don't know what it is you want me to do, but I'll not do it.' She lived at Hastings for many years after her retirement. A difference of opinion with a bomb during the Second World War resulted of course in her victory, and no doubt she said that Hitler must be severely punished. She survived to see this order carried out and died at a great age. Her successor as matron was a Nurse Hayes who is remembered as being equally alarming but in a more modern and theatrical idiom; she left for Africa in 1927, pleased to go and not much mourned.

In 1924 two doyens of the teaching staff also departed: C. E. Smyth after twenty-seven years, and Bam (known as 'Mr Evans *ma*' since the arrival of JFE) after forty. Smyth had spent most of his life, boy and man, at Summer Fields, and of a brilliant band of classical teachers in those days he was probably the best. He was equally efficient as a coach and referee at soccer and, had horse-racing been included in the curriculum, he would certainly have taken the scholarship

93 and 94. Bam in old age, bicycling down Mayfield Road and joining in Fifth Game cricket.

form! He retired in order to look after his Irish estate, and died three years later. He was a man whom people instinctively liked and trusted, but few could have claimed to know him really well.

Small boys are remarkably observant in ways, but are also capable of blinding themselves to what is apparent to others. 'Bam' had a definite Irish tinge to his voice, yet more than one of his pupils genuinely believed him to be French, that being what he taught exclusively. He had a very good knowledge of English as well as French literature, and was an unusually quick reader. He boasted that he had read the whole of Thackeray's novels in one Easter holidays and the whole of Dickens in another. He lived at Newton, and tended the roses in its garden lovingly, an occupation which he was permitted to continue after his retirement, emerging by invitation to judge the boys' gardens in the summer. He died peacefully in September 1931, between the turning-on of his bath and the return to his room to shave.

His retirement in 1924 heralded the arrival on the staff of Roger Jacques. RAKJ was himself an Old Summerfieldian and was destined to play an important part in the school's life for the next fifteen years. So was 'Bobs' Alington, who now took over the teaching of French as well as continuing to produce Shakespeare plays, with assistance from his brother Adrian, who seems never to have been officially on the staff but had a *pied-à-terre* in Mayfield. Several of his novels were published with some success during the 1920s and 1930s, and *The Amazing Test Match Crime* was recently reissued in paperback, to no little delight of the present younger generation. Bobs also wrote and published novels under the *nom de plume* of Hugh Talbot. Indeed, several of the staff were getting into print at this time, LAGS with both poetry and novels, and GB with *Aids to French Composition*.

Roger Jacques took over the supervision of the boys' gardens in 1925. They had been started in 1914, when Mr Buckingham, who looked after the school farm, had ploughed a strip under the pine trees beyond Second Game (now Colts) Pavilion. This strip was divided into sixteen plots, each being the garden of two or three boys, and it was suggested that flowers should be grown in the front part, with radishes, lettuces and mustard and cress sown in the back bed. RAKJ used to buy seeds and boxes of plants from the Summertown greengrocer, Mr Morris, whom he remembers as always smiling and never too busy to help. In addition to this and his teaching, RAKJ was in charge of Old Lodge from 1925 until 1937, at times having eight boys sleeping there, and at other times four boys and another master who was variously C. H. Barnes and H. M. Mullins.

An event that took many by surprise in 1925 was F. P. Penny's marriage to a Miss Wicks. One day in the summer, the staff were at tea on the verandah when Penny appeared dragging a majestic figure behind him, a tug towing the *Queen Elizabeth*. He approached Margaret Alington, seized her ear-trumpet and shouted into it, 'This is my latest indiscretion: I've persuaded her to marry me.' Aunt Margaret took some time to digest the information, and, when she had finally understood it, she remarked, 'I don't believe it;' but it was true, and the remaining weeks of the term floated by on a stream of champagne. Every time anyone opened a bottle in Penny's honour, he retorted by opening bottles in

95. Old Lodge, with an extremely bosky Drive leading down to the playing fields.

everybody else's. The wedding took place in August, and Penny continued to teach for two more years until he had completed 100 terms. Then he retired perfectly content to a house nearby, where he died some twelve years later.

The year of this wedding also saw a 'crossword craze' in the school. GB, always one to capitalize on boyish enthusiasms, included one in the April Magazine: the art of crossword-setting was in its infancy, but he cleverly made the black squares form 'S. F.'. Another budding hobby was photography: J. H. Max-Muller and R. K. Kay started up a club, held competitions and wrote about it with gusto in the August issue. It was in fact a glorious summer, and the Hay Feast was said to have been the outstanding success of the term. It may well be this one that LAGS had in mind when he used the Hay Feast in one of his novels, *The Last Enemy* (1936). Here is an excerpt from Part II, Chapter 2.

The annual Hay Rag was the year's one period of licence, the Feast of Misrule. Immediately after afternoon school, everyone, boys and masters, trooped down to the large hayfield, in which the hay had been ready cut. There they divided into forms, and each, with the help of its form master, built itself a fort out of the hay. Half an hour was allowed for this, and then the whistle blew for tea. The whole assembly lined up and received each a paper bag containing food, and a mug. The boys carried theirs off to the fort, where they sat peacefully and consumed it; while the masters either had theirs on the edge of the field, or, if they were young and enthusiastic, they too took it to their fort, and, vociferously welcomed, sat down and ate with their form.

After tea, which was a protracted meal, the assembly paraded again for grace, and then rushed off for the real purpose of the day: the Hay Rag. This was a fight on the good old principle of all against all. It began as form against form, one defending its fort against another, a regular alternation of sorties, in which the masters joined; but in a very few minutes all trace of order was lost, the forts levelled to the ground, and everyone scrapped indiscriminately. Old scores were paid off, and masters in particular had a rough time. It was the one occasion when they could be hit or slapped or rolled in the hay with impunity. Except on the rarest occasions, there was no malice, and the thing remained a rag, with the greatest good temper on both sides; but woe betide a really unpopular man, or one who was convicted by public opinion. He would be

96. L. A. G. Strong at the Hay Feast.

the object of concerted attacks: his face would be mercilessly rubbed in the hay, and the shirt would be torn from his back.

The Rag lasted till everyone was tired out – then there was a much needed easy, the boys trooping for more drinks, the harassed masters pulling hayseeds from their skins and mopping themselves up a bit. After that came the races; and, last of all, a period of quiet, when everyone lay in the hay, and held a kind of informal singsong, before linking arms and going off in one huge line across the field and back to the school. In struggling bunches they made for the gate, each crowd trying to get through edgeways without loosening their linked arms.

Once in the large school playing field, they all made one enormous line, and, at a signal, advanced towards the school, where, in the distance, the white aprons of the maidservants glimmered from the lower windows, and the smallest boys of all, who had been packed off indoors before the end, were clustered at the windows of the dormitories.

'One man went to mow, went to mow a meadow,'

bawled the long advancing line; and, as the song progressed, and the list of persons and properties grew longer, the singers became more and more out of breath and out of time, till, by the time they had reached the lawn, the song was in chaos. The french windows opened, and the headmaster appeared, benign and smiling. 'God Save the King' was sung, and then the head boy stepped forward and gave three cheers for all the staff. The entire school lined up for biscuits and lemonade, and the exhausted masters made their way to their own small dining-room, where a cold meal awaited them.

That was written in the mid-1930s, but only a few details have changed in fifty years: we have a queen rather than a king, and we don't have maidservants in white aprons; but the feast itself is very much the same, though the school is now too large to make an informal sing-song practicable. And probably it was just the same a hundred years ago. How soon after the school's foundation did it start? Or did it simply evolve from an informal picnic in July to watch or help the haymakers on the farm?

At the beginning of 1926 the leagues came into existence. They were the brainchild of Bobs Alington, and their purpose was to provide some *esprit de corps*, which it was felt had been previously lacking. On the whole the innovation was popular, and usually since then competition in league matches has been as fierce as in those against other schools. The names chosen for the four leagues, which each had thirty boys, were: Case, in memory of WSC; Congreve, after Billy Congreve OS, VC; Moseley, after the most famous OS scientist; and Maclaren after the school's founders. It is apparently fortuitous that the names make such a neat pattern in their abbreviated forms: CA – CO – MA – MO. An attempt in the 1950s to introduce a fifth league, possibly to be called Wavell, received the 'thumbs down' from the boys. So the leagues continue each to contain roughly a quarter of the school, though the actual number of boys is twice what it originally was.

Another innovation at this time was the Kinema show on Thursday afternoons. This was started by Bryan Buckley, who was very keen on the League of Nations, and many of these films were produced by them; the boys' reaction was not one of unmixed delight, but soon there were also comedies on Sunday afternoons between Tea and Chapel. The films were hand-projected first by RAKJ and later by Geoffrey Frodsham, who arrived in September 1926. At the end of this term BBB retired from teaching to become an Inspector of Schools.

97. William LaTouche Congreve, VC.

Two 'incidents' occurred in 1926: the Cottage Row, and the Great Catsmeat Rebellion. Both are fairly typical of life in a small, close-knit institution, and neither should be taken too seriously.

After his marriage, Bobs Alington lived with his wife Gill in a house in the Banbury Road. But his mother, 'Aunt Margaret', had ambitions for him and wanted to see him in charge of a house; had she reflected, she must have realized that, in a few years, changes were bound to occur which would give him his chance. Without consulting her husband, she induced Gill to approach John Evans, the housemaster of Cottage, with the astounding suggestion that he and the other Cottage masters should go and live in Banbury Road, while Bobs and Gill took over Cottage. This was a colossal blunder, and had many repercussions. JFE was deeply hurt and, though GB did his best to act as peacemaker, jealous feelings were aroused and many bitter things said. When the Bear eventually got to hear of it, he simply said, 'Who started all this rot anyway?' and vetoed any suggestion of a move. The row died down in time, and Bobs and Gill had only a year to wait before they moved into Mayfield, which suited them better than Cottage would have done. But Bobs and John never really saw eye to eye again; seeds of mistrust had been sown, which were to produce a harvest during the next decade. In view of this, it is a measure of Bobs' greatness and generosity of spirit that he wrote such an affectionate obituary of JFE in 1973.

The Catsmeat Rebellion was a more comic affair. In the early days of the school, Charlie Paine used to carve the meat as it was served out in the Dining-

Room: one hopes, *en passant*, that this use of the school carpenter was not a reflection upon the consistency of the meat! But later it was carved in the kitchen and put on the tables in pots, from which the master at each table would serve it; this came to be called 'catsmeat' by the boys, and was not popular. On one occasion the meat was served out, passed down, round and back up again, every boy saying as he did so, 'A clean plate, please, sir,' which he was entitled to do if he merely wanted 'veg'. Aunt Margaret was not unnaturally much fussed by this brilliantly organized revolution, and its success was due to the fact that no member of staff got wind of it before it happened. Only a Wavell could have masterminded such a campaign, and it brought about an instant change.

Llewellyn Jeffreys-Jones joined the staff in place of BBB at the beginning of 1927, a year which saw several changes. In April retired Nurse Bright, 'who has put in more years than she would like to mention of faithful service at Newton'; and in July J. C. R. Freeborn resigned after forty-three years as school doctor, being succeeded by Dr Hobson, who himself did more than thirty. But these departures were overshadowed by that of the Bear. He had anyway intended that the academic year 1927–8 should be his last, but early in October he had a stroke. He had been out shooting the day before, and in Chapel he 'blacked out' while taking the service. He soon recovered, but was told that he must give up work for good; he is reported to have said in reply to the doctor's orders, 'Thank heaven that I shall never have to beat a boy again!' Cyril Williams took over tactfully and calmly, handing over the editorship of the Magazine to GB, who also now took on Fifth Form, theoretically 'on approval', but in fact he did it for twenty-five years with signal success.

GHOSTS

Boys are inclined to tell one another ghost stories, and a large and rambling building such as a school provides a fertile background for these tales. In addition, one of the present staff is an expert story-teller and has created a number of stories which are fiction but have one foot in Summer Fields history. The tragic death of Theodore Meyer, for instance, provides the starting-point for one such story, but there is no historical evidence of his reappearing. Tom Coventon, who also died young, has a slightly stronger historical claim. H. B. von Arnim, a contemporary in 1913, wrote this paragraph in *A Century of Summer Fields*:

> My most unpleasant memory is the death in 1913 of Coventon, one of the four boys in my dormitory. We were all badly shaken, but he and I had been especially close. In fact it is possible that poor Coventon was, very briefly, a ghost. Shortly after his death I was awakened early one morning by the loud clatter of a boy's feet scampering down the stairs, exactly as Coventon used to scamper. But when I crept to the landing there was no one to be seen, although the clattering kept on.

A possible ghost of greater antiquity but no greater terror is to be found in the reminiscences of the 1870s from H. C. Hayter:

> Miss Maggie Maclaren had a dog called 'Beau', very nice but of uncertain breed. He died (fairly old, I should think) and his ghost was supposed to haunt a sort of glass-house and potting-shed, and for a time we were all rather afraid of going to the 'Vinery'.

This suggests that there was a period when the Vinery was used for both its original and its more recent purposes.

These, however, are mere bagatelles, the lightest of brushes with the supernatural. The only proper tale, both in proportion and in authenticity, comes from L. A. G. Strong's *Green Memory*.

98. Cottage, showing the door by which the ghost entered.

It happened in the summer of 1921, on a Sunday evening. Service had just finished in the school chapel, and I walked back to Cottage. The front door led into a hall. Immediately on the left was Case's sitting-room. He had not yet come out from chapel, where he had been playing the organ. The hall ran through the house to the back door. My room was at the back, on the left, and John Evans' on the right. Beside the back door, against the wall, was a cupboard where we kept our gowns.

I shut the hall door behind me, walked to the cupboard, opened it, took off my gown, and hung it on its peg. As I did this, I heard the hall door open behind me. I turned, and saw a man with a brown moustache, carrying music under his left arm, come in, close the door, and go into Case's room. Case had a moustache, and would be carrying music: so, naturally enough, for a moment I took the figure to be Case.

Then, after a second or two, I realized that he was not Case. His clothes were different. His moustache was different. His whole look was different. 'Who on earth – ?' I thought: and I went into Case's room to see. There was no one there.

I stood, staring, incredulous. I had not only seen the man go in, I had heard him open the front door. It was the sound of the door that had made me turn from hanging up my gown.

A strange, slow tingle travelled up my spine. Outside, the summer evening was radiant over the well-known scene, the roof of the cottage opposite, the flowers, the lawn, the little gravel drive. Everything that I was looking at contradicted this sudden chill of the unexplained. Then in at the gate came Case, his music under his arm, humming to himself. I met him in the doorway. He narrowed his eyes.

'Hullo! You look odd.'

'A very odd thing's happened.' I told him what I had heard and seen. 'Naturally,' I concluded, 'at first I thought it was you.'

He looked at me strangely through his glasses.

'What was he like?'

I gave him an exact description. As I was giving it, I marvelled that I had not instantly realized the stranger could not possibly have been Case. He turned away, and put his music down on the table.'

'Oh,' he said over his shoulder, 'that was Winford Alington. He was killed in 1917. He played the organ here before me. This was his room.'

It would seem that somehow, for a couple of seconds, I had tuned into the past, and seen the figure of Case's predecessor at the exact hour when he must so often have come across from playing in the chapel, with his music under his arm. But – this is the point that interests me most – I not only saw him, I *heard* him open the door. Did that door physically open and shut? Did I hear a physical noise, or did I translate to hearing, as well as to sight, a stimulus from the past?

99 and 100. Case and Winford Alington; they could easily have been mistaken for one another at a quick glance and against the light in a doorway.

101. School Photograph 1928. Cecil Day Lewis is at the extreme left of the top row; Llewellyn Jeffrey-Jones, Geoffrey Frodsham and presumably Clotworthy are in the third row down, with Roger Jacques in front of Clotworthy; John Evans, Strong and 'Liz' Lysaght are in the front row of standees; and the seated adults are the two Miss Hills (at either end), Hermione Williams with Ferelith, Cyril Williams, Bobs Alington and GB.

6

PENTARCHY AND DEPRESSION 1928–39

THE departure of Bear and Penny left the school with a young staff, Cyril Williams at forty-three being the doyen. He took Bobs Alington into partnership, and to serve them they had a team that was strong in talent as well as having youth on its side: L. A. G. Strong, the Rev J. A. C. Lysaght, John Evans, Geoffrey Bolton, Ralph Robinson and Roger Jacques formed the backbone, and the recent newcomers Geoffrey Frodsham and Llewellyn Jeffreys-Jones were also to contribute much over the next few years. The academic year 1927–8 saw C. Griffin Mullins on the staff and, even more briefly, a fine young musician called W. R. Clotworthy, who was soon being heard on BBC broadcasts, as was the other new addition, FPP's replacement, Cecil Day Lewis.

Fresh from reading English at Wadham, CDL was already writing and publishing poetry, but his *alter ego*, 'Nicholas Blake', the writer of detective thrillers, was to come later. When he did embark on this second career, he set his first novel in a school that owes much to Summer Fields, though it is fair to point out that he also taught for a year at Larchfield (with W. H. Auden) and for several years at Cheltenham Junior. Still, neither of those establishments has a hay-feast, leaving convenient hay-huts for finding small corpses in! His reminiscences, as recorded in his autobiography, *The Buried Day*, complement those of LAGS, particularly as to the treatment of new masters.

It was a great stroke of luck for me that Summer Fields should have been an exceptionally good school of its kind. As a nursery for Eton, where every year it won a number of scholarships, Summer Fields conveyed to the newcomer a sense of prestige and privilege. The small boys were, many of them, quick-witted and attractive, tending perhaps to be rather spoilt, but with an ease of manner and a charming touch of independence which reflected the homes they came from. As for the staff, in a few weeks they radically changed my attitude towards teachers and the teaching profession: both the younger masters and the older went out of their way to put me at my ease ... The older beaks were delightfully lacking in that self-importance or need for self-assertion which causes human beings to be regimental towards their juniors ... I had never imagined that schoolmasters were capable of such an intelligent interest in the young, or spent so much time discussing their pupils' work and characters.

102. C. Day Lewis at the Hay Feast.

It was just as well that morale was high, for the climate and accommodation left something to be desired. Since two or three families were drawing dividends from the school, its buildings had not been extended proportionately to its increasing numbers. The class-room in which I gave my first arithmetic lesson was not the only one in which two classes were taken simultaneously. The icy damp of the North Oxford winter gripped us for weeks on end, and from the draughts which swept the corridors I contracted a nagging neuralgia ... [It was] a world of bells and tattered books and football boots and crazes and blackboards and piercing screams; of ink smells, chalk-duster smells, smells of mud and mown grass, and the mousey smell of little boys; of draughts, radiators, chilblains, stringy meat and steamed puddings; of dismal walks in the rain; of boring jokes and catchwords endlessly repeated ... of days when everything went right, hours when to see the boys at cricket in the sunshine gave one the illusion of being blessed with eternal youth; a world of rewards and punishments, reach-me-down justice and covert partiality, of sadly unoriginal sin; a world where, under controlled conditions, the workings of the herd instinct may be observed in all their pristine innocence and mindless brutality, but where also, as in an accelerated film of plant growth, one can delightedly watch rapid unfoldings of intelligence, courage, inventiveness, sensitivity.

In his first term, CDL performed behind the scenes in *The Merchant of Venice*, which was 'by common consent regarded as the best yet'. This production was by GSF, assisted by LAGS; presumably AFA, embarking on his partnership with CAEW, felt that he might not have time to spare for other things. But his wife Gill once again did wonders with the costumes, as did RAKJ and CGM with the scenery; Mrs Strong 'again carried out her unobtrusive but effective duties at the piano' and CDL's fine voice was heard in an original setting of 'Tell Me Where Is Fancy Bred'. He also reviewed the play constructively, finding Ben Nicolson dignified and audible as Antonio but his brother Nigel not saucy enough as Nerissa. A. J. Shaughnessy, author-to-be of *Upstairs Downstairs* and many other television dramas, looked sinister as Old Gobbo and achieved the most penetrating

103. Deep End Bathing. The diving boards survived until the school stopped using the Cherwell for bathing in the 1960s.

whisper ever heard; but the *tour de force* of the production was the future naval captain John Wells's Prince of Arragon. None of this, however, should detract from the achievement of G. L. S. Batty, who learnt the part of Shylock in ten days and performed it admirably by all accounts.

This was, as Day Lewis noted, an era of crazes. The crossword craze has been mentioned already, and 1927 heralded a brief ascendancy of the 'banjolele and the ukalele', which must have made life quite tiresome for masters on duty, for the instruments were not all tuned to the same key. No sooner had this died than the first of many racing-motor crazes occurred, together with aeroplanes which worked on a gratifyingly noisy and deliciously smelly miniature petrol engine. Hours would be spent hopefully twiddling propellers until the glorious moment when the 'putt-putt' became a continuous drone. A few heady seconds of flight, and then hours would be spent in trying to retrieve the aircraft from the trees in the field; this occupation was said to have taxed RAKJ's agility in many breaks.

In September C. G. Mullins was replaced by his brother Hubert, also from St Andrews, Grahamstown, where their father was Headmaster, and Keble College; he stayed eleven years until the outbreak of the war. Another arrival was Edward Snell, who was to make a great impression in his three years here before he

104. Hubert Mullins and Llewellyn Jeffreys-Jones.

105. GB, Strong, John Evans, Edward Snell and Geoffrey Frodsham, with Gill Alington, Bobs' wife.

went to follow his father as Headmaster of Mowden School in Hove. (His son Christopher was to do the same in the 1960s). CDL had left to get married and, while ES as his successor may not have had his musical or poetic gifts, he was one of the most outstanding games-players that the staff has had, especially in the spheres of squash and rackets, both of which he played at international level.

In the ninth term of the League Competition, Michaelmas 1928, the only recorded tie took place – between Case, who had already won four times, and Congreve, who had won three. As with any tie, not everyone agreed with the 'umpire's decision', but at least it made for an exciting contest. It inspired two boys, N. M. Burney and J. C. Waterlow, to write:

THE BATTLE OF THE LEAGUES

Congreve and Case are fighting
    To gain the highest mark.
They draw and make exhibits
    And sew by light and dark.

The Football goes to Congreve;
    At Fives they set the pace:
But when it comes to Blackbook
    They leave the job to Case.

Case for their weekly papers
    Win excellent renown:
Yet black marks every now and then
    Have made their leaders frown.

Congreve and Case are fighting,
    And hotter grows the fight,
For each has scored the same amount
    – That's if they've counted right!

And what Leagues were the two young poets in? Moseley and Maclaren, of course! Their first verse suggests that league marks were scored for hobbies as well as games and weekly order papers. One may regret the passing of the Inter-League Sewing Competition!

Not only the League tussle provided entertainment in this term. Dr Williams himself gave a lantern lecture on his tour in Egypt and Palestine, and thirty boys went on a visit to the Morris Works at Cowley. There were also voluntary sessions of community singing, organized by Mullins, and a conjurer on the last Saturday of term. Another visitor was the Rev C. H. S. Gmelin, now in his last year as Headmaster of Holmwood School, near Liverpool, and soon to return to Oxfordshire to become Rector of Westcott Barton. He came to preach in Chapel, as did the Rev. Maurice Tanner, Gill Alington's father.

No magazine appeared at the end of Lent Term 1929, which was 'so broken up that we found ourselves at its end with little to chronicle', bad weather and disease being the culprits. But this year did witness the publication of the first School Register, begun before the war by the Rev C. H. S. Gmelin and appearing, at long last, due to the heroic work of GB. He was also now well into his stride as editor of the Magazine, and producing innovations, at first not too extreme. Four reproductions of younger boys' paintings in the July issue were a most praiseworthy idea, but this was not repeated: was the cost of half-tones too great in those days? Anyway, no more artwork appeared for forty years. GB also paid tribute to a magazine produced by the members of Fifth Form, *The Universal*, which was apparently not the first of its kind.

It is some time now since Fifth Form put forth a journal, with occasional assistance from New Room. We remember a very entertaining production in 1921, with very talented contributors [presumably John Lehmann *inter alios*]; but, unlike the 'Universal', it circulated more or less privily in manuscript, and members of the staff saw it only by special courtesy. For this there was good reason, as they were therein lampooned with greater freedom than some of them would have appreciated. But the 'Universal' is open to public inspection in the dignity of a noble typescript, and the first number promises well for others.

It did in fact survive through a succession of Fifth Forms, and GB plundered it gladly for material, always acknowledging his debt.

On 16 April, Dr and Mrs Williams celebrated their golden wedding, and the school was given a half-holiday to mark this anniversary later in the summer term. A sumptuous tea was provided upon the lawn, on the hottest afternoon of the year, when ices were particularly welcome. So were packets of sweets done up in golden tissue, and the grant of an 'Evening' (meaning no prep) in addition to the 'Half'.

At the same time the Comptons were retiring from running St Leonards after more than a quarter of a century. Mrs Compton, the model of a loyal and devoted headmaster's wife and vicarious mother to hundreds of boys, had been ill and had returned to work again before she was fully recovered. So they decided that it was time to hand the school over to the Barbers, and they retired to Rye amid expressions of admiration and regret and bearing a cheque in a gold and enamel box, a gift from the parents of past and present boys.

Having fired a preliminary salvo in 1928 and having interpolated an amusing little scene in 1929 (see opposite), GB revived the serious editorial in 1930 – which would have pleased EDC. His words in both the April and the July editions contain much wisdom which still applies today, the former being about the status of prep schools and the latter about the sterility of old-fashioned unreasoning

106. (*opposite*) Magazine, December 1929.

The Summer Fields Magazine

Mens Sana in Corpore Sano

Vol. VI | DECEMBER, 1929 | No. 11

CONTENTS.

THE CONSERVATIVE PARTY

SCENE: The Lobby. A change has been made in the time-table.

Boy. What is it next hour, sir?

Master (sententiously). What did the Head Master give out this morning?

B. (after thought). I didn't quite hear, sir.

M. You ought to listen.

B. Yes, sir. What is it, sir?

M. Look on the board.

B. Oh! Is it up?

M. I shouldn't tell you to look if it wasn't, should I?

(The Boy considers, head on one side. Evidently he is not sure. However, he goes and looks at the board.)

B. (to himself). Football colours — Special Preachers — Wanton damage — What does wanton mean, sir? (does not wait for an answer) — Carpentering, &c. — Boxing — (sighs) — What part of the board is it on, sir? I can't find it.

M. There, you ass.

B. Oh, *there!* (Looks.) I can't read what it says, sir.

M. Why, it's as plain as can be. French — F–R–E–N–C–H. What else could it be?

B. I don't know, sir. Only that didn't look like an F, to me. It looked more like a T.

M. T! Trench! Now, my poor ass, *is* there a subject called Trench?

B. No, sir. That's why I wondered, sir.

(Enter three or four more boys.)

B 2. I say, what is it next hour, anybody?

B 3. Greek. *B* 2. Greek?

B 3. Yes. Don't you remember? Old (sees master just in time) — Mr. Williams gave it out at Bible-reading. (The other boys, with accustomed tact, grin at the master, then at the speaker, to and fro, three or four times.)

B 2 (after a pause). But he didn't say *Greek*, did he?

B 3. Course he did.

B 4. That doesn't make any odds to me. I don't do Greek.

B 2. Oh lor! I shall have to go back and change my books.

M. (goaded). Of course it isn't Greek. Why don't you ever listen to anything that's given out?

B 3 (indignantly). I *did* listen, sir.

M. A fat lot of good it's done you.

Several boys. Why, sir, what is it, then?

M. French, you asses. *B* 2. *French*, sir?

M. French. French French French. Language spoken in France. French.

B 3, 4, 5, 6, &c. *FRENCH*, sir?

B 5. But it's always been Latin this hour, sir.

M. I know it has; but there's been a change.

B 5. (brightly) Why, sir?

M. Look here. The bell's going in two minutes. Next hour is French. It's been given out, and stuck up on the board. If any one comes with the wrong books, I'll shove him in extra drill. (Exit.)

B 5 (to the others). He can't. I'm on already. (They babble confusedly together, the word 'French' occurring frequently. The Lobby door opens. Enter another Master.)

B 1, 2, 3, 4, 5, 6, &c. (rushing up to him). Please sir — what is it next hour?

discipline. The April one sounds as though it was smarting under a Common Entrance failure or two, not because the boys concerned were inadequate but because the public school was oversubscribed. However that may be, 1930 was the first time for fifty years that we did not achieve an award at Eton, illness being a contributory factor in our failure. Our next blank year was not until 1983; so the end of the world had not come, as some thought it might!

The April 1930 Magazine carried, discreetly on its eighth page:

A NOTICE.

The following notice is being sent to parents at the end of this Term:

SUMMER FIELDS, OXFORD. Easter 1930.

Our respective fathers, the Rev Dr Williams and the Rev E. H. Alington, are now definitely retiring from active participation in the management of the School.

It will therefore interest our parents and friends to learn that three of the present masters are joining us as partners in their stead. These are Mr J. F. Evans (MA, Keble College, Oxford), who has been with us for fifteen years; Mr G. Bolton (MA, University College, Oxford), for ten years; and Mr R. A. K. Jacques (MA, Brasenose College, Oxford), who was a boy at Summer Fields himself. With such experienced men to support us permanently in the supervision and conduct of affairs, we may look forward with confidence to the continued efficiency and well-being of the School.

CYRIL WILLIAMS
A. F. ALINGTON.

That was the public notice, but GB gives a glimpse behind it.

In 1927 John Evans and I had been about to seek our fortunes elsewhere when Uncle Hugh's sudden illness forced him to retire. We stayed on for two years and then formally intimated that we were off. Bobs now took alarm; he knew that he could never run the school jointly with Cyril. They were poles apart in their beliefs and had never got on well. So it was Bobs (or so I've always understood) who went to the Doctor and said that we must be offered partnerships.

Of the discreditable negotiations that followed I will say little. Time and again they were on the verge of being broken off, for the Doctor's demands were really outrageous. One must remember that in his eyes we were interlopers and he feared that we should ruin *his* school by going all modern. But we felt that we had done the school some service and that this might be recognized when we were asked to pay for the privilege of continuing that service. Doctor, however, had never failed to have his own way in the 30-odd years since Mrs Maclaren's death, and he immensely disliked having to make concessions. Finally, a sort of agreement was reached, and in January 1930 we two and Roger Jacques were enrolled as partners.

It was not a happy partnership. Too many people wanted too many different things. Our weekly meetings revealed little unanimity and after a while were apt to resolve themselves into a monologue by John on the iniquities of his Latin form while the rest of us thought our own thoughts. My particular fault, a serious one, was that I was so happy in my own ploys of V Form, Soccer and Cubicles that I didn't bother enough about what was going on around me.

The new decade opened with distinction for Summer Fields cricketers. 'Gubby' Allen played for England, and Neville Ford represented Oxford University for the third year. In addition, Oxford's golf team was captained by Pat Marston, who was also in the Old Carthusian team that won the public schools competition. The school's own cricket season was good though brief. The First XI won most of their matches, but the Masters were unable to beat the Old Summerfieldians in a high-scoring match, which the latter won narrowly, largely thanks to 114 not out from a young man called Bowtell. He was in fact not an Old Summerfieldian at all, but the newly appointed School Secretary, who had joined us from Critchley, Ward & Pigott, the school's accountants, and who was to fulfil an interesting variety of roles here over the next half-century. He was immediately co-opted into Mr Bolton's XI to play against the Hon C. J. Lyttelton's XI, but was unable to rediscover his form, and the Worcestershire captain's team trounced the home one. Fearing a further defeat at the hands of North Oxford, the Masters stiffened their team with outside stalwarts, two of whom made nearly 200 runs between them, rather eclipsing the efforts of the genuine staff, though ES made 40 and GB took 5 wickets.

In the world of literature and the arts, OSS were also gaining notice. The drawings of John Merton were said to have attracted expert attention, and Victor Pasmore was exhibiting at the Royal Academy. Adrian Alington published his first novel, *Slowbags and Arethusa*, which was well reviewed, and Bernard Darwin wrote a delightful article in *The Times* about receiving and perusing his copy of the *Summer Fields Register*.

But 1930 was also the year when LAGS left teaching to take up writing as a full-time career. This had long been on the cards, and his marriage in 1928 to Sylvia Brinton had only increased the likelihood of his so doing. In his thirteen years on the staff, he had transformed the teaching of English; he was a fine schoolmaster, being a man of deep understanding with an essentially sympathetic nature. Boys could be sure that he would see their point of view, and their confidence in him was absolute. He revisited the school often after his departure, sent his son there, and came back frequently to read aloud to select groups of boys or to judge the poetry competitions right up to the year of his death.

Strong's replacement was C. H. Barnes of Winchester and Pembroke, Cambridge; Pat Marston joined the school permanently next year, upon the return of Edward Snell to Sussex; and at Christmas Charlie Paine retired after over fifty years as carpenter and maintenance-man. At the age of thirteen, he had come to assist his father, who worked as 'Booty', while his mother was cook-housekeeper until 1915. Charlie made the mahogany cabinet which still stands in the Headmaster's Study, containing important school documents. For thirty-four years he looked after the building and repairs of the various houses and lodges, besides teaching the boys carpentry.

A hut containing two (fairly small!) classrooms was erected opposite the gym in 1930, and painted a then popular shade of green. There it remained until the Music Block was built across the Lobby Drive in 1978, when it was dismantled to be re-erected as a pavilion in the far field. A more permanent building was the Squash Court, which was generously presented to the school by JPM in 1932 and has been in constant use ever since. At this time South Dor was converted into an Upstairs Library: GB had taken on a practically non-existent Library in 1926 and had built it up to respectable proportions over the years until two walls of Fifth Form Room were adorned with glass-fronted bookcases. The Upstairs Library was also a sitting-room for senior boys, and South Dor was ideal for the purpose.

107. The Upstairs Library, occupying what was both previously and subsequently South Dor.

The reason for the availability of this large room was that the numbers in the school were beginning to decline. The depression of the early 1930s had much to do with this; but it must have been apparent to many that the five partners were at variance, and word got about that Summer Fields was not what it had been. The situation was a difficult one for all concerned, but for no one more than Cyril Williams who, though by nature genial, had a rather hectoring manner and had ruffled some feathers in his earlier days. His father had enjoined him to be stern and rule by fear, but his mother wanted him to be popular; his avuncularity, cultivated quirks and oft-repeated jokes appealed to some, but others saw through his bluff exterior and found him unpredictable.

'He could sadly misjudge individual cases and miscalculate public opinion,' wrote Hugh Stubbs, who was at SF 1926–30:

In summer 1928 he determined to stamp out talking after lights-out. After a week or so, he announced that it would be a beating offence; shortly afterwards, the penalty was raised to TWO; then to THREE; finally, to his bewilderment, the irresistible cannonball met the immovable post – and it was raised to SEVEN. There was an impasse, which was further complicated by an incident when through a misunderstanding he flogged several boys for something of which they were not guilty. The school vibrated with protest; I remember seeing Hilary [CAEW's son, at that time a pupil in the school] in tears. At last, he plucked up courage to slip through the green baize door to the Study and explain the situation. I am not sure how the talking-in-dormitories situation ended; but CAEW certainly made handsome amends with salad lunches, lemonade, strawberry teas etc.

He made many improvements, not all of which were adequately appreciated. Hot water was more generously provided in the Changing Room, classrooms were multiplied and improved and, above all, the horror of the Vinery Rush was done away with. Roofed, porcelained, individually cisterned, a complete new apparatus (apart from the Fifth Form Vins, which needed no improvement) burst on our delighted eyes in 1929. ('And so NECESSARY!' I once heard a visiting parent remark, possibly meaning, 'And about time, too!') Even here, however, there was one odd deficiency: no bolts.

This same lack was acutely felt by Julian Amery when, as a new boy in 1928, he wanted privacy in which to give vent to his homesickness:

I found my way to the Vinery, as the conveniences at Summer Fields were known. Rather to my surprise they were in a kind of garden; to my consternation they had no doors ... There was no privacy to be found in these privies. My morale sank to my boots. I wandered disconsolately back towards my form room, the tears coursing slowly down my cheeks.

But there was a less spartan side to life, largely due to the influence of Cyril's wife Hermione, whom many remember with fondness. Indeed, some parents actually chose the school because of her. She was very much in the tradition of

Aunt Margaret, whom all the staff adored and who had looked after them with gracious maternal interest. Kitty Barber was held in similar affectionate veneration at St Leonards. All of these wrote wonderfully concerned and comforting letters to parents when their boys were ill.

108. Hubert Mullins and GB.

Numbers, however, continued to decline throughout the 1930s. In 1934 they sank below 100 for the first time since Mrs Maclaren's day, and, quite apart from the internal stresses of a staff in which almost half the men were partners in the school, it must have been hard to make ends meet. Roger Jacques recalls that one term, after all the accounts had been done, the partners' share of the profits was *10s 6d* (decimal equivalent $52\frac{1}{2}p$; actual purchasing power *c.* £20); 'Ruth and I spent it on a lunch,' he said philosophically. One of the many difficult aspects of a drop in the pupil-strength is that the staff, who have to be paid, do not necessarily show a corresponding decrease. Admittedly, in those days it was still possible to sack people; but it was a good and loyal staff that Cyril and Bobs led, and they would not have wished to treat them with anything less than fairness. On top of all the problems, there was also a capitation fee of £1 per boy per term to be paid to the Maclarens as long as the school had fifty or more pupils.

For all its difficulties, much that was splendid happened in this decade. We have no yardstick by which to compare school plays, but the 1934 *Henry V* and, even more, the 1935 *Richard II* were evidently out of the ordinary class. Produced by AFA and HMM, with Gill Alington and a skilful and enthusiastic team doing the décor, both plays provided a number of fine performances, notably those of Patrick Macnee and Robin Sinclair. The photographs of these two in *Richard II* adorned GB's desk in Cottage throughout the time that he was there. As editor, he reviewed both plays with high praise, and similar accolades came from Nevill Coghill.

The same term saw 'the best football season since before the war', in which the school played twenty-two matches all told, won sixteen of them and lost four. But the next season was even better, and, under the captaincy of Brian

109. The young Patrick Macnee, popularly known as 'Smee'.

110. Robin Sinclair as Richard II, with Brian Straton-Ferrier as the Queen.

111. The 1935 Football XI. *Back Row:* T. H. Barclay, W. M. Savery, C. E. McGrigor, I. J. H. Lewisohn; *Seated:* D. P. Macnee, M. K. Raikes, C. J. Crossley (Captain), B. I. Straton-Ferrier, J. J. Poole; *On the Ground:* Hon. J. L. Mackay and G. E. Seager.

Straton-Ferrier, this was 'the finest side and the finest season that we have had for very many years'. GB, who ran the soccer from 1927 to 1947, considers that the three outstanding teams he came across in that period were Cothill in 1933, Horris Hill in 1934 and our own of 1936. 'I am inclined, not without prejudice, to rate our 1936 side as the best of the three. What made us so formidable was, first, wonderful combinations and, secondly, the tremendous pace and scoring-power of our three inside-forwards, Straton-Ferrier himself, Gerald Seager and Tommy Carlyon. One match was scratched, a home game in which we could not have failed to score 10 goals; we scored 69 goals to 4 in the season, and no goal was scored against us on our own ground.'

Straton-Ferrier's own account of the last match of this wonderful season is worth quoting in full, for it evokes the best of school story-book excitement as well as the atmosphere of the 1930s Summer Fields, besides containing a brilliantly drawn and touching portrait of GB. Much has been written about his 'bates', his dedication, his likes, dislikes and aura, from Julian Amery, who remembers 'a tall, austere, bony classicist and cricketer, who hated foreigners and loathed Lloyd

George' to Hugh Stubbs's memory 'of GB's grin as he presided over an enormous bowl of strawberries and cream one lunch-time, looking rather like the friendly crocodile in the Russian comic.' But this account is a gem.

On Saturday 5th December 1936, we played Horris Hill at home, the last match of the season. So far we were unbeaten. Cothill – it would have to be Cothill – had managed to draw with us. Gerald Seager had had one of his very rare off-days and he missed a couple of sitters. GB swore he'd never seen anything like it since the famous day when David James skied the ball over the cross-bar from five yards in front of an open goal. [The evil that boys did lived after them. Poor David James, immortalized for generations by this single oft-told incident. Eternal infamy in this brief moment of zealous excess.]

None of us had been able to concentrate during that last week, and I was afraid lest one of the side should earn himself a whacking or be put in Black Book 2 for inattention, with disastrous effects on morale. In the event nobody got so much as a double-sided copy: I think none of the staff dared risk Boltosh's wrath by demoralizing any of his precious First Eleven. So Tark's gumpher-rod remained in its drawer, and Liz Lysaght's supply of History Picture sticks remained high.

In Fifth Form the tension was unbearable. That long, bony finger, and the jumbo yellow pencil, probed around the class much as usual, pausing now and then as one of us, too late, remembered the meaning of the vocab-book word a fraction of a second before it passed the lips of the next in line, while the familiar verse was sonorously repeated, as if for the first time:

'The moving finger writes; and, having writ,
Moves on; nor all thy piety nor wit
    Shall lure it back to cancel half a line,
Nor all thy tears wash out a word of it.'

But Saturday's match was in the forefront of all minds, and the whole of ancient literature seemed crammed with subtle references to the impending decisive battle. On the Friday evening we sang the psalm usually reserved for the day before Common E.: 'The ploughers ploughed along my back and made long furrows.' It wished us good luck in the name of the Lord. And finally Saturday came.

A few hurried last-minute conferences, and the plan of campaign was complete. 'We must have a goal *quickly*,' GB said for the umpteenth time, 'so get in there with everything you've got ὡς ταχ . . .!'

So there we were, trotting on to the field at last, neat adrenalin pumping through our veins. There was GB, his matchstick legs in long blue shorts and those crazy boots of his, his face trying desperately to register a referee's impartiality, and refusing to talk to us now we were under starter's orders. He looked grim, tired.

How that gaunt figure dominated my five years! I loved and revered him, and was terribly afraid of him, and now I wanted this triumph more, I think, for his sake than for ours.

GB blew his whistle and we kicked off. What immediately happened is a blur, but about thirty seconds later an image like a photograph impinged indelibly on my mind.

112. Costume as worn at Summer Fields in the 1930s. The two central characters in this picture are Robin Guinness and Hon. Montagu Robert Vere Eliot, who was a page at the 1937 Coronation.

In this picture we are attacking Horris Hill's goal, and Gerald Seager is poised high in the air like Nijinsky among a crowd of defenders, his clever head having found a good centre from the left wing. He deflected it in a high, slow lob towards the goalkeeper (a boy called Guy Lister: I knew him in the holidays). The goalie fumbled. The ball dropped on the line. He, two Horris Hill full backs, Gerald, Tommy Carlyon and I reached it about the same time. There was a great impact, and a moment later there were the two full backs, Guy Lister, ball and all in a heap at the back of the net.

I shall never forget Geoffrey Bolton's face as he came running up after blowing his whistle to register a goal. He was laughing, laughing in great uncontrollable giggles of glee, all pretence of judicial calm abandoned in this one moment of overwhelming victory.

For it was all over, and we knew it, and they knew it. We won quite easily after that. GB gave me a silver pencil engraved with the single word 'Invictus'. I don't think I ever valued anything so much. It broke my heart when I lost it my first term at Harrow.

In 1937 Cyril announced that he had had enough of being headmaster, his position was too difficult and he was going. Bobs summoned the other partners to Mayfield and told them very fully and frankly what his policy was going to be. Both he and Gill had 'modern' views on education and it was clear that, for better or for worse, the whole character of the school was going to be radically changed. John Evans and GB made it clear that they would have no part in such a future; so, to avoid further discord, Bobs very honourably resigned. He had a deep love for Summer Fields, but an equally deep dislike for much of what it stood for, and compromise was not really possible. He had some notable achievements to his credit. He raised the standard of French teaching to a remarkable height; his (and Gill's) productions of the annual play were outstanding; and he begat the League system which, after an uncertain start, proved of enormous value in spurring boys to corporate pride. It had not been easy for a second-generation Alington to live in harness with a second-generation Williams. The Doctor (now retired and living at the Royal Victoria Hotel, St Leonards-on-Sea) had never been keen on Bobs, as is witnessed by a letter he wrote to Anderson soon after his departure:

> This school [St Leonards] is bang full; and the Oxford one is improving, now that they have got rid of the youngest Alington with his modernside ideas and hatred of Classics; he is now in a good berth (thank the Lord) as an inspector of prep schools for a large district of England. Quite a nice fellow with a loyal wife – a Bateman Champain – who is clever and artistic, but of no use as a 'schoolmistress'. They have been thorns in Cyril's side ever since Hugh Alington retired in '28, and I wonder that the school has done as well as it has.

Cyril now withdrew his resignation, and for two uneasy years the school continued much as before. At the end of 1938 Cyril announced his firm intention of resigning in July 1939, having been twenty-five years in the school, the last twelve as headmaster. Roger Jacques followed suit; and so John and GB were left to face the Second World War with a school, as they thought, of some eighty boys.

The only other master to stay throughout the war was the Rev J. A. C. Lysaght. 'Liz' to generations of boys and staff, he is not credited with a Christian name, even in the Register, and was something of a mystery. GB believed that he had a large family, but his wife appeared seldom, and only his son Michael impinged upon the Summer Fields scene. Before the first war, he had built up a large tutoring practice in Oxford, but it folded in 1914, and he came in place of JFE, who had gone to fight.

Once at Summer Fields, he still spent most afternoons and every evening in coaching would-be undergraduates or graduates, and on Sundays he undertook, ten miles away, the duties of a vicar too lazy to do them himself. His means of transport on all occasions was a bicycle, which he rode at fantastic speed, but he was never really fit, suffering most of his life from sciatica and other painful ailments. Rumour, but rumour only, had it that he once tried to swim the Channel: he certainly rescued more than one boy from the 'hole' in the Shallow End bathing-place. Hugh Stubbs recalls one such occasion with a difference.

Once he jumped into the river to save a boy whom he thought to be drowning, though in fact the boy was simply treading water and wearing a rather peculiar expression. Taking prep that evening, Liz seemed to be in agony; he aroused widespread sympathy, and the boy – a cheerful, insensitive, athletic type – aroused universal indignation, though it was hardly his fault.

Liz was a delightful conversationalist, a gentle and lovable man and something of a saint. On duty, he would park himself at the far end of Lower School and devote himself to correcting papers, oblivious of the noise around him. There was an occasion when he was 'Taking Tea' – seated at top table correcting papers, technically supervising the boys – that one boy, tilting his chair too far, overset it and cut his head on a radiator. Bleeding profusely, he was escorted to Matron; but Liz, when asked about it afterwards, was unaware that anything untoward had occurred.

LANGUAGE: 1

Communities are prone to create their own languages, and schools are particularly apt to do so. The little paragraphs in *Private Eye* about St Cake's School are amusing because of their ring of truth: other schools' vocabulary does sound ridiculous. One thinks how affected it is of Etonians to talk about 'Halves' and Carthusians about 'Quarters' when they know perfectly well that they mean 'Terms' – until one becomes an Etonian or a Carthusian oneself, when it very soon seems entirely natural.

Yet idiosyncratic language is probably in decline, eroded by the mass media and the general trend towards communication. Winchester fights to maintain its 'Notions', as its peculiar language is called, but it is more a law unto itself than most institutions. As times change, so specific local terms become obsolete; an example is the Summer Fields word 'Squish'. No boy now in the school would know its meaning; equally, no boy in the school twenty years ago would not have known it. It was the school train, later the school carriage on a train, from Paddington to Oxford, and was presumably so-called because everyone had to 'squash' into a limited area.

A recent addition to the school's jargon is the acronym BOSFAM, which was invented by David Kidd-May to describe the team of 'Boys of Summer Fields and Masters' in the final rugger trials match to select First XV's in the late 1950s. Subsequently, it has also been applied to the annual golf tournament at the end of the Lent Term, and the 'A' Team of adults supplemented by a few First XI members which plays football against the Eton OSS. Its formation may owe something to the hideous Oxfam block, which had been built looming over Cottage garden in the early 1960s, and of which DJOKM would be made aware whenever he looked out of his window.

The Buzzer has long been the term for the school shop, whether housed, as now, in a hut beyond the Rose Garden or in the 'French Room'. The word is thought to be a corruption of 'Bursar' rather than of 'Bazaar', or could it be a 'portmanteau' of both? Jack Alington, Bear's second son, for a while fulfilled a bursarial role and was known as 'Jacky Buzzer'. In Victorian times there were Summer Fields cheque-books, and the master who looked after the boys' pocket money (Crofts, for many years) would also be in charge of the Buzzer. Of similar antiquity is the term 'Booty', which is used for both a member of the maintenance staff, especially the Clerk of the Works, and his office – for many years an antique shed next to the Vinery until this was taken over as a photographic dark room and Booty moved to the annexe of the old changing-room. The name derives from the fact that one of their main tasks in the early years was caring for the boys' footwear, and the innocent Victorian mind, whether master or boy, saw the possibility of calling them by the translation of '*praeda*', a word which every pupil soon met in his Latin vocabulary, even before he met the word in English.

Odd little bits of Latin persist in the sub-culture vocabulary (see Language: 2) as well as in the daily Grace before and after meals. But the expression 'Post' as proclaimed at the end of lunch is not the Latin for 'After', but marks the ghost of the time when the second post was distributed by the prefects in a more civilized age. Nor do we any longer have 'You may read if you've finished' at breakfast and supper, which persisted in various forms probably for about a century. GB used to rouse the Cottage boys to their cold baths by calling, '*Surgite!*', possibly on the assumption that hearing Latin first thing in the morning would do them good.

'Vinery' is self-explanatory; on its site was originally a greenhouse where, we are told, fine grapes were grown. As the school lavatory, it was at first still outside and in a garden, and the cubicles lacked doors. Only when the Dining-Hall was built at the turn of the century did it become possible to go to the 'Vin' without braving the weather. Another room whose name has a simple history is the Black Hole, where the staff have pigeon-holes for their books and correspondence and where stationery and duplicating equipment are kept. This was earlier in a room that no longer exists, roughly on the site of the central staircase in House, a room which had originally been a coat-room, and was dimly lit by some wire-meshed gaps giving on to the lower part of the Lobby. When the coats and boot-lockers were transferred to the changing-room area, the cage-windows were boarded and the first of a succession of windowless rooms created; not surprisingly, some wit dubbed it 'The Black Hole of Calcutta', and the name has been retained although the present Black Hole is admirably windowed.

Surely the oddest name is that of the cellar under House which is used as a heterogeneous dumping-ground, a heating control-room and an occasional drying-room: the Kipper Mine? This again, one suspects, must be some obscure Victorian joke; indeed, it has a whiff of Lewis Carroll about it: if one could set limed twigs for crabs, one could certainly mine for kippers. Possibly Victorian boys in their curiosity would ask, 'What is beyond this door?', and their mentors would reply with patronising amiability, 'Ah, now that is the Kipper Mine – where we dig the kippers for your breakfast, don't you know.' This would be analogous with the Potted Meat Horse, which used to pull the mower in the days before motor power and was widely believed to supply potted meat at certain teas (cf. 'The Great Catsmeat Rebellion', p.101–102).

7

FOUR SCHOOLS IN ONE
1939–45

JOHN EVANS was the first headmaster to buy, rather than to inherit, the school (indeed, he was also the last, as it had become a charitable trust by the time that he retired); he was also the first bachelor and the first layman to hold the office. Warm-hearted, snobbish and slightly eccentric, he won parents, boys and staff with his charm, and ever after held a special place in their affections. Many have imitated – but never other than fondly – his gurgling drawl, hands interlocked and kneading away at each other, suggestive of Lady Macbeth saying her prayers. In his younger days he was no mean athlete, a flyweight boxer and a passable cricketer; being the son of an Anglican canon and educated at Keble after Marlborough, he was extremely 'high-church'. Though wounded in the Great War, he continued to play and coach games with enjoyment, taught most subjects in his time but increasingly little towards the end, and was a devoted housemaster in Cottage, until he moved into the main building upon becoming the Headmaster.

It is no exaggeration to say that the Second World War saved Summer Fields. In its first three years, three other schools were evacuated from the Home Counties or the South Coast, and this of course pushed the numbers up again; they have never done anything but increase since then. The first to come, in September 1939, were 'Tubby' Stephenson, four staff and twenty-one boys from Farnborough; these boys included two Slades and a Naylor-Leyland – both families which have provided a rich crop of Summerfieldians. Indeed, the 1939 evacuee C. J. Slade *ma* was to become the 1979 chairman of the Governors, Sir Christopher Slade. Farnborough also brought with them a fine musical tradition and an excellent choirmaster in the person of A. W. H. Thomson, who, though he was generally known as 'Stodgy', very quickly had a tonic effect throughout the school. His coming coincided with the retirement of H. R. Annis, who had been the chapel organist since Case's death in 1922; apparently he never missed a service, Sunday or weekday, 'except for a very occasional visit to Henley during Regatta Week'.

Farnborough was a school of a very different character from that of Summer Fields [recalls Christopher Slade], the kind of school which could not possibly survive a war. It was set in a large and pleasant house just outside Sonning-on-Thames, with a magnificent garden and grounds and acres of woodlands sloping down to the river. All

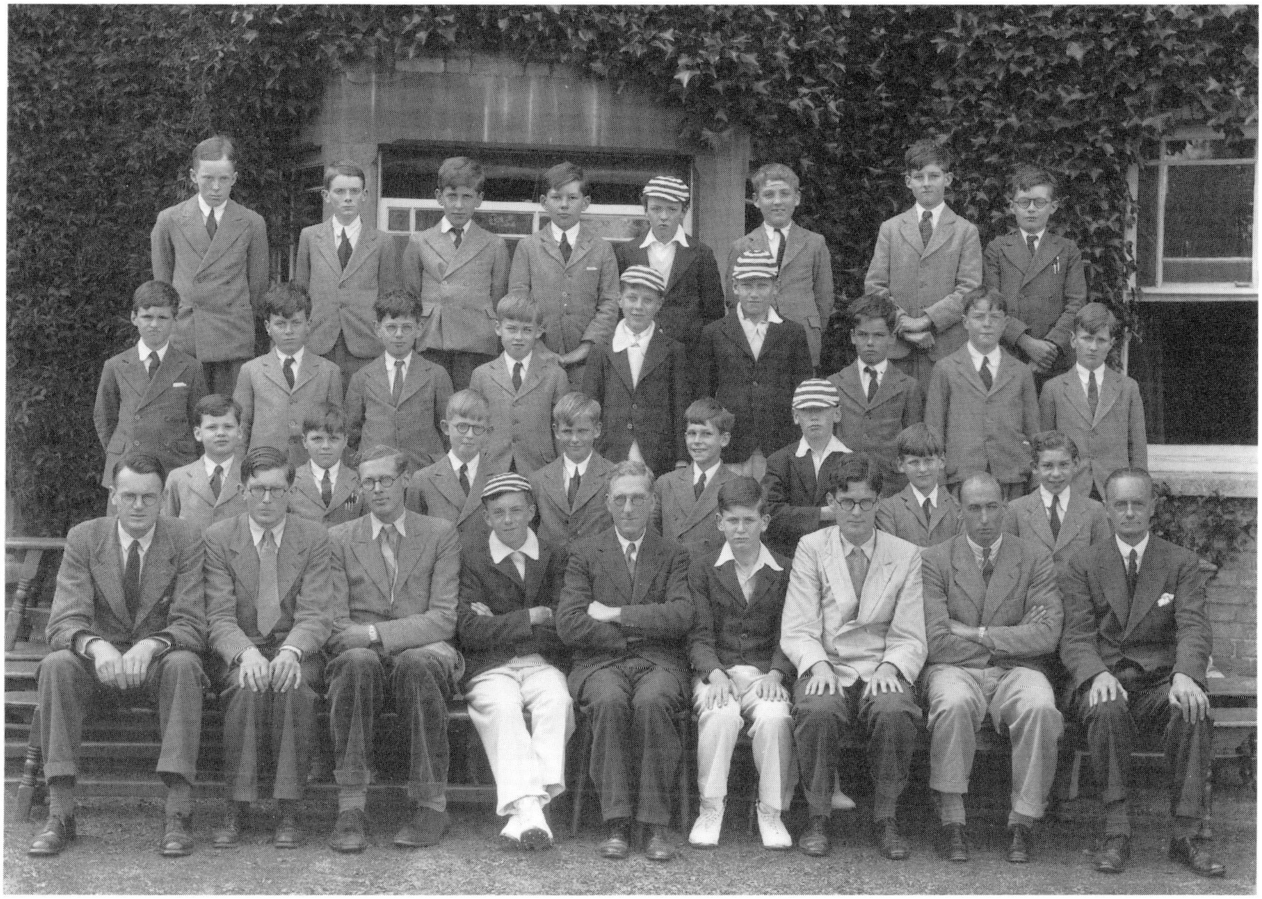

113. The 1940 Choir with 'Stodgy' Thomson seated in the middle, and 'Liz' Lysaght at the end on the right.

this for 25–30 boys. E. K. ('Tubby') Stephenson, who owned and ran the school, was a talented, perhaps somewhat dilettante, bachelor with many interests, sporting and artistic. He must also have been quite a rich man. He was supported by a staff of no less than five masters, all of whom were required to sing in the choir. With scarcely any exception, all boys were either choristers or 'probationers': to qualify as an exception, you had to be tone-deaf. The music was of a remarkably high standard. Visitors to the school received the impression of a country-house party: the atmosphere appeared as one of grace and leisure, unusual in a boys' school. However, it has to be said that the freedom allowed to the boys gave scope from time to time for bullying on a scale which would never have been tolerated or possible at Summer Fields, where there has always been more supervision. Perhaps, therefore, the end of Farnborough was not wholly lamented by all its pupils.

In September 1939, my brother Julian and I viewed the prospect of a transfer to a much bigger, strange school with some misgivings. We need not have worried. John Evans and GB, who were just embarking on their joint headmastership, and indeed all masters and most boys, could not have given us a kinder and warmer welcome. People put themselves out to make things easy for the nervous arrivals. Life at Summer Fields was rather more regimented than it had been at Farnborough; above all, there was a far more stringent scholastic programme.

To join Fifth Form under GB was, to begin with, a daunting experience. The cane no longer hung on the end of his desk, as we were told it had done only a few years before. However, his gaunt, hollow-eyed and skeletal presence, his quick temper and his bellow were alarming, until one came to appreciate his complete dedication to the school and, beneath a gruff exterior, his almost infinite kindness to those whom he considered worthy citizens – and there were many of them. Though no great scholar himself, he was a marvellous teacher of the Classics. We were given our grammar or vocabulary to learn before breakfast, at breakfast itself, and at other convenient gaps in the working day. But once we had more or less learned it, he devised the most imaginative ways of testing us. These included frequent cricket matches between the counties, when a mistake would cost the batting side a wicket. These matches were fun, save when the wrong side (Sussex!) lost, and GB's disappointment and displeasure were all too clear. He taught us to write simple Latin and Greek Prose and to translate into English, avoiding more than the minimum number of clichés. 'Down with parrot mentality!' was one of his favourite phrases, and he meant it. After the scholarship exams, in the middle of the summer term he introduced us to Homer with infectious enthusiasm. The school in those days was often accused of cramming. So far as he was concerned, the accusation would have been quite unjust. The same could not be said of the teaching of mathematics and history, which were at that time taught dismally badly.

The winter of 1939–40 was bitterly cold. The fields looked splendid with not only snow on the ground but icicles on the trees for much of the time. Life went on just the same. In Cottage, where I boarded under GB's tutelage, we were still woken every morning with his shout of *'Surgite!'* We then draped our towels round our middles, glanced at the water frozen stiff in the dormitory wash-basins, and descended to our cold baths. The food at that time was more plentiful and less unattractive than it became later in the War, but the school buildings were fearfully cold. Surreptitiously, and against all the rules, we used to fill ink-bottles with hot water and carry them round in our pockets. One day, an ominous and painful white patch appeared on the flesh of my right thumb. I suggested to the Matron that it might be frostbite, only to be told that little boys do not get frostbite in England. A fortnight later, when the patch had grown, I was at last allowed to see the school doctor, who said that it was indeed frostbite and there and then performed a most painful but effective operation.

The first few months of my brief year at Summer Fields coincided with the period of the 'Phoney War'. I occupied a week in the Sanatorium at Newton by composing anti-Nazi verses of greater passion than elegance. However, until Hitler entered the Low Countries, we were not very conscious of the War, except when we saw masters departing to join the Services or returning to visit us, like Jimmy Bell resplendent in uniform. When the Phoney War ended, GB told us that he did not expect the French to hold out much longer. I remember regarding such pessimism as unthinkable and almost

114. Winter Fields: 1.

unpatriotic; but he was proved all too right, and only a few weeks later the retreat from Dunkirk was to follow.

The strain for John Evans and GB, and indeed for all the staff, must have been very great, but it seldom showed. They did their best, and a very successful best, to keep things going as usual and to give us all a good time within the limits of fairly strict discipline. The sun never seemed to stop shining that summer. We bathed frequently in the River Cherwell, wallowing in the mud. We had our Hay Feast, and occasionally even had classes out of doors.

Man proposes: God disposes. The July 1939 Magazine had proudly announced:

We look forward to welcoming no fewer than four new masters next term. From Christ Church come Mr P. M. B. Savage, who has just finished reading Greats and will take Upper Remove, and Mr E. J. H. Dixon, the University Cricket Captain, who is also a first-rate musician and an historian. Cambridge sends us Mr J. B. Burrough, who is a PT expert, and Mr R. C. S. Trail, who specializes in French and English. No such infusion of new blood has taken place in the memory of anyone now on the staff, but we are looking forward to it and can assure would-be anxious inquirers that no violent revolution is in prospect or intended.

Hitler decided otherwise. The new blood was tragically destined to be spilled on the fields of Europe: of the four young men, only Patrick Savage was to return from the fighting, and that after being captured in Crete and made a prisoner-of-

115. Tom Allsop, school carpenter 1935–1978.

116. Charlie Simms, groundsman 1918–1982.

117. A Family Group taken at St Leonards at the outbreak of War; *Standing:* Perdita Marston with Jeremy; Hilary Williams; E.K. Barber; Hilary Barber; Rosalind Barber. *Sitting:* Hermione and Cyril Williams, Mabel Williams with Nichol Marston; Doctor; Kitty Barber. *On the ground:* Ferelith Williams and Brian Barber.

war. During the winter of 1939, members of staff were called up one by one, and replaced by undergraduates or older men. The school weathered the initial impact of the war well. An air-raid shelter had already been dug, and it was 'all hands to the black-out' as soon as war was declared. Hill and the maintenance staff, Gardner the Butler, Tom Allsop the carpenter, Charlie Fathers and Charlie Simms the groundsmen all worked flat out; so did Miss Bell the Housekeeper and the matronal staff, as well as the maids who voluntarily gave up their summer holiday and returned at the first summons. And Eric Bowtell was frequently in several places at once, possessing an uncanny gift for spotting chinks of light in the black-out and dealing promptly with them. The term had started with a staff of fifteen – rather over the odds for a school which still had less than a hundred pupils despite the Farnborough influx – but the war soon took several of them, and in the next year EKS, the Farnborough Headmaster, himself went to fight.

In September 1940, Ken and Kitty Barber brought four staff and thirty-four boys from Summer Fields St Leonards to Summer Fields Oxford, seeking sanctuary from the bombers. They had in fact evacuated Sussex early in the year, and spent a term and a half at Alderwasley Hall, a small Roman Catholic school near Matlock. They had not enjoyed the experience, because the school was haunted –

throughout, except for the room of Mr James, the Anglican chaplain: presumably it was a Protestant ghost!

The St Leonards staff included Jeffreys-Jones' younger brother Owen, who had been teaching there since 1929; David Mansel-Carey, who worked there from 1923 until 1958, Dennis Standring (1924–62) and Mervyn Dobson (1935–66). These three may be said to have formed the backbone of the staff for the best part of forty years, while the school was both 'at home' and 'away'. For Kitty Barber the move to Oxford was indeed a return to the nest in which she had been brought up, being the Doctor's daughter. By a sad irony, that winter saw the death at Rye of E. D. Compton, who nearly forty years before had set out with a handful of boys to start the new Summer Fields *mi*, and in the following March Doctor also died at the age of nearly ninety. He and Mabel had returned to Oxford by then, but only two years previously he had been leading an active life rather *à la* Gladstone at St Leonards:

> I keep very fit by working quietly at the school woods every morning for a good two hours, wet or fine, at the ivy and holly. I keep a tally every week of the trees whose lives I save for Posterity. There are about 5000 on the place, and I have cleared 1100 to my satisfaction since October the 5th. One has to be careful at 87, and I never cut very big boughs or climb the trees, but send the gardeners up! We have nearly fifty acres on the school grounds, and rather more than half are trees, some 100 years old.

* * * * *

118. Bohemia House, St Leonards-on-Sea.

This is a good moment to go more deeply into the history of the St Leonards school. After extensive searching in 1903, during which they seriously considered Battle Abbey *inter alia*, the Comptons and Wallace Maclaren found Bohemia House, a large mansion with fine rooms, in an excellent state of repair, spacious enough to hold from thirty to forty boys and within half a mile of the sea, but sheltered by its trees so that one was unaware of the town between it and the shore. Its grounds were in fact a paradise, the ideal of what prep school grounds should be, and they are remembered with affection and happiness by all who were there. Playing in the woods and making dams on Sunday afternoons were particular high spots of the week.

From the start, it was a less formal and more intimate school than the Oxford one, the reasons for this being partly its size, partly its geography (there was no 'private side', for instance) and

119. (*above*) The woods at Summer Fields St Leonards.

120. (*below*) How a cricket XI travelled to matches early in the century, Mr and Mrs E. D. Compton standing beside the bus.

121. PT and Drill on the St Leonards cricket ground.

partly the personalities involved. Wallace Maclaren's delightful and sympathetic character has already been commented upon; the Comptons were also a kind and concerned pair who took great care over their charges. EDC himself was said to be something of a snob; a distinguished figure with his dark hair and Elgar moustache, he would invite friends down to play golf and say, 'I've given you Lord So-and-so as your caddie.' Guy Boas, who loathed Oxford, spent two happy terms at St Leonards and remembers the Comptons' kindness. Sadly, EDC's harmless snobbery was to some extent his undoing, for one of his grander friends persuaded him to put money into some South American enterprise, which promptly swallowed it up and then folded up, as frequently happened in the 1920s and 1930. The school remained under the Doctor's management, and, when the Comptons retired to Rye in 1929, Ken Barber and his wife Kitty, Doctor's daughter, stepped into their shoes. The Doctor, when originally buying the house, had had to tap a number of sources to raise money, and the Barbers sensibly tried, to their own financial disadvantage, to buy out these friends and relations, so that they might one day pass the school on unencumbered to their son Hilary. Meanwhile, Cyril and Hermione Williams, now established at the head of affairs in Oxford, rather hoped that their son, also Hilary, might become at least a partner at St Leonards; these rival ambitions may have led to a certain amount of friction.

Relations between the two schools had not always been easy, anyway; perhaps the dictum about the UK and the USA, 'divided by a common language',

122. Summer Fields St Leonards Hay Feast; note the uniformed maids in the background.

applied. St Leonards boys tended to be more aristocratic than academic; and for a long time, if a boy showed any sign of being scholarship material, he was transferred to Oxford for his final grooming. This made nonsense of the valetudinarian reasons for the daughter school's existence, but explains why her top form was always called Upper Remove, and not Fifth Form. This continued to be the case, even when St Leonards started to win scholarships in her own right. Both schools had a school train to London known as the Squish, and both had an annual Hay Feast (at least, until it proved impossible to get anyone to cut hay in the middle of a town). But St Leonards never had a Black Book.

The Doctor always regarded Summers *mi* as his country house, and his family took it over every August, to the regret of the Barber children, who longed to stay there for the holidays. The gardeners of the very large garden traditionally timed their produce for August, and even many years after the war these habits persisted and it was difficult to get vegetables in term-time. As soon as the school broke up in July, Hook, the caretaker-carpenter-maintenance man, and his team had to clear most of the form-rooms and dormitories, which became drawing-rooms and bedrooms for the Doctor and his family.

During the war, though everyone 'did his bit' and put a good face on things, the amalgamation of the two schools cannot have been easy. The Barbers found it rather difficult to get on with John Evans (though they did with GB). No doubt, both having been in charge of successful schools, both sides felt jealous of their authority. Differences of churchmanship were also to blame: when the Archbishop of Canterbury announced that women might attend church without hats, Kitty Barber promptly did so, which offended JFE's high-church principles. When plans began to be discussed for the reopening of the St Leonards school after the war, JFE was not keen on the idea, and then suggested that, if it did reopen, it should do so under another name. This naturally hurt the Barbers.

But reopen it did, and it lasted for another twenty, mainly happy, years, first with Ken and Kitty Barber again in charge, then under their son Hilary, and finally under Ran Ogston, who joined the staff in 1951 and took over in 1959. Like Pat Savage at Oxford, he maintained that he never wanted to be a headmaster, and like Pat Savage he made a very good one, being a humanizing and civilizing influence. He and Pat set about bridging the gap that had occurred between the two schools, and they arranged a communal cricket match at Hurlingham as a convenient half-way point. At first Summers *ma* played against Summers *mi*, and later the two schools produced a combined team against a junior side from Eton or Harrow.

In 1966 the local council clapped a compulsory purchase order on the site in order to build a civic centre there. In fact, the school's having few, if any, local connections and the increasing difficulty at that time of travel from London probably meant that its days were numbered, anyway. Now, apart from the somewhat desecrated grounds, all is gone except the memorials to the dead of both wars in St Peter's Church, Bohemia Road, to which the school had walked, weather permitting, for Mattins every Sunday.

* * * * *

After Farnborough in 1939 and Summers *mi* in 1940, a third school was evacuated to us: St Cyprian's from Eastbourne in January 1942. Founded by L. C. Vaughan Wilkes, this school has been more written about than most prep schools: George Orwell, Cyril Connolly and Gavin Maxwell remembered it with little favour, but Henry Longhurst wrote affectionately of it. In 1939 the Eastbourne house suffered severe fire damage, and the school moved in September to Wispers, a large country house with magnificent grounds near Midhurst. But this house was taken over in January 1941 by the military authorities, whereupon the school amalgamated with Rose Hill, from Banstead, at Alderley in Gloucestershire. After a year in the Cotswolds, the Headmaster, W. J. V. Tomlinson, brought twelve boys with him to Summer Fields; and, with his wife and family, he moved into Mayfield, which had been shut up at the beginning of the war. One of the twelve boys was Peter Nathan, who recalls:

I myself joined St Cyprian's at Wispers on the outbreak of war, and there I came under the powerful influence of Mrs Wilkes, the Founder's wife, called by all boys at her insistence 'Mum'. She acted very much as joint Head during the School's wartime

123. Mayfield in the 1940s.

vicissitudes, and as a result of her direction Divinity was taught in depth to boys at an early age, often by her; many passages from the Book of Common Prayer and the Bible were to be learnt each week by heart, and not least one was required to recite the Collect for the Week. Her other speciality was History, to the extent that both T. T. B. Ryder and I were placed in the Townsend Warner History Prize competition even before arriving at Summer Fields.

On arrival in 1942, we were housed in Mayfield, where Bill Tomlinson became housemaster, assisted by his delightful wife Bud. She was the Wilkes' daughter, and the fact that the Wilkes family had intermarried with the Alingtons provided a Summer Fields connection. Similarly, Summer Fields' relationship with Radley was very much cemented when Bud's brother, John Vaughan Wilkes, became Warden.

My selection as captain of Cricket for my first Summer Term, with an old colour still in the school, was an embarrassment, but I was supported sympathetically and we won seven out of ten matches. These included two against St Bede's, ex-friendly-rivals from Eastbourne and now evacuated nearby. I had not played golf before coming to Summer Fields, and I played more like a cricketer than a golfer. Plus-fours were worn by many boys, but the nearest I got was wearing my trousers tucked into long woollen socks. This did not stop my winning the Dudley Medal, still a prized possession. My opponent, Carel Mosselmans (now chairman of Sedgwick Forbes PLC), had beaten me to win all four Golf Challenge Cups; because of the war, we received no replicas to keep, but National Savings vouchers instead.

One of many memories is of required study of the Classics before breakfast in Vth Form under GB, even Homer and Sophocles. Then, during breakfast, the master-in-

124. 1st XI 1943, with Peter Nathan as Captain.

charge would ring the bell and announce, 'If you have finished, you may read,' which was the signal for the Fifth-formers to study our Greek and Latin grammars at table prior to being tested immediately afterwards. The rest of the School opened their *Times* newspapers.

There was in those days a form called 'Modern Side', composed of those in their last year thought to have no bent towards the Classics. This was a mistake, as it made them feel thwarted and philistines. One who found Classics anathema and subsequently found work at Eton hard-going later became a Professor of Ceramics. Nowadays, the gifts of such a boy would be more likely to be discovered, since boys are encouraged to pursue interests of very diverse natures within or outside the curriculum.

Although I was there for only five terms, I owe a lot to Summer Fields. It was there that I gained a lasting love of Gilbert and Sullivan opera through GB playing his gramophone records of it. Eric Bowtell's film shows were always of the highest standard; nothing was ever too much trouble for him, and he even produced carefully prepared programmes of each show. This infectious enthusiasm coupled with the pursuit of excellence epitomised Summer Fields' contribution to my education: I am delighted that my son has just completed five years there.

The Lent term of 1942 was memorable for little other than bitter weather,

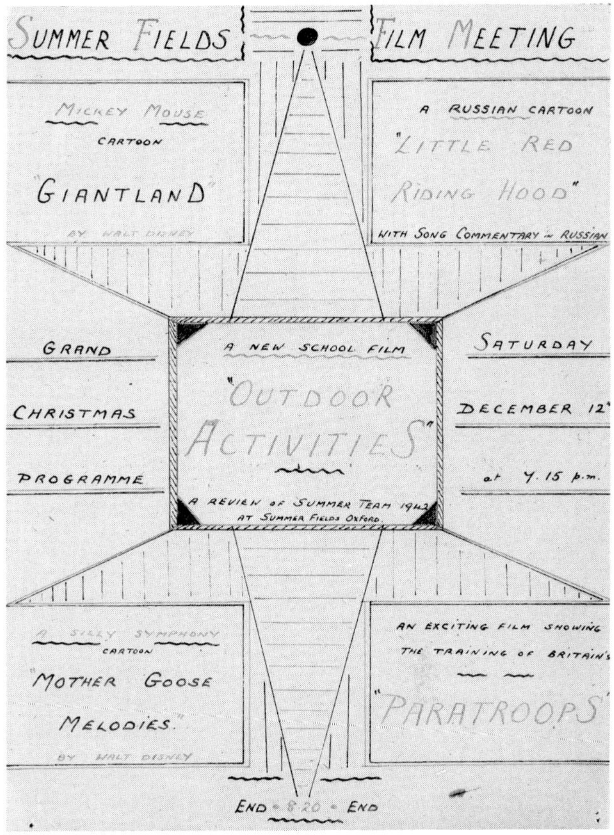

125. Eric Bowtell's film show for Saturday 12th December 1942.

chicken-pox and our first formal inspection by the Board of Education, who recognized the school as efficient, for it had by now settled down to a fairly normal routine, given the restrictions necessarily imposed by the war. Nights in the air-raid shelter became fewer, and plays were produced annually – except in 1943, when disease struck – but in the Dining-Room rather than the Gym. The leading figure behind these productions was Fergus O'Connor, a highly gifted master, and the performances of Julian Slade as Brutus and Peter Noble as Mark Antony in his 1942 *Julius Caesar* were admitted by the Magazine (i.e. GB) to be almost as good as those of Patrick Macnee and Antony Lyttelton in the halcyon days before the war. The postponement of *Henry V* from Michaelmas 1943 to Lent 1944 necessitated finding a new Henry, the original choice having left at Christmas; but Kerry St Johnston leapt into the famous breach to universal acclaim.

Travel restrictions meant fewer schools that we could play against, though we managed to reach Newbury to be trounced by Horris Hill in 1942. Our staple opponents at this period were the Dragon and St Bede's, whom we played at all three games; the cathedral Choir School and Cothill (cricket and soccer); St Edward's Colts (cricket and rugger); Swanbourne (soccer and rugger); and Winchester House, Harewood and New College at one sport each. The most remarkable sporting feat of the war occurred not in school matches but in the League cricket matches of summer 1943. Peter Nathan, captain of cricket for the second year running, made a century for Moseley against each of the other Leagues; whereupon, Moseley challenged a combined team of 'The Rest', and he made a century in that, too! His record is probably safe – though centuries are more likely to happen in League matches. The last century scored here by a boy was Benjamin Wood's for Case in 1979.

Throughout the war winters, Eric Bowtell kept the school entertained with a succession of splendid films on Saturday evenings and Sunday afternoons. In the Lent Term of 1942, he screened his first film of scenes from school life, the start of a succession which was to run on into the 1960s: much excitement for the boys in spotting their own brief appearances, riotous cheers for popular masters and barely suppressed hisses for the less popular.

On 1 December 1944 Mabel Williams celebrated her ninetieth birthday, and the school had a half-holiday, though she was unable to appear in person to request it, being laid-up after a fall. At Easter 1945, the Barbers took Summers *mi* back to St Leonards, and Miss Bell, who had been an admirable housekeeper since 1932, also departed. She was the first of many housekeepers who had to cope with the complexities of rationing, which went on in some forms for nearly a decade after the war, and in addition she had had to manage innumerable, and sudden, changes of staff.

There had also, not surprisingly, been a very rapid turn-over of teaching staff during the war: 'some rummish characters', as PMBS puts it:

> I remember a retired brigadier, who wore spats and was alleged to teach his French forms the technical terms used in roulette, and a non-practising clergyman, who wrote letters of protest to his colleagues in green ink. There was the excellent Miss Walford, known as 'Micky' after a celebrated 'Triple Blue' of that name. She was a Master rather than a Mistress, as she did Duty. A classic remark of hers was, 'Don't mock me, Davis, or I'll shake the liver out of you!' Bob James, who had been in my House at Westminster and a great pillar of the OTC, had a smart military moustache, but was in fact a conscientious objector. He was married to a Viennese wife called Lisl, and they lived in a caravan down in the farm fields with their daughters, who had botanical names like Bryony and Erica. Fergus O'Connor, strict but popular, taught music and played the organ, but had a terrible skin complaint, which he later went to Texas to have cured.

By 1945 the war was virtually over, and 'The Roll of Honour' appeared in the Magazine. As Patrick Savage has commented, we lost in each war a number approximating to the size of the school at the time, and it was particularly sad for him that the other three new masters of 1939 did not survive. Another casualty was Wing-Commander P. M. V. Lysaght, an old boy of the school and the son

126. The School at the end of the War.

of 'Liz' Lysaght; he had been married in October 1942 at St Michael's, Summertown, with the Summer Fields choir singing for the service. John Evans refused to make a war memorial the subject of an appeal for money; so no new buildings were put up – merely a wooden panel in Chapel engraved with the eighty-two names of the fallen, which was dedicated by the Bishop of Coventry, Cuthbert Bardsley OS, in 1951.

Apart from the innumerable birds of passage, some of greater duration than others, and the headmasters JFE and GB, the wartime staff had consisted of J. A. C. Lysaght, Ralph Robinson and the redoubtable Miss Hills: 'Rhoda and Mildred, appropriately dated Christian names,' writes PMBS. 'Miss Hill *mi* wore her hair like earphones. She was alleged to have been knocked over by a wave when bathing, and "never to have been the same again". They ran Manor, which was then a Lodge for little boys who had left House. They were known officially as Governesses, but they were much, much more than that. They taught the bottom two forms and brought their Latin up to such a high standard that they would have scorned the modern Common Entrance papers and might have made something of the Scholarship ones. Their firm foundations supported the whole fabric of the work in the school. They were never known as the Misses Hill, always as the Miss Hills, and for a long time after their departure, their little form-rooms still carried their names.' As 1945 drew to its close, others began to return: Pat Savage in December, Pat Marston in January 1946, and Jimmy Bell in February. Hubert Mullins did not in fact return, but married and lived nearby in the Woodstock Road at first, before returning to his native Africa.

At Easter 1946, GB handed over the editorship of the Magazine to Pat Savage. No more fortunate choice could have been made, nor more worthy successor found; though on the surface they might be thought to have had little in common, they were at one in their meticulous approach and delight in records; their sense of the school's history; their deftness in inducing old boys to write, or rediscover, their memoirs; and their encouragement of the young writer of both prose and verse. GB, in his valedictory paragraph, wrote of himself, 'After holding the position for sixteen years, he feels that he has by now committed all the errors of which an editor *can* be guilty and that it is time for somebody else to have a shot.' Pat began the next editorial with a delightful metaphor as well as a fitting tribute: 'It is only right that we should begin by taking off our hat to the late editor, as we step into his shoes. These, of course, he has worn so long and so well that they have grown to the shape of his feet, and it is for that reason the harder for another to put them on. Almost indeed it would be impossible, were he not still at our side ready with his help in doing up the laces...'

They were both being modest: the Magazine was passing from one Golden Age into another. If one could not quite say the same of the school as a whole, at least signs of post-war cheerfulness were beginning to appear.

LANGUAGE: 2

Nicknames seem to have had their day. Little more than a generation ago, every self-respecting boy had a nickname for every master, but since the war these have been increasingly few, and such as there are have been fostered more by the staff than by the boys. At the turn of the century, there were 'Bear', 'Crab', 'Bam' and 'Ping-Pong'; in the 1920s there were 'Sharky', 'Rhino', 'Boltosh' and 'String'; even after the war there were 'Ogre', 'Ticky' and 'Gibbers' (a verbal corruption of GB), but names tended to be simple adaptations of the surname, ending in either -o ('Bilo', 'Johno') or -ers, which still exists today ('Kidders', 'Langers'). This last is probably the final flickering of a branch of jargon which goes right back to the mid-Victorian period when the Prince of Wales, up at Cambridge, was referred to by the smart set as the 'Pragger Wagger'. This caught on, and came to be used for adapting both proper names (R. G. Pidcock was known as 'Pidder'; Willoughby Braddock in *Sam the Sudden* is called 'The Bradder' by his ex-school crony) and everyday objects, as 'wagger-pagger' for waste-paper basket, and indeed the word 'Rugger' itself. Elements of this are still heard in various spheres at Summer Fields, and never more resoundingly than on Friday mornings, when, as a change from Chapel, we have 'Congregagger Pragger'!

Schoolboy language proper is hard to keep track of; it is seldom recorded. Mention has already been made of Geordie Strafford's use of the word 'gut' for what was more officially called 'tuck' and what a later generation called 'guzz' (possibly a corruption of 'guts', and therefore the same word in essence?). As to the food provided by the school itself, a rich and varied menu of names, usually uncomplimentary and sometimes positively nauseous, exists in most such institutions, ranging from the starkly descriptive 'stodge' for those suety sponge mounds once thought so wholesome, to more imaginative flights of fancy such as 'matron's leg'. But these, as I have suggested, tended to be universal, rather than specifically Summerfieldian, terms for food which probably differed little from school to school: sago looked like frogspawn wherever you were eating it.

Almost as widespread, probably prevailing in most prep schools in certain eras and still alive in some, are a few concise Latin terms. *'Pax'* was a universal word to signify surrender, and one that both parties were expected to abide by. A typical exchange might go:

> 'You can't hit me now; you said "*Pax*".'
> 'Yes, but I had my fingers crossed.'

127. 'Guzz!' drawn by Haro Hodson in 1964.

This takes us into the language of gesture, or body-language even, and we shall meet it again; but first we must mention other Latin terms. *'Cave!'* can still be heard, and is interesting in that it preserves the 'Old', or Anglicized, way of pronouncing Latin; many boys in their time must have thought of it as 'KV', on the same lines as 'OK'. *'Quis?'* and *'Ego!'* remain in current use as a quick way of trading off unwanted objects. The more cautious used to reply, 'Ego decent' or even 'Ego decent to my liking' (a notable use of the gerund!), to safeguard themselves against having to accept an undesirable object. A stronger form of rejection lay in the word 'Fains!', which in various guises has been in use all over the country, and is a thoroughly Anglo-Saxon answer to a Latin question.

Terms like 'cad', 'oik' and 'bully' were once part of the currency of private education, only the third being still in use. 'Oik' (could this strange word have a Greek origin?), which says as much about the person using it as about those it is used to categorize, has been replaced by the equally unattractive 'yob' or 'yobbo'. 'Cad' has a charmingly nineteenth-century ring to it; at Summer Fields it has been used also as a verb, to 'cad' meaning to fight unfairly by schoolboy conventions, especially shin-hacking or pulling the hair. It was not looked upon as 'wet' to 'blub' if one had been the victim of such 'cadding'; indeed one's tears could pass for righteous indignation rather than weakness in the presence of pain.

A 'bate' (which does seem a more distinctive spelling than 'bait'), whether on the part of a boy or a master, was always something to provoke gossip and feelings of awe or sadistic delight if one was not the immediate target. There were set tactics for causing certain boys to erupt, the commonest being to goad them with clumsily ironical remarks like, 'Fan down! Fanny, fanny, don't get batey, dearie!' This would become a chant, accompanied by fanning gestures with hands outstretched towards the wretched victim, until his endurance broke and he would charge into the attack or collapse in tears. If a master then appeared to ask what the matter was, schoolboy honour forbade the unfortunate to 'sneak', but boys with authority (and this included, for instance, Lower School prefects) might sometimes acceptably 'report' others.

The Molesworth books of Ronald Searle and Geoffrey Willans contain a number of terms that have been used at Summer Fields. 'Chiz' and all its variants may possibly derive from '(Hard) Cheese', i.e. bad luck; its parallel 'swiz' perhaps incorporates elements of 'swindle'. One might also say 'swizzle' and 'swee', suggesting a French pronunciation of the root form: 'I claim big swee!' or 'I claim chiz!' were common cries at the injustices of fate. 'Bish' is a relatively common prep school word for a mistake, but how many other schools used 'skiv' to denote, not the domestic staff, but a boy who became (theoretically) subservient to another for payment?

'Be my skiv for half a sweet-ration a week?'

Skivs and slaves, who were unpaid but bound by loyalty, blackmail, or fear, were expected to do the bidding of their masters, and this was one of the ways in which gangs were formed. But such arrangements were often of short duration, the verb 'bunking' being capable of transitive and intransitive use in both grammatical and practical senses. Feeling secure in his freedom, the liberated one might turn and 'cock a snook' at his erstwhile lord, a gesture performed by thumbing the nose and twiddling the fingers – admirably expressive and often accompanied by some such derisive chant as 'So derdle erdle er to you!' Thumbs were also used to express gratification, very much on ancient Roman lines: the announcement of an extra half-holiday would be greeted by frantic pistoning up and down of the clenched fists with thumbs raised. No emperor or vestal virgin ever put so much energy into their 'thumbs ups'.

128. 'Chiz!' drawn by Haro Hodson in 1964.

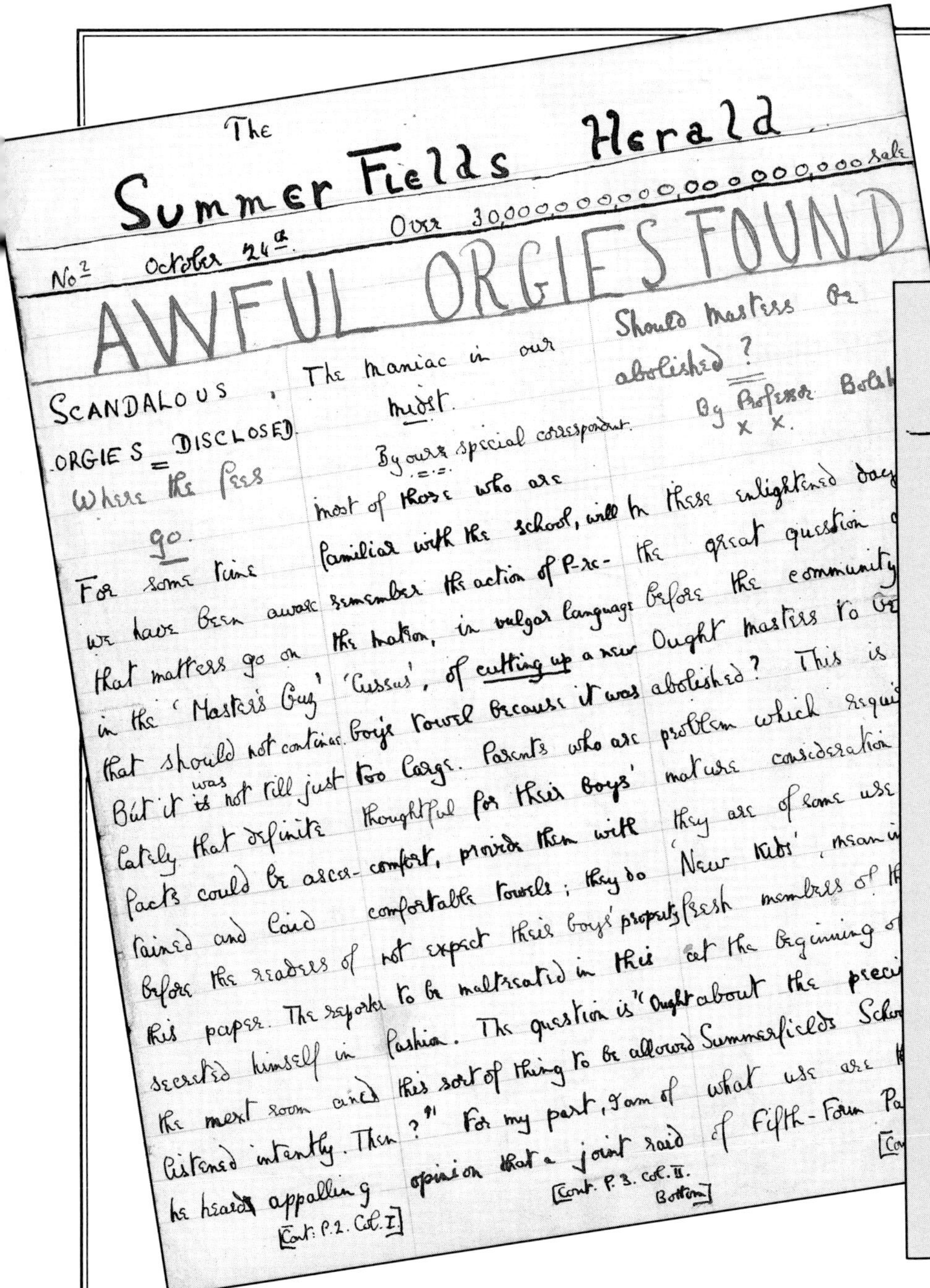

The Summer Fields Herald

Over 30,000,000,000,000,000,000 sale

No 2 October 24th

AWFUL ORGIES FOUND

SCANDALOUS, ORGIES DISCLOSED. Where the fees go.

For some time we have been aware that matters go on in the 'Master's Guz' that should not continue. But it was not till just lately that definite facts could be ascertained and laid before the readers of this paper. The reporter secreted himself in the next room and listened intently. Then he heard appalling [Cont: P.2. Col. I]

The maniac in our midst.

By our special correspondent.

Most of those who are familiar with the school, will remember the action of P-rc- the nation, in vulgar language 'Cussus', of cutting up a new boys' towel because it was too large. Parents who are thoughtful for their boys' comfort, provide them with comfortable towels; they do not expect their boys' property to be maltreated in this fashion. The question is "Ought this sort of thing to be allowed?" For my part, I am of opinion that a joint raid [Cont. P.3. Col. II. Bottom]

Should masters be abolished?

By Professor Bolsh[illegible] x x.

In these enlightened days the great question before the community Ought masters to be abolished? This is a problem which requires mature consideration. They are of some use [illegible] 'New Kids', meaning fresh members of the [illegible] at the beginning of [illegible] ought about the prec[illegible] Summerfields School what use are [illegible] of Fifth-Form Pa[illegible] [Con[illegible]

129. The *Summer Fields Herald* (1920), a delightful racy publication, of which four numbers have been preserved. It is full of mildly subversive comments about the Bear, Case, JFE, Penny and Miss Peirce.

130. *Pinnacle*, the Shell Magazine (1950) depicts on its front cover a caricatured Wilfred Williams being stung on the nose; its contents are a fictional tale, much in the Billy Bunter idiom with SF setting, ('Swisher Lorrington, the tyrant master of the Lower Fourth') and a strip cartoon about 'Mr Uranus the tec' – the work of Christopher Miles and Brinsley Turrell.

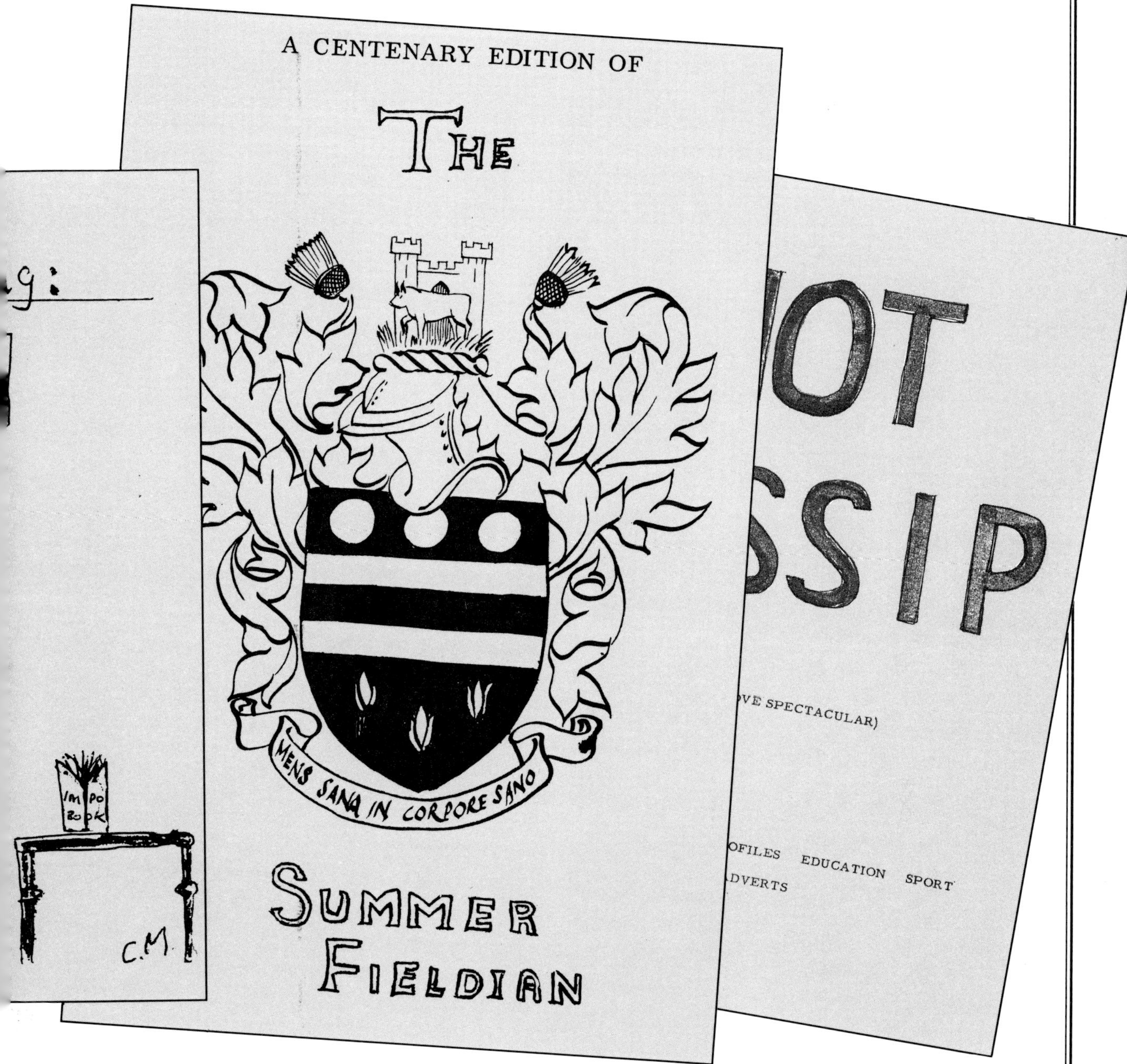

131. More respectful, the *Summerfieldian* in the early 1960s was started by Adrian Ward-Jackson and taken on by Charles Lowndes. It contained reproduced photographs, and such articles as 'An Introduction to the Caribbean' and 'The History of Skiing' as well as school news.

132. *Hot Gossip* (1981) was produced by Timothy Lezard and his colleagues in Middle Remove. It barely lived up to its name: its most sensational report was of a boy being hit in the teeth by a kite; but it contained a judicious mixture of interviews with school news, a little history and some mythology.

8

FROM AUSTERITY TO THE END OF AN ERA
1945–60

THE war ended. Summer Fields *mi* had gone back to St Leonards in Sussex, but Farnborough and St Cyprian's never started up again. R. W. G. Robinson retired after twenty-five years, but still reappeared for three days every term to invigilate the Common Entrance candidates: his unfailing kindness must have calmed many nerves. He really enjoyed these brief returns, arriving in time for breakfast at Top Table, where, it is said, he made tea-time conversation. An even bigger gap was caused by the departure of the Miss Hills, who between them had put in eighty-four years' service. They would have retired earlier, but loyally stayed on to see the war out. Liz Lysaght retired after thirty-five years in 1949 and died in the following year. The stage was set for a new generation of young masters under John Evans and GB.

John and GB. 'They look like two monkeys,' said Miss Walford once, looking closely at a school photograph. 'Different kinds, of course,' she added. Indeed, JFE's nickname among the boys was now Ticky from some supposed likeness to

133. 'They look like two monkeys!' This group from the 1946 school photograph shows, apart from the boys, Bets Terry-Bevan (Matron), GB, John Evans, Miss Walford and Mrs Beadon (Sister).

the monkey in a French book called *Ticky & Tacky*. GB didn't have a nickname. It had been a friendly convention that masters called each other by their Christian names, but GB was always GB and never Geoffrey at Summer Fields.

GB had some likes and dislikes that did not seem consistent with his innate conservatism. He ate strawberry jam at breakfast instead of marmalade, and there were some quite innocuous things that were anathema to him, such as onions, nutmeg and cats. It was a special mark of appreciation that he allowed Miss Morgan, who was his 'Dame' at Cottage for a dozen or so years, to keep a cat – white, allegedly deaf and apparently nameless. GB wore a faded sports jacket and baggy grey flannel trousers almost all the time. He even refused an invitation, when he was at Eton with the Scholarship candidates, to dine at Windsor Castle with the Governor, because he would have had to change into evening dress.

John was very peculiar about money. It embarrassed him and he did not carry cash around with him. It was always said that Matron did his shopping for him and that he had never been known to travel by public transport. He had some amusing turns of phrase: for instance, 'That boy is just sheer congealed smell.' He contemptuously described anything remotely innovative in education as 'raffia-work in the nude'. 'Minus a million' was his measurement of disapproval. He always held up the letters that he received (and seldom answered) to the light, to see if they had a decent watermark; but he only grunted without saying anything if they hadn't. He used the Evelyn Waugh phrase 'hired assassins' to describe masters bringing teams from other schools.

His own staff who returned from the war were Pat Marston, Patrick Savage and Jimmy Bell. Over the next five years, they were joined by H.W. Clayton, P.J.H. Johnstone, H.W.L. Hartley, the Rev. W.H. Jarvis, C.H. Hossell, W.A. Williams and R.N. Porthouse. Bets Terry-Bevan, who had arrived during the war, continued as Matron until 1952, when she was replaced, after a most unfortunate successor who lasted a bare month, by Nancy Lovett: she came to help out for the rest of the term and stayed for twenty-two years, taking over the additional role of Sister upon the retirement of Mrs Beadon in 1957. The faithful Hill remained in charge of 'Booty' until Christmas 1958, being succeeded in the new year by his equally faithful right-hand man, Jack Edmonds, who occupied the position for twenty years. Tom Allsop returned to the carpenter's Shop, where he continued until 1978; so, apart from absence at the war, he had been school carpenter for over forty years. In the school's century and a quarter there have been only six 'Chippies', one of whom lasted less than a year.

Another who served the school for many years was the butler, Gardner, a slightly shadowy, even sinister figure to both boys and masters, who saw touches of Philbrick in him. Ashen-faced and seldom smiling, he progressed up and down the long passage between the front door and the Kitchen, in a far from clean tail-coat, which smelt of sardine oil. He once went into the Study and announced Scotland's premier duke to JFE with the words, 'There's a man called Hamilton wants to see you.' His successors during the 1950s tended to be short-lived and to depart in the small hours with various items of cutlery.

134. The Ogre.

For some years after the war, Pat Marston was often absent ill; but in 1952 he was finally cured, and from that date countless 'Modern-Siders' have reason to bless his name. He it was who bellowed, stamped, fumed, praised and cajoled the weaker candidates through Common Entrance. He, with others, revived the interest in golf and raised the standard of cricket and enjoyment on Second Game, making it one of the most idiosyncratic and unforgettable experiences a Summerfieldian could have. Captain after captain received the inimitably scrawled set of instructions signed 'Ogre': 'Will bat ... Will bowl ...' A Third XI victory over the Dragon put him into the best of humours ... until the next 'Black Monday' when Modern Side had a Latin grammar test. Wearing his 'bate tie' and wielding a strange weapon known as 'booly-barker', the Ogre glowered over the form, enunciating his questions in a loud staccato: 'Number Eight: Genitive plural ... genitive plural of: *rex, dies, mare* ...' only to pad into the Lobby growling, 'They know nothing!' and then return to Middle School for 'Number Nine ...' It was mainly due to Ogre and to Pat Savage that the 'old' pronunciation of Latin, which most schools had ditched between the wars, if not earlier, was retained at Summer Fields until the 1970s. For his fiftieth birthday, Ian Kellie (maths master 1956–9) composed some doggerel which aptly captures the Ogre ethos:

The Ogre's in the Lobby, lads;
    The Ogre's in his lair.
He may push you through the window,
    So let those shout who dare!

Watch Ogre in the Lobby, lads,
    For weather foul or fair.
The Borvan barometric mood
    Reflects the Abingdonian air.

When it's 'Ugh!' or 'Grunt!' look out!
  The Ogre's got a hate ...
And 'Wah!' and 'Grrr!' – it might be *you*
  If Ogre's in a bate.

There goes Lord Borva with a scowl;
  The sky grows surely darker.
Many boys are sure to howl:
  He's got his Booly-Barker!

But when the Third XI's won a match,
  Or M. Remove are sane,
And Ogre's in the Lobby, lads,
  The world's all right again.

Now only Ogre gets away with such
  A strange sartorial hobby
As slippers on the playing-field
  And hob-nails in the Lobby.

And Ogre wears plus-fours, my lads,
  When Ogre's dressed for golf.
And Ogre wears the trousers,
  So don't you dare to scoff ...

and more of the same kind. That last verse, incidentally, shows that many people still did call the game 'goff' before the media stereotyped it as golf.

Patrick Savage was the antithesis of Ogre: tall, spare, meticulous and aesthetic, at first painfully thin from years in a POW camp, he at once appealed to boys by his entertaining but highly disciplined teaching, infectious laughter, beautiful handwriting, ingenious word-play and endless doodling. In the days before 'graffiti' had become part of the common man's language, he defaced and decorated dull old textbooks. 'Shortbread Eating Primer' was not enough for him: *CLIVUS*, a beginners' Latin verse book, was transformed into first *OBIMUS* and then *GROBIMOSHY*, and *COMPARATIVE ATLAS* became *BOOM-BARABIMBO BABEAST*. He did not in fact teach geography but classics, especially Latin verses, French and most notably English, which he took over from Bob James in 1949 and ran in a most lively manner, enticing generations of boys to enlarge their vocabulary, improve their script, enjoy good authors and try their hand at both reading and writing poetry. Pat's own poems were published in more than one post-war anthology; his cartoons and witty sketches enjoyed a more select but highly appreciative public.

If the two Pats knew the value of amiable dottiness, Jimmy Bell was equally

135. 'GROBIMOSHY'.

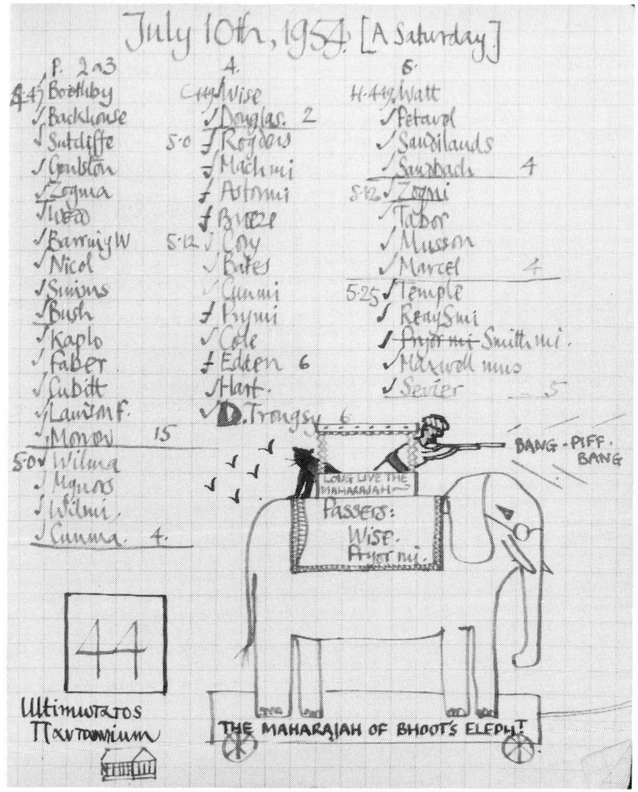

136. A page from the Bathing Book, in which the boys who swam each day were recorded, together with much else in the imaginative treatment of Patrick Savage.

MUSIC, BY PATRICK SAVAGE (1944).

It is the last of all the metaphors
When words have failed. It is the ultimate
Most splendid transformation into time
Of the eternal nameless things that space
Cannot enclose; sadder than sorrow is
And soaring over joy. It is the truths
Of mathematics, but with beauty added
In such designs as darken into nothing
The exquisite unities of coloured contrast
And counterpoise of shapes, or the precision
Of intricately twisted glass and stone.
It is the paradox that has resolved
The paradoxical: repose in movement,
Depth that uplifts, and satisfaction even
In disappointment. And it is, besides,
Across the boundaries of difference.
The only common language left for sharing
All the unformulated private worlds
That men have dreamt of, going on for ever.

137. (*left*) 'Music', by Patrick Savage.

138. (*above*) Jimmy Bell and Wilfrid Jarvis at the Hay Feast. c. 1949.

individualistic, but in a more workmanlike vein. Himself a member of GB's 1932 Fifth Form and a scholar of Radley, he took on his mentor's mantle in 1952, so well-versed in the school's classical tradition that he knew exactly what to preserve and where to introduce a more modern and elastic approach. From the first he was a success. Popular without ever courting popularity or pandering to the second-rate (he could use his wit to blistering effect if one fell below the expected standards), he was for many years the producer of the annual play, of which sensitive declamation and simple effects were the hallmarks. Phenomenally well-read, he introduced his pupils to the joys of Maugham, Saki, Maupassant, Oscar Wilde and many others. As a boy he had represented the school at both cricket and rugger, and as a master he ran the latter for several years. He and Pat Savage were GB's lieutenants in Cottage, and a more interesting trio to amuse the young scholar's leisure hours would be hard to imagine.

Harold Clayton was another original. Gifted as both a musician and a mathematician, he was stimulating and unpredictable. During the 1960s he teamed up with D. N. Straker of Downsend School, Leatherhead, to write a best-selling maths course, published and ably marketed by the Pergamon Press of Robert Maxwell, who had four sons at the school. In singing lessons, no instruction as to how to sing was ever given (probably this was the prep school norm at that time, apart from choir schools), but much enjoyment was had from chorally roaring out traditional songs ancient and modern, which subsequent generations have never had the chance to learn, to their sad loss. Harold lived at Old Lodge until his marriage in 1952 to his cousin Margaret Charlton, who also later joined the teaching staff; they then bought a house on the Banbury Road, a mile to the north of Summertown.

Philip Johnstone ran the French, and his wife Joyce took over the youngest form after the departure of Sheila Herdman for Canada. Phil loved minutiae and tricky points, was in charge of the Buzzer after GB gave it up, and always used tiny pencils, seldom more than an inch long. Was it true that he cut up new pencils to produce these? Quite possibly. Together the Johnstones looked after Mayfield for fifteen years and then became the first occupants of New Lodge

139. Joyce and Philip Johnstone.

on the Front Drive. The French results of thirty years of Fifth Forms are a testimony to PJJ's skill as a teacher: with PMBS and JLB, he produced a textbook, *Preparatory French*, which was used for many years throughout the school, and no doubt GB approved of this successor to his own French book.

Harold Hartley OS was a traditional schoolmaster, who dealt with history and geography in the days when these were still taught as groups of facts to be memorized. Methodical and strict (with himself as much as with his pupils), he overawed some by his inexorable methods; but not a few came to bless him when, at their public schools, they found that they had at their fingertips all the important dates and events in British history – an invaluable framework upon which to hang the clothing of politics, characters and theories. Harold, speediest of right wings, was in charge of First Game football for nearly thirty years and managed some fine teams. With his wife Joan he took on Newton when it reverted from being a Sanatorium in 1958. He tilled its lovely garden with dedication, while she made a gracious home for two dozen middle-school boys.

140. Newton, for many years the school's sanatorium, under a succession of Sisters, culminating with Sister Beadon; it reverted to being a Lodge in 1958.

Wilfrid Jarvis was a chaplain after John Evans's heart. Steeped in the impeccable Anglican tradition and possessed of a tuneful voice, he conducted services of deep devotion with the full regalia of vestments and frontals, bells and genuflection, but stopped short of incense. A friend of John Betjeman, he taught English as well as what was then called scripture, and he was a good teacher. Less orthodox but more amazing was Charles Hossell, a first-class all-round sportsman who ran the cricket for some years. But it was his maths lessons that were unusual. The syllabus was taught, and well taught, in about half the term, for the rest of which he read to his forms: Saki, Arnold Bennett, Dornford Yates, Eric Linklater, whatever took his fancy. It was outrageous, and the authorities would surely not have approved, but it worked.

Wilfred Williams and Richard Porthouse became the staple residents of Old Lodge for many years. Wilfred taught history in a way that was more relaxed than, but not incompatible with, that of HWLH; he founded and organized the train club; but his overwhelming passion was classical music – a love which he transmitted to many colleagues and pupils. He arranged for notable musicians to visit and play at the school on several occasions, particularly the conductor Charles (now Sir Charles) Groves, who was most encouraging to our budding musicians, including 'The Scholars'. 'Porty' taught most subjects in his time; his degree was in English, but he is more frequently remembered as a PT instructor and raconteur of Munchausen-type tales featuring his own military exploits in India. 'Porty of the Punjab' was an *alter ego* in which perhaps even he himself came to believe, but he was really the kindest of men.

So it was a cultured staff with touches of eccentricity combined with real intellectual power, keen sporting interest and ability. Nobody worked harder in the post-war 'austerity era' than GB. John Evans suffered breakdowns in 1943 and 1953, taught less and less, and became a squirearchical figurehead. Still lovable but more remote, he would stroll down to the farm or watch football matches, clad in plus-fours, co-respondent shoes and a great teddy-bear coat, his simian smile just visible beneath a cloth cap, and his high-church voice occasionally lifted in exhortation or execration. In the Study, smelling of cologne and turkish cigarettes, he failed to answer letters unless they were deftly fielded by Eric Bowtell, sometimes beat boys (though more often he left this to GB), and even more occasionally handed out pay-packets to the staff. He would walk round for several days at the end of term, his pockets bulging with little brown envelopes, which the staff knew contained their salaries but which he found it hard to bring himself to hand over. Finally, 'Here's tuppence ha'penny, my dear,' he would gurgle deprecatingly, as if financial transactions were sordid but to be got through with graceful good humour.

Physically, the school changed little under John's headmastership, though the steady increase in numbers over the period meant the occasional shuffling around of the various uses to which buildings were put. Often as many as three forms were taught simultaneously in New Room, and two in the Gym, sometimes two in Middle School; and for certain periods GB would have Fifth Form and, say, Middle Fourth at the same time in Fifth Form Room. Fifth Form under JLB was taught round the long table in French Room, which also housed the Buzzer-cum-stationery-cupboard. Lessons were taken in the Green Hut opposite the Gym, and in 1950 a 'Garden Hut' was erected behind Old Lodge to serve as an extra classroom. These huts were not noted for their warmth in winter; the rooms in the main school building had open fires, and the Gym and the Changing-Room were heated by monstrous black stoves. The work of coal-heaving and fire-lighting was done by the uncomplaining maintenance staff.

Throughout this period films were a regular feature of the week in the two winter terms, and Eric Bowtell, through his connection with the Scala Cinema in Walton Street, was able to get the latest and best full-length feature films for Sunday afternoons as well as a cheerful assortment of 'shorts' for Saturday evenings. These were projected in New Room, which was set up as a cinema with benches and desks rearranged by the New Room Vergers. Early-Bedders and Non-Timers saw roughly half the Saturday evening show (unless they were in the Black Book), the former coming down from their dormitories in dressing-gowns and slippers. Half-Timers and Whole-Timers saw the complete programme. EFB also made an annual film of school life, first in monochrome, later in colour, which particularly featured the River Feast, the Hay Feast, the Sports and the games. Other seasonal entertainment was provided in December with the Carol Service, modelled upon that of King's, and the latest Bell production, often with a curtain-raiser performed by First and Second Form. The main plays in this era were *Androcles and the Lion, The Critic, Tobias and the Angel, The Boy with a Cart, Macbeth, A Midsummer Night's Dream, Julius Caesar, Ajax* and *Lady Precious Stream*.

141. Eric Bowtell, whose films delighted generations of boys in the 1940s, 1950s and 1960s.

Academically and culturally, the school continued to flourish. Its sporting record was satisfactory, though not brilliant. Its weakness was in its care for and comfort of the boys, both physically and emotionally – not so much the medical

142, Changing for Break in the 1950s.

care: when one was ill, one was usually well looked after, though Dr Hobson did have an unfortunate tendency to look upon an enema as a panacea – but in the actual living conditions and what is now called the pastoral side. The place could still be a bear-garden for the weak, the shy or the unusual boy. Food was inadequate in the post-war years; impetigo, veruccas and chilblains were rife. The school was cold in winter, and the Changing-Room stank in summer. Bullying was not unknown, and physical violence to some extent condoned. Prefects would frequently knee one's back and pull one's hair with great force: in most cases they merely thought that they were doing their job, which in fact consisted of little more than herding the school at certain hours of the day, using these methods to preserve order and a semblance of silence. Gangs existed, but seldom committed any real atrocities: the fun lay more in the organization – the hierarchy, the 'bunking' and promotions, and the secret plans. On one occasion of an unpopular boy's being taunted and booed in the boxing ring, John Evans, when it was suggested that he might stop the outcry, said, 'I like to think that it's just their way of clapping, my dear.'

Many of the staff were approachable, and most of them were genuinely interested in the school and their charges. But there was too little feminine influence – nearly all the staff were bachelors – and too little communication between the Study and the Prefecture over things that mattered. The scholars were cosseted and driven, the games-players were admired, the weak candidates were helped and dragooned; but the 'boy-in-the-middle', who was none of these things, was comparatively neglected. There was a lot of free time, which some used constructively, but others took as an opportunity to make mischief. Thirty

143. Fifth Form about to settle down to afternoon school in Fifth Form Room, which doubled as the Library from the 1930s until the 1970s. Identifiable in the picture are (*left to right*): Peter Kay, Graham Evans, George Breeze, Harold Dobbin, ?Christopher Alderson (in foreground), Patrick Wedd, ?George Chamier, Adrian Arnold, Edward Mynors and Patrick Hudson.

years earlier, they were given no such opportunity; thirty years later, their life was so busy, in addition to having so much to try out in licensed extra-curricular activity, that the Devil would find less chance. But this was the interim time: in many cases, it made the boys develop an admirable capacity to amuse themselves, but for some the week-end stretched ahead as a boring, and often chilly, blank. Life was easier in summer, though.

Despite steadily increasing numbers, John's bonhomie and love of the school and GB's loyalty and hard work, the machine was in danger of running down – and there was nobody to succeed. As GB puts it, 'We were both bachelors and heirless: whom were we likely to find ready and able to take on not only the school, but the mortgage which we had incurred in buying out the Williams–Alington interest? Moreover, we had yet to buy out the Maclaren interest – if we could raise the necessary money. Clearly we had to become a Trust with a Board of Governors who would ensure that the school would carry on. With much care we chose our Governors and, after protracted legal negotiations, we finally became the Summer Fields Trust Ltd in September 1955. What Mrs Maclaren and the old Doctor would have thought, who can tell? But "Mrs" by all accounts was a most progressive woman and we can but pray that she would have approved.'

The first chairman of the Governors was the Rt Rev. Robert Mortimer, Bishop of Exeter, who had known the school for some time, having had two sons there. His fellow-governors were six OSS, five of whom had also recently had sons in the school: Lieutenant-Colonel A.M. Borthwick, Admiral Sir William Davis, Viscount Lambert, The Rt Hon. Harold Macmillan, J.H. Max-Muller and T.G. Usborne. Two more OSS were added in November 1955: Sir Roger Mynors and the Hon. G.R. St Aubyn. Johnnie Max-Muller later became the second chairman, when the Bishop took the title of 'Visitor'. Giles St Aubyn served on the board for over thirty years, retiring in 1986, when, having finished teaching at Eton, he went to live in Guernsey.

The creation of the Trust was virtually John's last act as headmaster. In the Easter and Summer terms of 1956 he became less and less fit; he fell seriously ill in the first week of the Michaelmas term, and it became plain that he would never again he able to do the job. On 15 October the Governors appointed GB as his successor. GB's tribute to John is of interest. 'This was a sad ending to a career which had started in 1914 and to seventeen years of headmastership in particularly difficult circumstances. It is true to say that Summer Fields was the only mundane interest in John's life. He gave everything that he had to the school, and in his retirement he must have been conscious of work well done. I shall not pretend that in our long association we always saw eye to eye, nor will I deny that he could be very difficult to work with; but of his single-minded devotion there can be no question. I do not think that, when things were going wrong in the 1930s, either of us ever doubted that the luck would turn; he, more than anybody, was responsible for the fact that it did.'

If the generation gap was showing badly towards the end of John's period as headmaster, it was unlikely to improve under GB, for he was over sixty when he succeeded John. But he wisely co-opted Patrick Savage as his partner, and Pat persuaded GB to make some useful reforms during his four years in office. He abolished Bible-Reading, a New Room ceremonial when each boy stood up and read a verse in turn, causing more mirth than religious edification; he cut down on Sung Eucharists ('Long Chapel', as the boys used to think of it), and had the master-on-duty to read the lessons, which before had been monopolized by JFE's pious monotone. He gave the prefects more prestige and privileges, including the Prefects' Dinner; and his first set of prefects – Ian Schmiegelow, Anthony Letts, Basil Eastwood and Christopher Purchas – responded to this treatment in an exemplary manner. He also introduced distinction ties for prefects, scholars and 1st team players, and an annual dance with the girls of Greycotes. For many years, more or less coerced boys had been steering one another round the french-chalked dining-room floor on Thursday afternoons to the tinkling strains of the accompanist, while Miss Lane intoned, 'And – left, right, together; right, left, together . . .', and now at last there seemed to be some point in it.

But, more than all this, the first Appeal was launched with a Dinner on 14 November 1957 at Claridge's, presided over by the Bishop of Exeter. The health of the school was proposed by the Prime Minister, Harold Macmillan, and replied to by GB. By subsequent standards, this appeal was modest and amateurish, but it led to the first proper overhaul that the school had had for half a century, and that alone made it a landmark. The old six-seater desks, with their generations of ink-runs and hieroglyphics, were replaced by more up-to-date ones; and floor-lockers were removed, except in New Room. The form-rooms were repainted, and strip-lighting was introduced, as it had been in the Dining-Room in 1951. The playground was given a bitumen surface, and its ruinous fives courts pulled down; the Gym was re-roofed, the Carpentry Shop extended, and showers (at last!) and a boot-room were added to the far end of the Changing-Room. A new and larger Lobby was built, with a niche tailor-made for the portrait of Harold Macmillan that was later transferred to the Library. The plan to build six new form-rooms, however, had to be deferred through lack of funds.

The Cricket season of 1958 was one of the best ever. The First XI contained two superlative players, Rupert Daniels and David Calvert-Smith, and several very good ones. Daniels, the captain, was the mainstay of the bowling, taking 64 wickets in 16 matches. Calvert-Smith rarely failed with the bat, and made two 50s in the week that he won 5th scholarship at Eton; he is arguably the best all-rounder that the school has had since the war. These two, with support from Michael Faber and others, saw the team to nine victories, their only defeat being at the hands of Bradfield Colts.

It was not a vintage summer in terms of weather, though, and the Hay Feast had to be cancelled. But to compensate there was a visit from the Prime Minister and Lady Dorothy Macmillan, during which he planted a tree on the Masters' Lawn. This was the beginning of a period of great activity in the gardens and grounds, which had perhaps not always had the attention that they deserved. Under the guidance of Governor Tommy Usborne and Groundsman Frank Ricketts, a programme of planning and planting was started, which was to culminate in the Centenary Year with the opening of the gardens to the public. Mr Usborne presented a number of interesting and decorative trees, and Frank managed to obtain the remains of Miss Nancy Lindsay's unique collection of roses. The surrounding of the near fields with climbing roses certainly reintroduced the 'paradise' atmosphere that Lady Burne-Jones had noted a hundred years before.

Patrick Savage having been appointed assistant headmaster in 1956, and having produced a sumptuous Diamond Jubilee edition in 1957, handed over the editorship of the Magazine to Harold Hartley in 1958. Harold and his wife Joan also took over the running of Newton at the same time, when it became

144 and 145. The changing face of New Room. Above: As it was until the 1950s, with the open fireplaces and the massive six-seater desks. Below: c. 1960: new desks, new lights and more space.

146. The corner of the Playground, looking up Summerfield Road to Summertown, and through the gate towards Borva.

147. The Playground in the 1960s, as seen from Cottage, with the Cubicles block and the Gym beyond it.

148. Lobby interior, shortly before it was converted in 1960. Here Harold Macmillan and GB are making an almost royal progress towards the front door, past the oft-remembered shoe-lockers and over the uneven red and white tiles.

149. Prime Minister Harold Macmillan planting a Tulip Tree, assisted by Head Groundsman Frank Ricketts, June 1958.

a Lodge, and the sanatorium was moved to the top of House. This meant the pensioning off of the Newton Bus, a remarkable vehicle in which generations of ailing boys had been wheeled to Newton by Hill or Edmonds. Hill retired in the same year, after more than fifty years of devoted service in, and later as head of, the Maintenance Department. His single-minded loyalty and deep knowledge of how the school worked made him indispensable in the particularly difficult periods before and after the war; but Jack Edmonds, who succeeded him, showed the same qualities for the next two decades.

150. Hill – the faithful steward.

Harold Hartley produced some interesting magazine editorials between 1958 and 1964, in which he examined the status and role of prep schools and what they offered. Though himself an Old Summerfieldian and an Old Etonian, he was politically inclined to socialism; it was a source of entertainment to colleagues that on election days the Hartleys went off to vote, he Labour and she Conservative, and so they cancelled each other out. In his articles, he never pulled any political punches, but he did invite his readers to look at the school from a less complacent and conservative (with whatever size of C) viewpoint. His editorial at the beginning of a new decade begins with a noteworthy warning.

For Summer Fields the 1950s have ended with the superb triumph of Mr Macmillan's return to further power, which guarantees the future of this and other schools for another period, while the size of his majority and the manifest trend seem to offer a glimpse of even further-reaching approval. At any rate, at this moment it is difficult to look ahead into the 1960s and foresee (or, truth to say, wish to foresee) the worries and dangers.

All history tells us such an attitude is dangerous; the prophet entering 1910 might have felt nothing would go wrong in that decade; despite the Wall Street slump of October 1929, the prophet entering 1930 might only have foretold steadily improving years, nor have foreseen the heart-rending descent of that now much execrated period; but yet the prophet of 1890 or of 1900 or of 1920 or of 1950 was in fact in for a good

151. GB lining up the Leagues for tea at his last Hay Feast.

ten years, in each case ten years of prosperity and happiness, garish happiness those who grew up in the '30s are inclined to say, unhealthy happiness they rather like to sneer: because the '30s and '40s ruined and annihilated so many lives, and withdrew the rewards of lives just opening to grasp them, these generations, who were formed in them, hardly expect 1970 to enter without the unexpected and the unpleasant having happened, and the careless having been surprised.

Within three months, the unexpected had happened. GB's doctors forbade him to spend another winter in the Thames Valley, because of the state of his chest. So, after only four years as headmaster, he had to leave the school to which he had given forty-one years of his life. During that time, there was no year in which he had not had a profound effect upon many young lives – mainly in the form-room, often on the soccer pitch or cricket field, sometimes in Cubicles and Cottage via his beloved P. G. Wodehouse or Gilbert and Sullivan. Nobody could sit under him and not be affected: some were antagonized, some were frightened, but all were educated in depth, and a few began to realize what a remarkable teacher he was, even before they ceased to be his pupils; many came to recognize this afterwards. Shy and gauche in some ways, he was not a misogynist, as has sometimes been alleged: more than one mother chose Summer Fields specifically because of him. He is an impossible figure to encapsulate, but Bobs Alington came as near to doing so as anyone is likely to manage, when he wrote his obituary a few years later for the School Magazine.

I suppose he thought of little other than Summer Fields and Summer Fieldians, cricket and cricketers, Gilbert and Sullivan operas and their casts, the Classics and classical authors, with occasional excursions into the worlds of French, P. G. Wodehouse and football. It was his delight to introduce generations of boys to these worlds of his. But, though he loved cricket and everything to do with it, he was a very indifferent performer; though he loved the Classics, he was not a real scholar; though he loved Gilbert and Sullivan, he was quite unmusical. And this was his glory. He had but two talents, and he went and gained other two. The quality of his knowledge was the result of determination and hard work: he made himself an expert – not a scholar, but an expert. If he had had more scholarship, he would not have been such a great teacher.

To generations of Summerfieldians he was a figure of awe – tall, gaunt, white-haired, apparently arthritic, frequently turning his left wrist and arm over in the air, or playing imaginary strokes with an imaginary bat and a flat left elbow. His bark could be alarming, but was he really in a 'bate'? Eight times out of ten – no! On the other two occasions he was probably exasperated, for he was a perfectionist. Failure on the part of those with whom he had so thoroughly identified himself maddened him. It was like his own failure.

GB was essentially humble. He realised his limitations and accepted them, and made the best of what he had got, which was enough to turn him into a great schoolmaster – one who put the boys first, the school second, his teaching third, the rest of life fourth, and himself a bad fifth. Humility and experience had made him wise.

I like to think of him organising cricket on the Elysian Fields:
Odysseus, caught Aeneas, bowled Bolton, 0.

153. Summer Fields c. 1960, the Tennis Competition in progress.

'I hope you are a Communicant and that you play Bridge,' were the closing words of Dr Williams's letter confirming John Evans's appointment as an assistant master in 1914.

Luckily, JFE was able to reply in the affirmative to this dual qualification, but not all prospective masters had such a smooth entrée. Both GB and LAGS have commented upon how in the early days new members of staff were very much left to find their own feet. When 'Bam' Evans arrived in 1884, Mabel Williams asked him what he had come to do at Summerfield. He said that he had come to teach the boys French.

'You won't,' was the encouraging reply.

Similarly, upon Bam's departure, Bear Alington, having interviewed Roger Jacques and given him the job, said afterwards to John Evans, 'He's a nice chap, but I don't suppose he'll teach them much.'

Employment of staff was mainly haphazard and done more by word of mouth or by knowing the right people than by anything so vulgar as advertising. Patrick Savage had decided as a boy at Westminster that he wanted to be a schoolmaster. So, towards the end of his time at Christ Church, he was beginning to approach Gabbitas and Thring, famous for their rubric, 'Write promptly yet carefully to ...' But he also mentioned his plan to Francis Egerton OS, who won the MC in the war and later became chairman of Mallett's. Egerton, hearing that Pat wanted to teach, said, 'You must come and see John.' John was of course JFE, who was busily engaging four new masters for September 1939.

So we canoed up the Cherwell, and landed at the Shallow End. It was a marvellous late May afternoon, and we strolled up through the fields in the sunshine until at last we reached the farm gate, and, across the playing fields, for the first time I saw *SUMMER FIELDS*. I shall always remember that great moment, and I still think that the proper way to approach the School is from the country, and not through the increasingly suburbanized Summertown. At that time, the view can hardly have changed since the days of the Foundress, and it fitted in with the old address: 'Summer Fields, *Near* Oxford.'

John Evans was the 'Master in Cottage' then, and that was where we went. He could not have made things easier for me, and we clicked in no time. I have a letter from him, dated May 21st. It is the only one that ever began, 'Dear Savage ...' and it offered a 'salary of £60 a term ... with full board and housing (that sounds better than "lodging") and also laundry ... I hope that you will enjoy life here; in fact I do not doubt for a moment that you will do so.' He was bang right there!

154. David Kidd-May, who has taught at SF since 1955.

Similarly, some years after the war, David Kidd-May's letter of application from Worcester College arrived on the morning that John Evans and GB happened to go down for a stroll in the Parks to examine the cricketing talent for the new season. There they met J. C. Masterman, the Provost of Worcester, who was also keen to see how the young hopefuls were shaping in the first trials. As a result of this fortuitous meeting, David was invited to lunch with JFE and GB.

I remember little about the occasion now, except that it was out of term, the rooms and seemingly endless passages echoed emptily to our footsteps and I was surprised by the amount of glass overhead. We had lunch in the private dining-room (where the administrative offices now are) and, as I sat looking out onto the lawn and the mulberry tree, I was acutely aware of the different aura surrounding each of my hosts. John sat at the head of the table and did all the talking, I on his right offering my modicum, GB on his left saying virtually nothing, but exerting the curious effect of making me more careful not to commit some *faux pas* or other to satisfy *JFE*'s demands rather than his. It was a peculiar influence, which has fascinated me ever since.

After lunch, we walked round the fields and down to the river. By the time I left, it was somehow clear that I was being offered a job, since I seemed to measure up to some degree of satisfaction and, anyway, John Ralphs was departing to a school nearer the centre of Oxford and needed replacing. And my appointment there and then would save the trouble of advertising.

No mention had been made of salary. This, to the vulgar and impecunious me, was a matter of no little importance; to JFE, one felt, it was a subject to be avoided at all costs. Since no-one else seemed willing to bring it up, I summoned the courage to request a second interview in order to put the crucial question personally. It was an embarrassing moment for all concerned, unexpectedly so when I felt bound to mention that the figure offered was less than the amount my old prep school was prepared to give me. The consternation created by this reply was unmistakably unnerving: the idea that my little prep school should be in such a position was obviously untenable. The normally sauve, but now shaken, JFE was only able to say that he was sure he could equal, or even better, what I had been offered. Thus it came about that my arrival at Summer Fields was a popular event: everyone's rise in salary saw to that. My star had been launched on the sort of ascendancy that could only result in a burn-out.

155. Duncan Williams, master at SF 1955–63.

That story and the next one lent colour and substance to the picture which the younger members of staff had of JFE as an unworldly throw-back to another age. The image was one of a member of Boodle's who never carried any money on him and, when he wished to leave the premises, would ring up Bot (Eric Bowtell) in his secretarial-cum-bursarial office in Manor to apprise him of the fact. Bot would then appear at the front door with the Daimler and a wallet stuffed with notes.

When Duncan Williams came for his first interview in Michaelmas 1955, he was driving a car he shared with a colleague at Little Hampden Manor; but it was his friend's turn to have the car when he was summoned a second time. That he was now without his own transport was not apparent to JFE until the time came for departure. On learning that he had to cover some of the return journey by bus, John showed considerable signs of disquiet, clutching Duncan's arm several times with the earnest enquiry: 'Are you sure you'll be all right, my dear?' and insisting on accompanying him to the bus-stop. On the way, he frequently returned to the subject of Duncan's well-being, and showed deep concern about the whole risky business. But, as they approached the stop, it seemed that part of the reason for John's coming too was to display his knowledge of the stop's whereabouts, for the note of pride in his voice was unmistakable when he pointed it out. As the bus drew up, John was still wondering about this dangerous undertaking. In a now somewhat doubtful state himself, Duncan boarded the bus and looked back finally upon the trim, tweed-suited figure waving hesitantly, a confused expression of alarm and admiration almost overcoming the polite smile of farewell.

In the following term, Ian Kellie had a most agreeable interview and tour of the school, after which he and John returned to the Study. It was confirmed that he had secured the job, and John finally enquired if there was anything that he would like to ask. Ian searched desperately in his mind for the kind of question which would at the same time reveal the broad scope of his intelligence, the astuteness of his perception and his overwhelming suitablity for the job. The long seconds dragged by and, not wishing to remain unimpressively dumb, he found himself asking rather falteringly whether there were any special rules about smoking – where he ought not to do it, for instance. John was obviously determined to do justice to the profundity of this question and puckered his brow in long and serious consideration of its implications. 'Well, my dear,' he eventually replied, 'I think that perhaps – if you don't mind, that is – it might perhaps be better if you don't smoke in the Chapel.'

There are fewer anecdotes about sackings; the principal characters are less likely to feel that they appear in a good, or amusing, light. It is hard to assess the proportions of what is true and what merely *ben trovato* in those that have survived; anyway, their protagonists had better remain anonymous. One young master, after a disagreement in the Study, had the *Railway Guide* thrust across the desk at him with the words, 'Would you like to choose which train you will leave by?' But the young master kept his head and called the bluff, taking the book and looking up a train with every appearance of seriousness; whereupon the headmaster capitulated completely, and presumably conceded whatever point had been at issue.

Another master was sacked for general slackness and disloyalty, but he was extremely popular with the boys, usually being cheered all the way to and from the wicket in the Broomstick Match. He was reinstated after assuring the Headmaster amid tears that he would never regret a change of heart. He survived for nearly twenty more years, but he was finally sacked by the next Headmaster.

A very colourful character numbered a way with words among his charms. These charms had led to an entanglement with one of the matronal staff, and the unfortunate outcome was not unpredictable. Word got about that Miss —— was 'in an interesting condition', and these were the days when such a state of affairs meant dismissal for both the interested parties. The Headmaster tactfully refrained from doing anything until the Summer Term ended, and then the matter was taken out of his hands. The master stormed into the Study and delivered an impassioned tirade which lasted for ten minutes and ended with the words, 'I resign!' He then burst out of the Study, declaiming to the intrigued and not unsympathetic colleagues who had remained within earshot, 'The b*****'s sacked me!'

156. Winter Fields: 2.

9

INTO THE SECOND CENTURY 1960–75

MANY men join the teaching profession because they want to become headmasters: Patrick Savage was not one of these. He guided the school ably and imaginatively through fifteen of its busiest years, but always maintained that he had not wanted to become headmaster and that he never enjoyed the job. Under these circumstances, he was fortunate in having a strong support team: the moment that the Governors appointed him, he asked for Pat Marston and Jimmy Bell as assistant headmasters. This had the added advantage of bringing Perdita Marston into the running of the school. Not only did she provide a much-needed feminine influence in a still largely bachelor establishment, but it gave a pleasing sense of continuity to have a member of the foundress's family among those in authority once again. She mothered the little boys, read to them on Sundays and sometimes came to tuck them up at night, as her great-grandmother had done eighty years before.

PMBS took over just when a number of the building operations resulting from the Appeal were reaching completion. The most obviously striking was the

157. Patrick Savage, Head Master of Summer Fields 1960–75.

158. Jimmy Bell OS, Assistant Headmaster 1960–78.

159. Painting of Harold Macmillan by Joseph Oppenheimer, which originally hung in the new Lobby, but was later moved to the Goelet Library.

new Lobby, which was twice the size of the old one and more practical as well as more imposing. The familiar, fondly remembered and unevenly worn red and yellow tiles were replaced by black and grey plastic ones, a recess was prepared for the portrait of Harold Macmillan, and the shoe-lockers were exiled to beyond the Changing-Room, which had also had something of a face-lift, and where the new showers spouted plentiful and unaccustomed hot water.

New kitchens and store-rooms were built at the end of the passage, where previously a mere scullery had adjoined the Dining-Hall. The old kitchen was converted into a Science Laboratory and Lecture Room, largely through the generosity of Captain Robert Maxwell, whose four sons were at the school in the 1950s and 1960s. His main enterprise at that time was the Pergamon Press, and this gave its name to our laboratory – a nice blend of classics and science. The Lecture room was furnished through part of John Evans's bequest, but later the two rooms were reunited as one large physics and chemistry area. This

160. The old Lobby, a view which ceased to be in 1960.

161. The new kitchen (1960) with the chef, Martin Dornig.

resulted in an amusing (and rightly preserved) anomaly: if one enters from the north, one is going into the Evans Laboratory, but from the south it is the Pergamon Laboratory. To have a science lab was quite advanced for 1960, and we were one of the first prep schools to do so.

The summer of 1961 saw the completion of New Lodge, the first house to invade the garden and orchard of Old Lodge. Philip and Joyce Johnstone were its first occupants, having given up Mayfield after twelve years to Duncan Williams. TDDW had arrived in 1956 after working for some years as an Assistant District Commissioner in East Africa. He took over First Game cricket, which he ran for half a dozen years with an assortment of keen young assistants – mostly Sussex martlets whom GB had pointed in the direction of Summer Fields. David Mordaunt was the first of these; he had played county cricket for Sussex and Berkshire, and was long remembered for his lusty hits in staff matches, using his great height to advantage with both bat and ball. He went on from Summer Fields to Stowe and thence back to his old school, Wellington, where he became the housemaster of Beresford.

Next came Chris Saunders, *en route* for Cambridge, where he was only kept out of the cricket side by a young man called Brearley; but he later played cricket for Oxford, while reading for a Dip. Ed. As well as being a fine wicket-keeper, he was an enthusiastic and talented soccer coach. He was subsequently a housemaster at Bradfield, whence he would come over regularly to referee our matches, and then Headmaster of Eastbourne. Chris Snell followed in the footsteps of his father Edward, who made such an impression here in the 1930s. A Wykehamist of great sporting ability, he ran our cricket with both Duncan and

162. David Mordaunt and Chris Saunders, masters at SF in the early 60s who both went on to distinguished teaching careers at public schools; DJM at Stowe and Wellington; CJS at Bradfield and then Eastbourne as Headmaster.

then John Murray before returning to Sussex in 1966, to assist Edward at the family school, Mowden, and then to take it over upon Edward's death.

163. A view from House of the League PT competition in 1964.

The 1962 cricket XI was an outstanding one, captained by Massimo Brooke and having the record-breaking Dennis Tabor as its main bowler. His 82 wickets at just over 3 runs apiece in 15 matches is likely to remain unchallenged, as fewer matches are played nowadays. He also made 352 runs in the season, with Rupert Parsons, the wicket-keeper, not far behind him at 323. Mark Brooke and Mark Faber each made nearly 250, and another five scored more than 100 in the season. The batting failed to reach over 100 on only three occasions, and in fact Brooke declared in 10 out of the 16 matches. Our totals over the season were: 128, 152–2, 138–7, 128 (having been 22–5), 163–4, 146–9 (in reply to Swanbourne's 193–2 declared), 137, 55, 157–8, 86, 207–9, 88, 193–6, 120–8, 151–9 and 128–9. With such batting and Tabor bowling, the only defeat was against Bradfield Colts, the one match that Tabor missed. The cricket remained in a healthy state through the mid-60s, with first Mark Faber and then John Barclay, both of whom became Sussex county cricketers, the latter ending up as captain.

Two Old Summerfieldians joined the staff in the early 1960s. Larry Rawstorne, the son of a Lancashire rector who had also been here, had been in the soccer XI for four years as a boy and later played in the Public Schools Soccer Trials. He helped greatly with the sport before emigrating to Australia, where he still lives. Nicholas Aldridge was on the staff from 1962 to 1966, during which time he initiated the printing press and managed the school's pop group, 'The Scholars', which was formed early in 1963. They gave several concerts with changing personnel over the next three years and made a record in the Centenary Year, which rapidly sold out. One of the group, Nick Horne, enterprisingly made his own electric bass in carpentry.

The centenary was celebrated with suitable éclat and in diverse ways. The preparations are amusingly recorded in the daily log-book kept in meticulous nautical manner by Commander Eric Hitchens, who took over as Bursar from Bill Acworth in 1963. Sadly, the splendid new Pool, donated by parents and friends, was not ready until September 1965, but the Vinery was enlarged and refurbished,

164. 'The Scholars', the school's pop group, which made a record in 1964; (*left to right*): Nick Horne, Oliver Lee, Mike Thomas (*behind*), Nicholas Polunin, Charles Marling and Martin Gore.

165. The Swimming Pool, which in 1966 finally replaced bathing in the Cherwell.

166. Eric Hitchens, bursar from 1963 to 1975.

and half a dozen new form-rooms were built or created from existing rooms. It was a sprucer, up-to-date school that greeted the Old Boys who returned, many for the first time in years, for the school's hundredth birthday. Pat Savage masterminded a string of Events and Occasions with great skill and resounding success.

In collaboration with Sir Anthony Wagner, Garter King of Arms, Pat designed a coat of arms for the school, and it was officially recognized in 1964. He used the red-white-red-white-red of the flag as his basis, and upon this he added three bezants (gold coins) symbolizing St Nicholas, to whom the Chapel was dedicated in 1962, and three lilies, in honour of our long Eton connection. He did not, of course, have to search for a motto, as Archie Maclaren's 'Mens Sana in Corpore Sano' predated the school itself. Besides this and helping with the production of the Scholars' record, Pat induced Haro Hodson to draw some cartoons relating to the Centenary Sports Day for the 1964 Magazine. As well as producing regular cartoons for the *Daily Mail* et al., Haro and his wife had produced an admirably athletic and poetic son, Peregrine, who won most of our competitions in both these spheres and has gone on to become a traveller and writer of international repute. His book *Under A Sickle Moon,* about the Afghan War, is compulsive reading.

In addition to these, there was the book of reminiscences, *A Century of Summer Fields* (see pp. 186–7), and in due course the Summer Fields Rose, raised by the celebrated John Mattock on the suggestion of Frank Ricketts, which finally appeared in 1969.

The first Event of the Centenary Year was a dinner on 3 April, in the Hall of Balliol College. Nearly all of the Best and Greatest Summerfieldians were there, and speeches were made by the Bishop of Exeter, chairman of the Governors, by Harold Macmillan and by the Headmaster. John Evans, Ran Ogston, Roger Jacques, Ralph Robinson, Edward Snell and Bobs Alington were there as well as 150 OSS, but GB was not.

Danny,
Hurstpierpoint,
Sussex.

My dear Pat,

I have just been carted off to Cuckfield Hospital, no private ward and a bloody row. I won't attempt to describe my feelings. Obviously I now have to scratch next week. I'll say as little as I can, but I don't think I've ever minded missing anything so much before. You will please give them all my love and say how sorry I am. I don't know if they're going to do anything for me here: if so, I shall hope to be up for the Australians and on June 19. Tell Harold, please. May you have the happiest of evenings.

Yours ever,
GB

Three weeks later he was dead.

167. Top Table in the Balliol Dining Hall for the Centenary Dinner, 3rd April 1964. The Bishop of Exeter presides, with Harold Macmillan on his right, and beyond them Patrick Savage and Ran Ogston. John Evans is at the far end of the table, and Bobs Alington at the near end.

168. Governor Tommy Usborne with Cuthbert Bardsley OS, Bishop of Coventry.

On 19 June a sherry party was held for local notables, friends of the school and former staff, and the following day served the dual role of Centenary Commemoration Day and Sports Day. A service was held in St Michael's Church, at which the address was given by the Rt Rev. Cuthbert Bardsley OS, Bishop of Coventry. At the request of GB's family, rather than having a special memorial service, the school used this Commemoration Service, when so many OSS were present, to pay respect to him. Then it was out into the sunshine, for a splendid Sports Day in the finest tradition of the no doubt rose-tinted memories that many of those present preserved. It was in fact a splendid summer; the press, both local and national, were mainly kind. The hard work of the two Pats, Jimmy Bell and Eric Hitchens paid off: the celebrations passed with admirable smoothness.

Pat Savage invited Cecil Day Lewis back to Summer Fields, and during the 1960s he and his wife, famous in her own right as the actress Jill Balcon, regularly came to judge the verse-speaking competition at the end of the summer. They would spend a day and a night or two at the school, listening to the boys' readings in the afternoon and then giving an informal but highly professional reading of their own in the evening. These occasions seemed to be enjoyed immensely by both performers and audience, and it was a very special privilege to listen to such an artistically chosen and movingly delivered anthology, from two of the most musical voices imaginable. The visits ended with CDL's death in 1972.

The year 1964–5 saw the arrival of four masters who between them have already put in nearly 100 years at the school. After serving with the Gurkhas and doing a stint in the City, Charles Churchill decided upon a teaching career. He arrived for interview with a car full of assorted dogs and Siamese cats, which

171. (*Opposite*) 'The Ghost of Thark', staff play 1966; not a very clear photograph, but the masters are in fact (*left to right*) N. J. Chapman, N. E. Aldridge, C. ff. Churchill, Rev. J. O. White, J. L. Bell and H. G. Jones.

169. Pat Marston and Charles Churchill judging the fielding competition.

170. Nigel Chapman, cricketer and master at SF 1965–1988, when he became Headmaster of Lockers Park.

appealed greatly to PMBS, and started work in January 1964, teaching mainly Latin in those days; he also founded the school's Photographic Society. Having a Cambridge golf blue, he helped Ogre in that sphere, and he took over the cricket from Chris Snell in 1967. Nigel Chapman, who came in the following year, also had much to offer the cricket, having captained Felsted for two seasons and being an Essex Second XI player. He was the captain of the Rest in 1964 when Rupert Daniels captained the Southern Schools, in a match in which they both made centuries. He it was, too, who stirred up some of his colleagues to stage the first Staff Play for twenty years: *The Ghost of Thark* (freely adapted from the Aldwych farce). This was to be followed over the years by *See How They Run* and *Pools Paradise*; all three were somehow kept secret from the boys until the performance, and all three were notable dramatic triumphs for the producer and for Jimmy Bell, doyen of the cast, revealing a talent that his pupils might not have suspected as a drag-artiste!

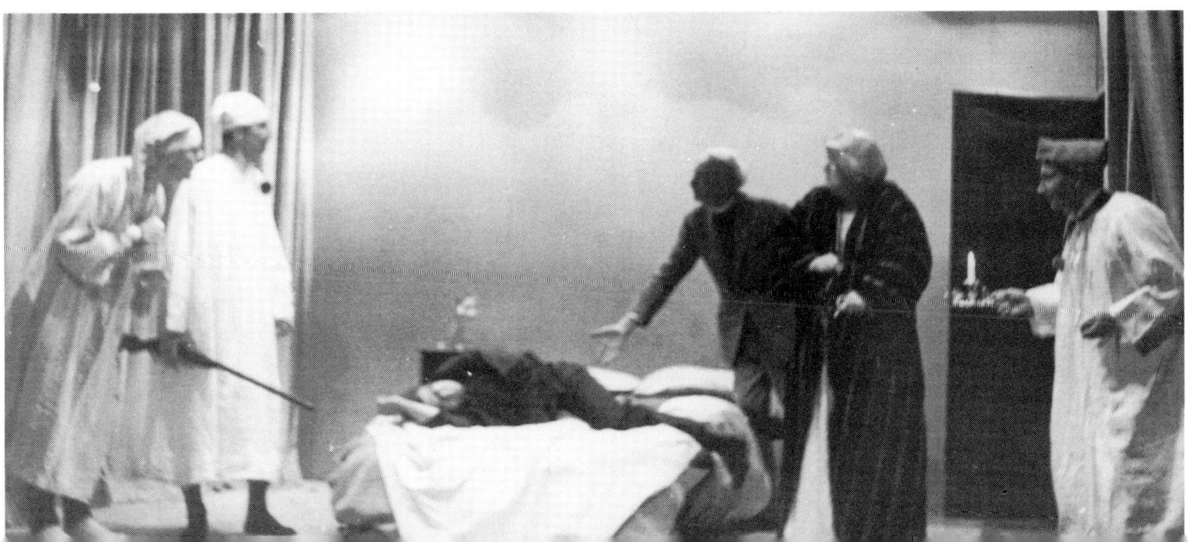

In January 1965, Nigel Talbot Rice arrived to do the teaching practice part of his Oxford Dip. Ed. He had already taught for three years at Papplewick after graduating from Oxford and was sufficiently impressed by Summer Fields to return on a permanent basis in the following September. He was soon in charge of the swimming (as bathing became, once we had a swimming-pool), and spent hours with a stalwart band of workers painting the sides and bottom of the pool; another of his projects was a scale-model of the school made by the Leavers of Lent 1966. David Langdon also joined the permanent staff in September 1965. Summer Fields music had had its ups and downs over the years, but it would be no aspersion on many excellent musicians to say that we were not really a musical school until he began to make us into one. In 1965 David was the music master, organist and choirmaster; Cynthia Hartwell and Miss Harris taught some piano pupils, and that was it. Twenty-four years later, David is director of music, with an assistant director and a teaching staff of twenty: boys learn more than twenty different types of instrument, including the organ, bassoon and harp; as well as

172. Model of the school (1966) made, under the guidance of NTR, by leavers (back row, left to right), Bruce Hector, John Austen, Michael Thomas, Richard North-Lewis, Ian Breminer; (front row) Charles Ingestre, Peter Flach, Richard Chute and Anthony Kirk-Duncan.

an orchestra of thirty to forty, there are three choirs, a madrigal group, and every conceivable instrumental ensemble.

The 1960s were a period of rapid social change, which was reflected in education, even in the private sector, traditionally perhaps less prone to innovation than the maintained schools. Apart from the new buildings already mentioned, other important changes at Summer Fields included the introduction over the decade of a number of new activities, and a reassessment of the existing systems of rewards and punishments. Teaching methods also changed: the 'new maths', welcomed by pupils but bemusing for their parents, had already appeared. Nationwide, English became less a matter of grammar and literary study and more a heuristic pursuit of imagination and creativity. This happened at Summer Fields, where David Kidd-May, the new head of English, welcomed the innovations of young men like Ian Dunbar, who was a great source of inspiration and ideas during his five years. Some of the old guard derided lessons spent lighting candles and watching their flames, and no doubt sometimes the new methods went 'over

173. 'The Italian Straw Hat' (1972), produced by Ian Dunbar. A bevy of temporarily female beauty represented by Jeremy and Nicholas Stafford-Deitch as Wedding Guests, Hubert Gibbs as Annette, Andrew Johnston as Helen, Simon Wade as Virginia and Antony Gardner as Clara.

the top'. Certain passages in the Magazines of the late '60s are a little cloying. But the air let in through the newly opened windows was certainly fresh and had an invigorating effect.

Boxing ceased to be offered in 1964, upon the departure of Jack Morley, who had succeeded his father as gymnast and boxing coach in the mid-1930s: each of them had given thirty years to the cause of *corpora sana*. But emphases had changed, and indeed memoirs of many who had suffered at school had been published, suggesting that, rather than making a man of one, being hit on the head and body might have a deleterious effect on both the mind and body. Badminton made a civilized alternative for those who wanted to use the Gym, and gymnastics continued with revamped equipment. The bursar's log contains the following note for 30 August 1966:

British Rail collected vaulting horses. Apparently delay was due to mistaken impression that they were *live* ones!

As well as the printing press, the photographic dark-room and the new swimming-pool, various societies came into being. A Natural History society ensured that we continued the Holman-Hunt tradition, and birds and even badgers were watched on various occasions. For several years a number of our boys went on the IAPS Educational Cruises in the Mediterranean, under the guidance of David Langdon; and Charles Churchill arranged a ski trip, which has become an annual event for boys and their families, with more than 100 skiers in many years. The Architectural Society (and where better to study architecture than in Oxford and Oxfordshire?) was instituted by two masters who joined the staff in the late 1960s, Ran Ogston and Henry Thorold.

R. A. L. Ogston had started his teaching career at Cothill and after a short spell there went to Summer Fields St Leonards; he became its headmaster in 1959 and guided it through the last seven, by no means easy, years of its life. When it closed, he and a few of his pupils came to the Oxford school. Glad to have shed the mantle of authority, he immersed himself in various activities, starting the Weather Station and assisting with the music. The Rev. H. C. Thorold OS came in 1968 as chaplain, having previously been a housemaster at Lancing, a school with a commendable Anglican tradition. It was Henry's proud boast that he altered nothing in the Chapel during his seven years here: his services were seemly and reverent, but enlivened by his own unique style of preaching. He drove an ancient Bentley, and he took on the task of bringing the Register up to date. Since retiring from Summer Fields, he has lived at his family home of Marston Hall in Lincolnshire and has continued to produce extremely well-written and popular guidebooks to counties and their antiquities.

A committee, convened in 1967 to examine the system of rewards and punishments, abolished both the Imposition Book (a punishment book of some antiquity, and known to the boys as the 'Impot Book') and the Discipline List: one's name on the latter for a minor behavioural lapse meant running up and down the drive for ten minutes in Break. The Black Book retained its century-old status, and a new system of 'minuses' covered the lesser infringements. As an incentive, a Conduct Cup was presented by PMBS for the League with the fewest minuses in a term; and, from Lent 1968, a sumptuous Feast with party games was given on the last night of term for the members of the winning League. The positive side of this is laudable, but, in a material age, there is inevitably a regrettable aspect to it, in that boys now consider that they are competing for a feast, where before they were merely competing for a cup – valueless in itself, but much prized for its kudos.

Harold Clayton retired in 1968, so that he could spend more time breeding labradors, his passion, as well as maths, music and gardening. He and Margaret went to live no great distance away, near Witney, and many fine Summerfieldian dogs are offshoots of their kennel. Harold will be remembered not only for his five-volume *Natural Approach to Mathematics*, but also for his publication of an up-to-date Register in 1960.

Two years later, Ogre and Perdita departed to a tranquil retirement at Benson.

174. The feminine touch in the 60s and 70s; Perdita Marston, Patsy Boon and Joan Hartley.

She had spent her entire life at the school in one capacity or another, starting at quite an early age to add a decorative note to the Summer Term photographs and, latterly, after bringing up six children of her own, providing a motherly and organizational persona that did much to put small boys and mothers at their ease. He first entered the school as a boy in 1918 and had been involved with it on and off ever since. His larger-than-life personality was inevitably missed, and nowhere more than on Second Game cricket. He reappeared from time to time, always welcome and comparatively unchanged, until his death in 1981: he had fulfilled his three-score-years-and-ten, but not much more.

Nigel Talbot Rice was elevated to maintain the triumvirate, and his wife Joanna admirably fulfilled the maternal role. If these two stepped into the official shoes which Ogre and Perdita had occupied, the arrival of Willie Pryor on the staff in that autumn helped to ensure a continuity of OS 'characters': WLAP would be hard to equal for originality of teaching style and diversity of interests. Ordained into the diaconate in 1975, he has done much to revive links between the school and Summertown, both by his non-stipendiary auxiliary ministry at St Michael's, and by his 'clearing up and cheering up' the community as Great-Uncle Bulgaria, Head of the Wombles. Wombling has become a well-subscribed activity for Lower School boys who enjoy picking up litter in return for gobstoppers.

In 1970, an Appeal Campaign was launched with the vital but unromantic aims of paying off the school's liabilities, especially those to the Foundress's successors, and instituting a proper staff pension scheme. The former was not easy, as by now some of the Stuart-Maclarens were in the West Indies. Under the able direction of Air Vice-Marshal Charles Moore CB, OBE, the campaign raised more than £100,000, which far exceeded the original target; but it must be borne in mind that these were the days of galloping inflation, so targets tended to need to be surpassed. The incompetence of the government and the strength of the trade unions were felt at the end of the next year, when the miners' strike led to power-cuts, which meant specially rearranged and improvised timetables. In the event, the school was not too badly hit; it certainly brought out the ingenuity in many people, and reminded one of Carrying On in the War Years.

The Magazine of 1971 differed from its predecessors in size (quarto), general style and the fact that it carried several illustrations and photographs as well as a Gallery of Boys' Own Art. This has been the basic pattern for subsequent issues to date, with a further slight increase in page-size (A4), a large increase in the number of photographs and the adoption of a two-colour cover. PMBS somehow managed to find the time among his headmagisterial duties to edit this new-look magazine, and the four issues over which he presided were as enjoyable as the seventeen of his previous editorship.

In 1972, Cubicles, the scene of many happy memories of GB's evening reads,

175. The Goelet Library, imaginatively converted from Cubicles in 1972.

ceased to be a dormitory and was converted into a Library of magnificent proportions, through the generosity of the Goelet family. This was the room's third use, for it had originally been the Dining-Room: it made an almost collegiate library with its bays and tall windows. The plan had been to surmount each bookcase with a bust of some literary ancient above a coat of arms of a school benefactor. The arms are in place, but the busts never appeared. The oil-painting of Harold Macmillan, however, makes a good focal point at the upper end of the room.

But the major structural project of that year was the building of Beech House, as a family house in which some small boys could also sleep: a home-from-home very similar to the original Summerfield. This was the brainchild of NTR, who initially financed the project and was later reimbursed by the school. The site chosen was that of the sandpit in front of the Mayfield greenhouses, and beside the magnificent tree which was to give the house its name. Jimmy Bell had dubbed it the 'Palazzo', and for a long time 'The Old House' was entertained (a) because it resembled, *mutatis mutandis*, the Old House at Windsor, and (b) analogously with New Room, because it was not at all old. But the joke would have been hard to live with, once the newness had worn off! It was designed by Francis Johnson, and upon its completion Nigel and Joanna Talbot Rice moved in with their daughters Sarah and Caroline and eight boys. Though they had intended to give up the boys when their family increased, they still occupy it today, with four daughters, one son and ten boys. It is one of the more gracious buildings in a school

176. Beech House (1972).

not renowned for architectural beauty, and makes a suitable Headmaster's House.

Grace, however, is a feature of the school grounds, and that summer its gardens were opened to the public as part of a national scheme; this reflected great credit upon Frank Ricketts and his gardening and ground staff. Their tremendous contribution year by year in providing not only playable pitches but attractive surroundings would be hard to praise sufficiently, as would that of those who keep the school clothed, tidy, healthy and fed. In 1971 we dispensed with outside caterers, and it was readily agreed that our own team of Mrs Taylor, Martin Dornig and Mrs Ricketts did every bit as well as they had done. In 1972, two men retired who had each given thirty years' service: Bert Stockford, who originally worked on the farm at the beginning of the war, but later moved to the booty, and Willie Gardner, diminutive and cheerful, who had been cleaning shoes and passages since 1942.

Upon Ogre's departure, Second Game was exiled to the far field, and the Under-11 Colts took over Second Game Pavilion and what many consider to be the best wicket in North Oxford, a move in tune with the 1970s cult of youth. In the same year, David Langdon introduced sailing for a select few, and it has remained a much-coveted 'extra' to this day. Michael Rice took on the printing press, and over the next two years he produced printed work of more than professional quality.

177. Chapel during Sung Eucharist in the 1960s.

John Evans died in October 1972, being over eighty, nearly blind and probably not unwilling to go. He had been very ill a year or two before and, thinking that he was at death's door, had wanted to pray, but in his state and to his distress he could not remember the words of the Lord's Prayer. He had a deep and simple faith and was responsible for the 'high-church' character which Summer Fields religion maintained for so long. He always sought high standards and quality, and made friends with all conditions of men, women and boys: to him, they had all equally been 'my dear'. A Memorial Service for him in Chapel in March 1973 was thronged with Old Boys, staff, parents, matrons and countless others who had known and loved him. As Henry Thorold had said of his eightieth birthday party, 'this was a wonderful chance for many of us to pay tribute to him – to honour a beloved headmaster, a most endearing friend'.

That year was a successful one in all three sports, and its success was in no small measure due to the captain. Peter Morris is unique in having captained the school's teams for four successive terms; he also won the tennis, the victor ludorum trophy, five Fifth Form prizes and a scholarship at Eton. One cannot really quantify such achievements, but this looks like an unbeatable record. In recent years, Nicholas Evans-Lombe has come close to a similar achievement. It goes without saying that both boys were Head Prefects – or Captains of the School, as PMBS preferred to call the office.

John Evans's bequest to the school was used to embellish the Chapel which he had loved so much. In retrospect, it seems both sensible and aesthetically pleasing to have whitened the walls, which had previously been bare brick, the yellow Oxford brick which even the fondest heart could not call attractive. The Chapel was wholly repainted and refloored, and red carpeting laid between the new choir stalls, which were given new lights and chandeliers. All this was planned and put into effect by PMBS, a labour of love both for the building itself and for John, to whom he had been almost *in loco filii*.

In January 1974 the great elm on the Masters' Lawn was blown down in a night of such violent storms that its crash was not heard. Some of our elms had already been felled in the 1960s, and the remainder were to fall victim to the Dutch elm disease over the next few years. A symbol, perhaps, of a time of departures, for in 1975 the Headmaster, Matron, Bursar and Chaplain all retired, together with Wilfred Williams, who had been teaching at the school since 1949.

Nancy Lovett had been Matron through nearly a quarter of a century and was all that one imagines the best type of school matron to be. She put her work before everything else, and her Great Ormond Street training and hospital experience meant that she was a thorough professional. Her calm kindness was always a comfort to sad or ailing boys, but she was not gullible: the malingerer stood no chance.

178. The collapse of the Great Elm, which also removed part of the low stone wall separating the Masters' Lawn from the Drive.

179. Wilfred Williams.

180. An art lesson in the 1960s with Jackie Black: Henry Elwell, Jonathan Grey and Charles Denman.

Pat Savage decided to retire a year earlier than his statutory time, as he felt that he would by then have done all that he could and wanted to do as headmaster. This would also enable his successor to assemble his own team of Matron, Bursar and Chaplain; one major change-over would be preferable to a drawn-out process. For someone who did not feel in his element at the head of affairs, he has a remarkable list of achievements to look back upon. He began the physical modernization of the school, while introducing a number of humane and civilizing measures. Notices written in his splendid hand always carried an extra cachet and often contained a characteristic wit. He injected this sort of style into the school as a whole, with coats of arms, honorary OS Ties and a whole range of reasons for awarding boys Distinction Ties or for flying a flag above the Pavilion. He moved with his housekeeper Resy, remembered by more than one generation of Cottage boys, and his Cavalier King Charles spaniels to Burford – near enough to be in touch, but, thoughtfully, not so near as to inhibit his successors.

At a meeting in March 1974, the Governors had unanimously decided to offer the headmastership to Nigel Talbot Rice, and he accepted it, thus becoming the first married headmaster for thirty-six years.

Nigel Talbot Rice was born in 1938. He was educated at Lambrook, Charterhouse and Christ Church, and served for two years in the Coldstream Guards. He taught at Papplewick for three years and then took a Diploma in Education at Oxford University. He joined the staff of Summer Fields in 1965, and has been with us ever since. He married Joanna Manning, daughter of Air Commodore Manning, in 1968.

The Governors have the utmost confidence in his ability to lead Summer Fields through the years ahead and look forward to working with him to maintain the standards and traditions which Patrick Savage has so ably fostered since 1960.

March 1974 C. H. Christie

A CENTURY OF SUMMER FIELDS

That the school should be a hundred years old in 1964 was felt to be a suitable cause for celebration, and, under the masterly organization of PMBS, a six-month programme of events went off extremely well. But the most impressive product of the centenary was the anthology edited by Richard Usborne and called *A Century of Summer Fields*. It was a remarkable compilation, put together with such art and taste that it distilled 'Essence of Summer Fields' from every page. When the author Gillian Avery visited the school in 1986, she said, as she entered the hall, 'I've never been here before, but I feel I know the school very well. I keep *A Century of Summer Fields* by my bed and I often dip into it.' It is an encouraging tribute that a book deliberately put together for a specific readership should nevertheless appeal to 'outsiders'; and this was the feeling shared by most of the newspapers that reviewed it.

The book appeared in the summer, 1,500 copies being printed and the price being 30s. Usborne and the publishers, Messrs Methuen, took great trouble over its production, and it was later chosen as one of the best-designed books of 1964, and exhibited at the National Book League and overseas. The only disappointment was that it was bound not in the school's own bright red, but in a rather dull, if distinguished, brown. To thank Richard Usborne, the Governors rebound a copy in Summer Fields red leather, complete with gilt edges. The School Library now also has a red-bound copy, which makes it to some extent theft-proof. For the book is sought after: with hindsight, one can see that it would probably have been safe to issue 2,500; there would have been a slow but steady sale over the next two decades. The original run of 1,500 was sold out within a year, and a surprising number of people now find that they have lent their copies to someone, but they cannot remember to whom or when. A secondhand copy cost £4 or £5 in early 1988, and was cheap at the price.

Eight national papers reviewed the book: their comments were on the whole favourable, but they showed a forgivable tendency to review the institution rather than the book that described it. Philip Toynbee, whose *Observer* article was occasionally hostile, frankly admitted, 'I was sacked from two of the four private schools which I attended, and my memories of that long incarceration are almost uniformly horrible.' He then went on to criticize the school's lack of humility (he was not alone in this), fatuous snobbery, exclusiveness of all but the very rich, conformism, philistinism, priggery and cruelty. 'What this school really needs,' he concluded, 'is Smart-Alec for headmaster, Grimes to take the fifth form, Foulenough for Bursar and the late André Gide as cricket coach.'

In the *Sunday Times*, George Melly commented upon 'the English upper-class obsession with its school-days', but found our book more fascinating than a Salopian Anthology which appeared at the same time. He also complained with some justice that 'you get the impression that the *raison d'être* of the place is to win scholarships to Eton,' but added, 'the book contains a fair-minded but authoritative attack on this aspect by a grandson of the founder and one-time master and partner at SF, who left to become a School Inspector.' The *TES* contained a detailed and somewhat equivocal (anonymous) article called 'Grey Serge Elite', laudatory in tone but cynical in overtone. 'This delicious anthology holds a preparatory school between its covers. Here are its character and its testament. Here are its record and its raison d'être ... Bow your head, A. S. Neill, and be off with you. This is Summer Fields, not Summerhill. We English like the boy to be an all-round boy. You only wanted him to be himself.'

Anthony Burgess in *Country Life* disingenuously lambasted the prose style of a passage of deliberate parody and then, pleased with his perception, informed his readers, 'That comes straight out of the school magazines that brighten the lives of Graham Greene exiles ...' Too right it did: it was written by one of the better-informed students of the genre! H. F. Ellis, author of the A. J. Wentworth stories beloved of many SF masters, concluded his paragraph in *Punch* by stating that 'the interest lies rather in the occasional cold douches of criticism that have wisely been permitted to refresh the generally cosy, congratulatory chorus'. Peter Vansittart, who compiled one of the most fascinating anthologies in our language, *Green Knights and Black Angels*, quoted Bobs Alington at length and then asked his readers if these strictures were only part of a vanished period-piece.

Several newspapers commented upon Harold Macmillan's having acted the Prime Minister in *Rumpelstiltzkin* and reproduced the photograph which shows him with longish hair. Charles Greville in the *Daily Mail* was eulogistic: 'I am against Prep Schools. But I fancy that, if I had gone to a famous Prep School on the outskirts of Oxford called Summer Fields, I would probably be in favour of them. It is an extraordinary and unusual place ... [The book] makes completely fascinating reading – even though I never went there ... Young Macmillan obviously enjoyed it. And having dipped into this astonishing, rosy, unclouded, summery past – so did I.' William Hickey in the *Daily Express* retold the story of the origins of the Dudley Medal Golf Competition. In 1907 the future Lord Dudley had cajoled the future Lord Norrie into letting him win the Golf Championship, partly to mitigate his father's likely wrath over a bad report. Lord Dudley was predictably delighted and resolved to present a silver medal each year for the competition.

Apart from full and friendly coverage of the school's Centenary Events in the local press, there were one or two interesting mentions elsewhere. The *Heraldry Gazette*, in introducing the newly acquired coat of arms, went on to mention the Eton connection and concluded amusingly with 'The parallel bars seem to have an obvious significance, as perhaps the bezants have also.' In fact, the press found in our centenary and our book what they wished to find: lots of good stories and a confirmation of their prejudices one way or the other. One bitter memory was not included in the book, but has hung for years in the Headmaster's Study, a reminder that not everybody may be finding it all such jolly fun: 'To me Summer Fields was a prison, not a school. Thank goodness I enjoyed Eton. We had no funny jokes in Greek there before breakfast.'

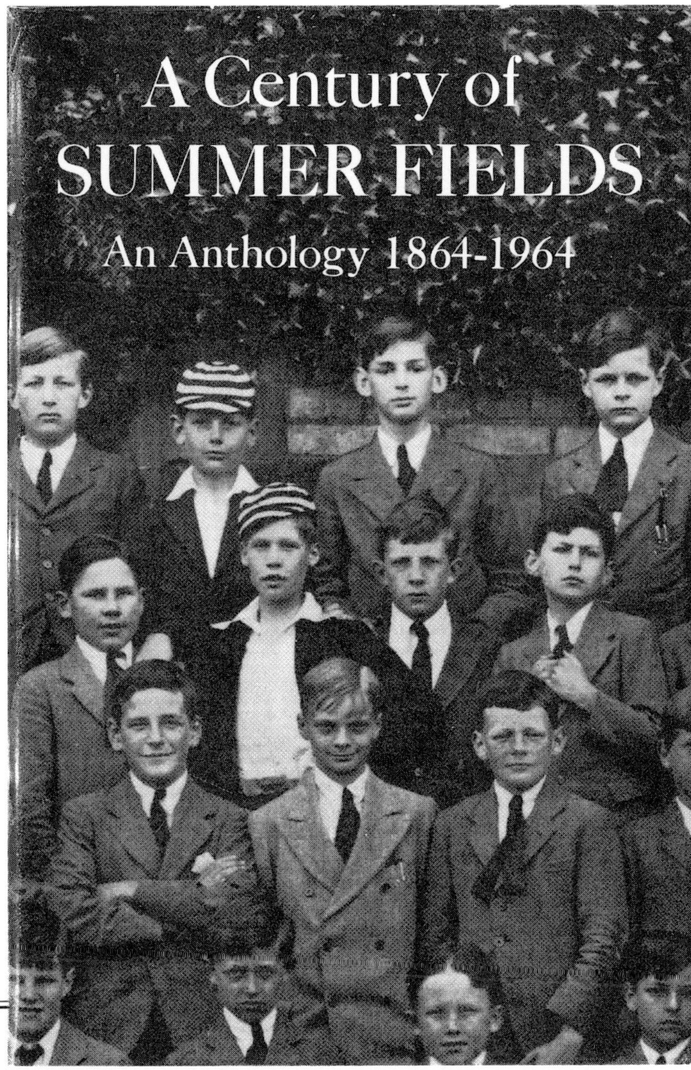

10

EXPANSION, 1975–89

NIGEL TALBOT RICE brought immense energy and organizational skill to the job of headmaster. Within six years, he raised the number of boys in the school from 180 to 220, and over the next six years to 240, which the Governors decided was quite big enough. The conflicting forces here were those of economics versus spirit. In the 1970s, a word that was resurrected from apparent obscurity to sudden fashionableness was 'viability' – and this was the justification of the economic argument. To keep the school to a manageable size (and what that size is must always be a matter of opinion) and preserve its spirit, intimacy and contact might be to risk the school altogether in financial terms. So, as is usually the case, the economic argument won the day, and, in a welter of new buildings and increased 'facilities', inevitably some of the prized atmosphere has been lost; but many OSS, parents and grandparents who revisit the school comment with delight upon what has been preserved. Though much is taken, much abides – and in the late 1970s the school became solvent for the first time in decades.

The introduction of a tutorial system did much to counteract the risk of the school's becoming too impersonal. Each boy was allotted a tutor, with whom he would have a private session of ten minutes every week. This has turned out to be a helpful way of seeing that everyone receives attention; often the session is little more than an exchange of news, but it does provide a chance for the boy who feels victimised, misunderstood or lonely to unburden himself. The system means that there is always somebody who is going to be sympathetic and interested in hearing that one has just got a SUG or a Black Book, that one's hamster has had babies or that Mummy and Daddy have gone to America for a month.

At the beginning of the new regime, discipline was tightened and, though the working day was slightly shortened, everyone was made to work harder: the leisurely gaps soon became filled, both for the pupils and for the staff. Terms of employment and working hours began to be stated, where before they had merely been assumed. This could hardly be otherwise in an era when people started to watch clocks and to expect time off. A schoolmaster's or matron's job had never been 'nine-to-five'; indeed, in boarding-schools it has not been a job so much as

181. Nigel Talbot Rice, with Joanna, Sarah, Caroline and Rebecca, 1975.

182 and 183. Between 1975 and 1977, a new uniform was introduced. The tweed jackets and viyella shirts as worn by Giles Nevill and Alexander Paine were replaced by navy blue guernseys and aertex shirts in league colours, as seen below. Note also the substitution of new metal-frame desks for the wooden ones.

a way of life, and therein have lain both its strengths and its weaknesses. No professional training can match total commitment; but equally, those who are so totally committed run the risk of having little life of their own, and so in time becoming blinkered to the outside world.

Another modern trend was the regular appeal for money, with which to repair or modify existing buildings and erect new ones. The playground was sold off to a speculator, and almost immediately resold to become an old people's home; this left Cottage and its garden as the only area that the school now owned on the far side of the Mayfield Road. The playground would not be greatly mourned by some, but its valuable space as a car-park was missed at plays, leave-outs, etc. A few years later, an equivalent area with five hard tennis courts, which could also become a small hockey pitch, was created after the Mayfield Wood was felled. This allowed the soccer pitch to remain where it was and to retain its north-south axis; but, sadly, it put the cricket field firmly into the town, when previously the view from the pavilion had been only school buildings, the roof of the parish church and trees.

Front Lodge, which was beginning to need serious repair, was a listed building; a preservation order forbade its demolition. It was sold in 1979 and immediately altered from a haphazard pre-Victorian cottage of some charm to a yellow-pebbledashed box, such as can be found on most modern 'exclusive' estates. The front gate to the school, withdrawn twenty yards, was henceforth usually kept locked.

The late 1970s saw the departure of several stalwarts of the teaching staff. In 1978, Jimmy Bell officially retired after forty years, excluding the war, during the last eighteen of which he had been assistant headmaster as well as running the classics, Fifth Form and Mayfield. The last-named of these was taken on by Nigel and Lindsay Chapman, and his other roles by Nicholas Aldridge, also an OS and once a member of JLB's first Fifth Form, who had returned in 1975 when NTR took over. Jimmy continued to teach part-time and did not finally retire until 1985, when his wit and inquisitorial

184. Front Lodge before its modernisation.

sessions in the Lobby were much missed.

Philip Johnstone ran the French for a quarter of a century with great success. His wife Joyce had for several years been a junior form mistress as well as looking after Phil, their son Ian and Mayfield. Harold Hartley and his wife Joan had at first lived 'out' in their cottage at Headington, called 'Huggins', before they took over Newton. Harold taught some Latin to 'Modern-Siders' in his early days, some geography, but especially history, of which he had charge for thirty years. Ran Ogston had been with us for only thirteen years, but, with his St Leonards period, his total Summerfieldian connection had been more than a quarter of a century. He did a marvellous job as librarian and also with House, which in those days contained over seventy boys – no light assignment at the end of a heavy teaching day! The Johnstones retired to Swanage, the Hartleys to Cornwall, and RALO to Ludlow, where he was soon back at the organ-keyboard in the lovely St Lawrence's Church, and even did some part-time work at a local prep school.

With these and other departures, NTR began to build up a staff, many of whom have by now been at the school for a decade. Oliver Lee OS, Richard Balding, Anthony Browne and Henry Riches started the new vintage of a younger generation of masters, as had happened in 1896 after the death of Mrs, and similarly after each of the great wars. A senior element was provided by Tom Flynn and Rodney Blake, both of whom had been headmasters in their time; but

185. Joyce and Philip Johnstone.

186 and 187. Two aspects of Harold Hartley: (a) Active, with the starting-pistol and smart boater; (b) Pensive, with Ran Ogston.

they were not as old as some boys evidently imagined. Tom was once asked, 'Are you the ancestor of that other old man who takes us for Rest?' Fred King, an ex-RAF padre noted for his brilliant sermons, was chaplain for five years, while his wife Suske took care of the youngest form. They were respectively succeeded in 1980 by Fergus Capie and Clare Hollander; and these were joined by Jonathan Bush in 1980, by Gavin Hannah and Mark Johnson in 1983, and by Brian Ogilvie, Henry Phillips and Jane Butler in 1984. Thus, a comfortable balance has been achieved and maintained in the 1980s between experienced and younger staff; for there has remained a 'core' of Messrs Kidd-May, Churchill, Langdon, Pryor and McNeile, together with Stephen Cox and Nigel Chapman who left in 1986 and 1988 to become headmasters, and Patsy Boon, who has taught a junior form since 1966 and who is now better known as Patsy Logan since her marriage in 1977.

188. Oliver Lee, Rupert McNeile and Anthony Browne timing Sports heats.

189. Tom Flynn.

The 'feel' of the school changed somewhat. Like the staff and boys, every area was made to work to justify its existence. Rather tired form-rooms were given new uses, being replaced in a two-phase operation by two blocks of custom-built teaching-rooms in 1977 and 1983. This double-block of sixteen carpeted, white-boarded rooms was called Bolton in memory of GB and was sited where once the Shrubbery, scene of so many games of 'Salamanca', had separated the new kitchen from the playing-field. This involved the demolition of the air-raid shelter, unused for thirty years and disappointingly devoid of any period 'treasures'.

The Gym, completely redecorated and given a false ceiling, became much more cheerful as Macmillan Hall; it was opened by its great namesake at Prizegiving in December 1979. A Music Block and Gallery were added at the south end, replacing the second gateway to the road and two huts. The 'Tool Shed' was re-

190. The new form room block, soon to be called Bolton.

191. Harold Macmillan returning from opening Macmillan Hall, December 1979, accompanied by his son-in-law Julian Faber, NEA, JTR and NTR.

sited in the Rose Garden, and the Green Hut was made into a pavilion for the further games-field. It had not been used recently for teaching, but had housed the Secretary and Bursar. These moved into new offices created by partitioning the old Headmaster's Dining-Room (subsequently the Upper School Library and then the Prefects' Room) on the left of the front door.

Highly successful fund-raising appeals were held in 1977 and 1984; the former was organized by Col. Archie Noël, and the latter by Bernard Ashford. In addition to the buildings already mentioned, these meant that all the Lodges could be redecorated and given heating, and that various buildings could be adapted for more worthwhile purposes. Notable among these have been the Mayfield and

Newton Barns, running for fifty yards along the north-west boundary of the school property, which were used as a hatter's and blacksmith's in the last century, and later to store coke, trunks, the Newton Bus, tractors and much else. Their imaginative conversion consisted first of accommodation for four bachelor masters, and subsequently of maisonettes for three married couples.

While NTR was the master-mind behind these extensive developments, tribute must also be paid to Bill Dixon, who was bursar from 1975 to 1986. He saw to it that every penny which the school earned made interest and was accounted for in the most useful way. A genial ex-RAF Group-Captain, he was a positive personality, whose watchword was 'No problem!', and indeed problems placed in his hands immediately seemed to lose their menace.

A large building was added to Old Lodge, dwarfing its symmetrical proportions and subsequently annexing the name of Front Lodge, as the previous owner of that name had become a cookery school. Though the new Front Lodge is not the most attractive building in North Oxford, it is at least functional, relieving the congestion of House by giving dormitory accommodation to forty boys and a comfortable flat for their housemaster. One must also say in its favour that its muted colours are a restful contrast to the rather strong red brick of the Music Block which faces it. It is perhaps a pity that these two buildings are the

192 and 193. 'Scylla and Charybdis.'

first that most visitors see of the school; but, once they have passed between Scylla and Charybdis, they come to *rus in urbe*.

The major new building of the present era is the Indoor Swimming-Pool. This was financed separately from the 1984 appeal by a handful of generous parents, and it has made a great difference to the life of the school. The Centenary Outdoor Pool, though undoubtedly beautiful, was unlikely to be used for more than six weeks, even in the best of summers; but an indoor pool, attached to the main building by a new Changing-Room complex, can be used every day of the year, and is ideal for wet half-holiday afternoons. The siting of the new pool in front of the east end of the Chapel has changed the aspect of the familiar eastern elevation of the school; but, considering that swimming-pool buildings are not normally noted for their beauty, this one is at worst inoffensive and at best complementary to what goes on above and beyond it, and each year it blends a little better, as the shrubs and creepers grow up round it. Perhaps its architect's greatest achievement is to have built something that, from the outside, does not look like a swimming-pool! It was opened in May 1985 by HRH the Duchess of Gloucester, and christened by a race between the bursar, Bill Dixon, and his grandson Ben, who was the captain of swimming. It was a close thing, but youth just won the day!

So much for buildings. The other major alteration to the school's appearance has been the loss of many trees, mainly elms, over the past fifteen years. There has been a certain amount of amateur and professional replanting, but, unlike buildings, trees take time. The drive leading down to the Farm is just beginning to look like an avenue again, but the farm-fields themselves are horribly stark,

194. The New Indoor Swimming Pool, 1985.

having lost hundreds of elms and also many hedges through neglect. Of the roses planted around the near fields in the early 1970s hardly a vestige remains; but what is left of the Front Garden and the Rose Garden are again receiving loving attention and cannot often have looked better than they did in Summer 1988.

Against this background, an increasingly busy school life has been led from year to year. A tear had to be shed for the last Squish, which ran in April 1976; since then a coach has proved a simpler and more practical form of transport for the London contingent. The summer of 1976 was extremely hot and dry – as summers are in nostalgic memory, but this one resulted in a virtually hayless Hay Feast. Noble were the efforts of any form whose fort-walls rose to more than a couple of feet! A number of new activities flourished, including one called Other Activities, which was the ungamesy senior boy's alternative occupation on two or three afternoons a week. But for the hardy, there were the increasingly popular judo (filling the space left by boxing) and orienteering around Oxfordshire on several Sundays, with special trips for the most proficient to Worcestershire and Wales. This was arranged by NJC, who also master-minded Expedition Day, which first took place in 1977: a day on which the whole school departs in several coaches and different directions.

This was also the year of the Queen's Silver Jubilee. We commemorated the occasion with an Evensong followed by Dinner in the Field. All the dining-room tables had been carried outside and set up in order, and the evening sun shone on a truly festive occasion, with a roast sucking-pig fresh from the spit being the central feature of a sumptuous meal. Every boy had a menu, printed by the School Press, with a Jubilee coin attached.

The 1977 football XI was a memorable one, though its record was not quite that of Straton-Ferrier's 1936 team, as it lost to Horris Hill in its very last match. But nothing became the members of this team like their demeanour in their hour of disappointment; that they could be so sporting as well as aggressive and entertaining said volumes for NJC, their coach, and for Robert Eden, their captain, as well as for the whole side.

The deaths occurred in the same year of two men who had been significantly connected with the school. Much has already been said of Bobs Alington's innovatory genius, and his understanding and love of the written and spoken word can be seen on several pages of this book. His integrity drove him to leave the school that he loved when at the height of his powers, but his influence remained for decades. When he visited the school in the 1960s, he expressed admiration for the changes that PMBS had made, saying, 'If I had been allowed to do what you have done, I should still have been at Summer Fields.' A

195. (*top right*) Orienteering. Simon Gardiner, Julian Booth, Tommy Butler, Jonathan Bruce, Philip de May and Jamie Carr in the new School Minibus, the money for which was raised by various sponsored undertakings in 1979.

196. (*centre right*) The end of the trail. Two orienteers return after a ten-mile hike around the hills of Radnorshire.

197. (*bottom right*) Jubilee Dinner al fresco, June 1977.

198. Robert Mortimer with Patrick Savage.

compliment to treasure, and a comfort to feel that progress had received a blessing from the other side of the Foundress's family.

The Rt Rev. Robert Mortimer DD, formerly Bishop of Exeter and first chairman of the school's Governors, had played a crucial role in the early days of the Trust. His two Summerfieldian sons have also achieved distinction, Mark as a classicist in the Ronald Knox tradition, and Edward in journalism. When they were boys at the school, their father cut a fine figure in the family race on Sports Day, black stock flapping in the breeze or, in later years, gaiters adorning the running legs. Articulate and extremely able as a chairman, he was quick to grasp a situation and could be relied upon to show genuine understanding. Yet an almost casual manner belied his commitment, as Patrick Savage describes.

He used to slope in, with his hands in his pockets, at about twenty nine and a half minutes past two and find us, with emptied coffee cups, waiting. 'Isn't it about time that we got on with this meeting?' he would say; and we followed him in exactly as the clock struck half-past. Round the table we sat, while Bob, fed with the facts by Johnnie Max-Muller, would, without giving offence or being in the smallest degree pompous, politely let everyone say just what was needed, stop them from rambling and extract the essence. We were released, equally punctually, yet not feeling in the least rushed, at fifty nine and a half minutes past three, in time for tea.

199. Part of the Summer Fields Big Band, 1987: trumpeters David and Elaine Andrews, clarinettists Annabel Arnold, Carol Gibbs and Richard Balding.

Nowadays, Governors' Meetings are held *before* rather than *after* lunch: a meal in prospect concentrates the mind wonderfully. Today's meetings are allowed an hour longer; but similar powers of control and direction have been shown by four succeeding chairmen, first Johnnie Max-Muller, then Henry Christie, whose period covered the change of headmastership, and then Christopher Slade and Micky Jones.

In 1977 and 1979, musicals were performed in the parish church: first, *Noyes Fludde* with half the school as animals; and then, from the comparatively sublime to the wildly popular, *Joseph and the Amazing Technicolor Dreamcoat* with our own five-piece staff band, under the guidance of Richard Balding. RGRB, a professional clarinettist and saxophonist, has done wonders for the appreciation of, and involvement in, light music among both staff and boys. In a number of concerts and musicals, he has trained up the 'Summer Fields Big Band' to perform as the final part of the Music Society's annual soirée, when members of staff show some unexpected talents.

Joseph could not have been staged in the Gym anyway, because 1979 was the year in which it was undergoing conversion into Macmillan Hall. This was the start of a period of experimental and home-grown drama, with plays written by members of staff, notably Robert Barnes, Jonathan Bush, Henry Riches, Henry Phillips and Nicholas Aldridge. At the same time, major 'straight' productions,

200–203. Plays of the early 1980s: 200. The New Faustus, with Julian Edwards in the title role; 201. Oliver, a rare boys-and-staff musical; 202. The Ballad of Salomon Pavey, with Hugo Heimann and James Maby; 203. Julius Caesar: Rory Barnett as Cassius, and Oliver Page as Brutus.

ustus

.... JASON HOWARD
.... JAMIE CARR
..... ANTHONY BUXTON
.... OLIVER PAGE
... ALEXANDER BERTIE
ADAM JANKIEWICZ
TIMMY LEES
MARK LITTLE
JAMES MACKENZIE
RORY O'NEILL
TOM PITMAN
NICKY POWELL
BENJAMIN SHAW
PAUL SLOT
.... JAMIE CARR
. RICHARD MIDDLETON
...... THOMAS WYATT
. ANGUS MALCOLMSON
... CHARLES OLIVIER
... JASON HENCHMAN
.... JULIAN EDWARDS
.... SIMON GARDINER
...... HUGH POWELL / JAMES EADIE
.... WILLIAM NOTT
...... PHILIP TURNER
.. EDWARD SEYFRIED
LUDO STIRLING
MATTHEW WILKINSON
.... RUPERT EVE
...... STEVEN GRIGG
.. CRAIG PHILLIPSON
ALEXANDER MANISTY
MARK MAXWELL
SEBASTIAN MORLEY
HUGH THOMPSON
EDWARD COOK
JONATHAN BRUCE
ALEXANDER WRIGHT
JASON HENCHMAN

Acolytes .... THOMAS BYNG
ALEXANDER MACDONALD-BUCHANAN
Cardinals .... PIERS COVILL
ADAM HIBBERT
Friars .... MAURICE ROCHE
MARKHAM DARBYSHIRE
GERVASE THORPE
WILLIAM CAZALET
ANDREW BENTLEY
DICK OVEY
The Pope .... MARK FLYNN
The Archbishop of Rheims .... WILLIAM COLEY
King Raymond of Hungary .... RICHARD FITZGERALD
Tim, Jamie, Rory } Three Boys .... { TIMMY LEZARD, JAMIE MIDDLETON, RORY HOWARD
A Barman .... GILES ANDREWS
An Old Drunk .... JAMES CATTO
Grot, Twit, Pewk } Three Roughs .... { CHARLES GARDNER, KIPPER EADIE, CHARLES LAMBERT
Helen of Troy .... JASON HENCHMAN

Prompt: Jonathan Hannay, Dick Ovey and Hugh Powell
Scenery built by Keith O'Connor, and painted by Tinker Stoddart and her artists
Costumes created, organised and arranged by Joanna Kidd-May, assisted by Tinker Stoddart, Patsy Logan and Joy Barrett
Masks by Tinker Stoddart
Make-up by Nicholas Aldridge, Anthony Browne, Rachel Sharpe, Elizabeth Ormrod and Rosemary Jankiewicz
Stage Crew: Nicholas Macdonald-Buchanan, Michael Burton
Sound and Music by Henry Riches, David Macaire & Michael Mackay-Lewis
Lighting by Rupert McNeile & Piers Covill
Photographs by Charles Churchill
Front of House Management: Anthony Browne, Stephen Cox
Stage Managers: Michael Feben-Smith and Hugh Thompson
Assistant Producer: Philip de May
The Play Produced by Nicholas Aldridge

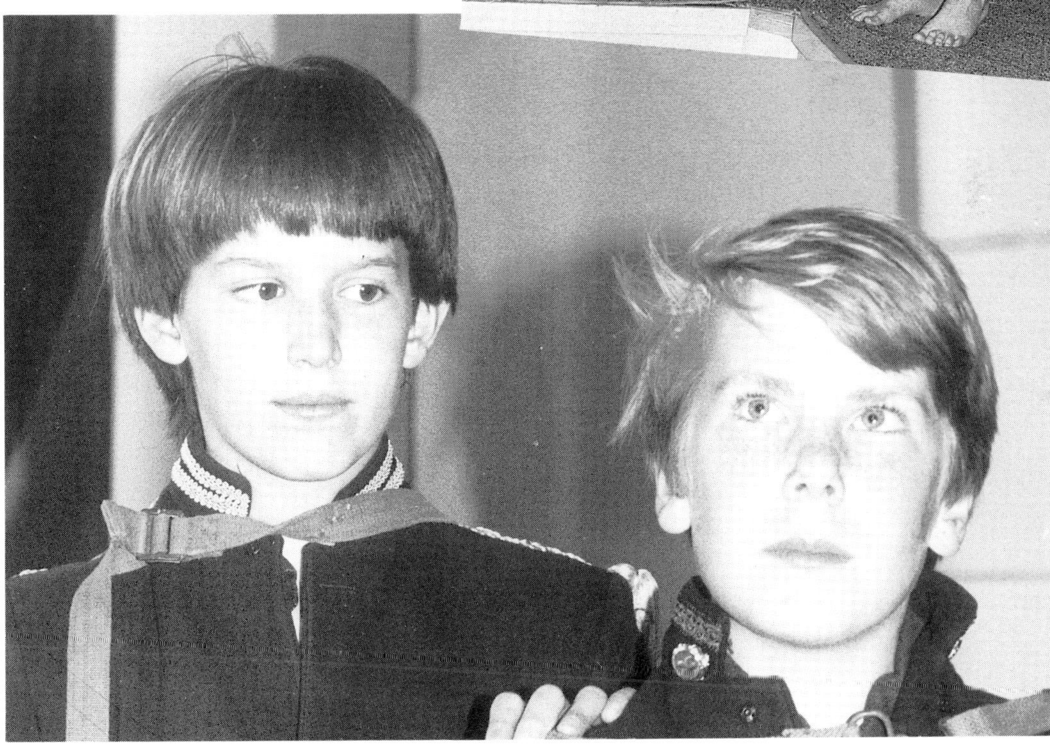

such as *Faustus* (1980) and *Julius Caesar* (1984), alternated with musicals like *Oliver!* (1981) and even our first Gilbert and Sullivan, *The Pirates of Penzance* (1985). A high spot was reached in 1987 with Henry Riches's own *Jumbo Carr Does His Bit*, with music organized by the combined talents of Messrs Langdon and Balding.

204. 'Jack' Edmonds, 'booty' for 35 years.

In 1980, Donald Richards retired from being School Doctor after nearly twenty years, and was succeeded by Roy Spilling, whose elder son was just then entering the school. In the same year 'Tinker' Stoddart gave up the art, into which she had put much inspiration for seven years, as has Judith Lane, who returned in 1983 and now educates boys in a splendid variety of media, pottery being arguably the most popular.

The new decade also witnessed the retirement of 'Jack' Edmonds from running the maintenance side, after a working life of devoted service. Originally, he had worked under Hill, and then taken over from him, and there was no area of the school that he did not look after: he had to cope with everything, from power-cuts and floods (the old Lobby was prone to direct water straight into Lower School) to small boys wanting string for their conkers. The school has been blessed with not a few men of Jack's calibre: mainly unseen and far too seldom acknowledged, their part in the daily routine and the maintenance of the fabric is crucial to the place's existence and cohesion, and it is heart-warming that so many have served the school for so long. At the present time, the three gardening and ground staff, Graham Person, Roger King and Ray Bennet, have between them averaged more than twenty years and seem well set to follow in the footsteps of Charlie Fathers, Charlie Simms and Frank Ricketts. Not much shorter has been the span of Mario Marchi, whose Italianate suavity has added distinction to the role of butler, both in the Dining-Room and on Special Occasions in the 'Front', and his wife Jennifer, whose cooking has kept both boys and grown-ups contented in an age where school food has become an art form in its own right.

Statistics and records were in the forefront of several people's minds at the beginning of the new decade. Since 1880, the only year in which a Summerfieldian had not won a place on the Eton Election Roll was 1930. The superstitious

Part of a bird's-eye view of the School in 1988, painted by Richard Sorrell.

The Staff of Summer Fields 1987. This was an attempt to gather all the adults who are involved with the school. The Governors are absent, as are a few of the domestic and

music staff; but otherwise this is it: teaching, matronal, house-parents, bursarial, secretarial, domestic, kitchen, maintenance, groundsmen and visiting staff.

Nigel Talbot Rice and his family.

205. Cricket on First Game: a 2nd XI match in 1988.

suggested that the figures 80 and 30 were unlucky for the school and predicted a barren year. So it was pleasing when they were confounded in some style by two KS, two OS and five at other schools – the best 'bag' quantitively since 1943. But perhaps the Cassandras were half-right and 8 and 3 were figures of ill-omen, for in 1983 we did draw blank at Eton (though we felt a little aggrieved at Nicholas Hoffman's not getting anything, and both he and Marcus Jiggins proceeded to win internal OS awards for distinctions within a year of going there). Perhaps it was salutary to have the succession broken: it is not healthy to feel that we must inevitably win something.

On the games-field, our rugger XV of 1981 produced the best record ever, winning all eight of their matches, with 117 points to 8. This fine achievement was due to the dedicated coaching of Stephen Cox and Rupert McNeile, and to a superb pack led by the captain, Philip Turner. There were some criticisms that the team did not play particularly attractive rugby, but RAHMcN rightly pointed out that they always played to their strengths (the forwards), that it is easier to coach forwards than outsides at this level, and that the team never approached a match with a 'We mustn't lose' outlook, but always aimed to win. They did, with scores ranging from 26–0 (twice) to a nail-biting 4–0 in the final match against Lockers Park. No cricket scores, simply a lot of well-drilled excellence. The next year's team were in many ways equally good, though they had neither the

206. The Croquet tradition goes back a long way, probably to 'Mrs' herself; the 1988 first-formers Sam Michell, Oliver Bowes, John Down and Henry Morton Jack uphold the tradition of competitive sportsmanship.

unbeaten record nor any really outstanding players; but, under the quietly efficient Simon Welsh, they won 10 out of 12 matches, drawing 0–0 v Stubbington House and losing by a mere two points to Ludgrove.

Tennis, under the direction of Anthony Browne and coach Tony Beale, became an increasingly important and successful game during this decade. Five new hard courts built on the site of the Mayfield Shrubbery enabled regular group tuition to be given during games periods, and the standard improved rapidly. A little further afield, camping provided a highly popular week-end activity, down in the river-meadows by the Cherwell and sometimes elsewhere. JFE had been deeply suspicious of anything that involved tents, and had set his face firmly against the school's having a Scout or Cub Pack; but Henry Riches soon showed what valuable training and enormous fun camping can be.

The school has in general got out and about rather more of recent years. Apart from Expedition Day, there are excursions to theatres, concerts and museums. WLAP is particularly faithful in patronizing both the Ashmolean and the Pitt Rivers with junior forms. On one memorable occasion, he instructed his young flock to stand back and let two ladies pass. They turned out to be French, and rather formidable.

'You should not teach ze young such chauvinism,' hissed Madame.

The boys gazed in some awe as the ladies passed, while one whispered, 'Please, Sir, what is chauvinism?'

'It's French for Good Manners,' came the swift reply.

Indoors, the Debating Society, revived in 1975, flourished, with both senior and junior meetings as well as father-and-son and balloon debates, under the chairmanship of Oliver Lee. An annual public-speaking competition helped to foster similar skills, and a cup was presented for this in memory of Giles Sedgwick OS, who died tragically young in 1983. The theatrical productions settled into a comfortable routine of one every term with occasional variations, notably a Staff Revue in February 1983. It is a pity that, as at many schools, these do not take place regularly, but it is a matter of finding both the time and the inspiration. Anyway, this one was enthusiastically received, and amazingly it had been kept secret. There was really quite an air of apprehension when the HM announced in his sternest manner at supper that every boy, no matter what his commitments, would take a chair to Macmillan Hall and wait there in silence. A hushed school trooped down the passages under the grim gaze of patrolling prefects, and sat in great awe until it became clear that a staged 'Staff Meeting' was a bit of buffoonery, and was not going to decree death for some newly unearthed wickedness.

Two similar occasions have seen a collective hoodwinking of at least some of the boys. At the Celebration Lunch for the Royal Wedding in 1981, the school was honoured by a visit from the elderly Princess Alice of Gutenberg, who, after lunching at Top Table, surrounded by staff and prefects, addressed the boys in a somewhat squeaky and Teutonic tone, which caused a mixture of mirth and embarrassment among her audience. Later in the afternoon, she threw away her stick, veil and wig, and re-emerged as Felicity Fletcher-Campbell the cello-teacher.

The other episode concerned the game called 'Bombers and Fighters' which had evolved at first as a way of occupying 'the Rest of the School' during Confirmation, and had then become a regular end-of-Michaelmas game for everybody. It is similar to 'Prisoners' Base', but each year a fancy-dress theme is chosen. However, in 1985 a member of staff was injured, and it was announced that there would be no 'Bombers and Fighters' in December 1986. Knowing smiles turned to frowns when the school was confronted with a Lecture on Nelson instead; this lecture ran for over ten minutes (and very good it was, too!) before the dais was invaded by pirates pursuing Lady Hamilton, and all reverted to end-of-term bonhomie.

207. David Langdon and Michael Feben-Smith as Hinge and Bracket.

208. Headmaster and Chaplain in unfamiliar roles.

In 1983, the build-up was an important announcement: the school had recently been inspected, and the inspectors had stated that Summer Fields must start to take girl pupils. A mixed reaction: many guffawed, some were stunned, and one boy burst into tears! But, once the audience had recovered some of its composure, everybody enjoyed the remarkable wealth of talent that appeared. Messrs Langdon and Feben-Smith made a convincing Hinge and Bracket, Messrs Capie and Riches showed equal polish when surrounded by a bevy of lovelies in 'What a Swell Party', and the Headmaster did not quite win the title of 'Miss Summer Fields 1983'. But he was subsequently persuaded to exhibit his charming *altera persona* at the Dewdrop Inn round the corner; what would once have been done as a 'dare' was now done for charity.

Charity has become a constant presence in our lives, and each Lent a very large number of boys forgo their sweet rations to contribute to a chosen Good Cause. This takes place in addition to regular Chapel collections and occasional appeals of a specific nature. Since 1982 we have contributed through Action Aid to the education in Kenya of Fred Mamai – in the tradition of the assistance that we gave under PMBS to a Greek village school in the North Euboean Foundation.

209. Sir Christopher Slade, at a dinner held in his honour when he retired from being Chairman of Governors, with NTR and JTR.

The boys themselves are more aware of the world outside school than was the case even thirty years ago. As has been said, the school has become more outward-looking; and one of the signs of this has been a shift in the balance of the Governing Body. Originally it was composed entirely of Old Summerfieldians, but a gradual dilution occurred in order to include parents of Summerfieldians (Bishop Cartwright, Lady Fox, William Wilkinson and Julian Faber) and headmasters of other schools (John Carleton of Westminster, Henry Christie of St Edward's, and Canon Pilkington of King's, Canterbury, and St Paul's). By the 1980s, Old Summerfieldians were in a minority, and, when Sir Christopher Slade resigned the chairmanship in 1986, he was succeeded by Micky Jones, the Bursar of Radley – a school which has close links with Summer Fields, and which has provided a fine example of how to combine progress and tradition successfully in the present age.

Traditionalists may have mourned some of the changes made in Chapel to bring the school's worship into line with current Church of England practices. In 1975, weekday evensongs and evening prayers were abolished, and *Hymns A & M* adopted in place of the *English Hymnal.* This was soon joined by *100 Hymns for*

Today, and in 1980 the Summer Fields Prayer Book was produced, containing a selection of prayers, hymns and popular songs, as well as shortened versions of Morning and Evening Prayer and a form of Series Two for the Communion Service. A gradual reduction in the number of visiting preachers has been matched by a great increase of boy-participation in the services. In 1987 the Authorized Version of the Bible was replaced on the Boys' Clothes List by an anglicized edition of the American 'Good News Bible'.

Though one can chart such changes in the Governing Body and in Chapel, it is much harder to assess to what extent the school's clientèle has altered over the years. The Bentleys, Daimlers and baby Austins on the front drive of yesteryear have become Mercedes, Porsches and BMWs, but what sort of people now send their sons to Summer Fields? Once, such a question meant 'What does your father do?' or, if he was very important, simply 'Who is your father?' But in the 1980s, often both parents have jobs, and indeed a parent may have several jobs, or jobs that are hard to define: many of them are probably management consultant executives. And does Daddy describe himself as a farmer or a landowner, when he is self-evidently both?

The presence of day-boys since 1976, and the establishment of bursaries and an entry test, may have helped to alter the mixture a little, at any rate in terms of maintaining academic standards. An interesting yardstick might also be how many OSS send their sons, but that in effect would be more of a reflection upon the school as it was twenty-five or thirty years ago. In those days, the mixture of parents was possibly still dominated by the 'landed gentry' – a term not at that time suspect, and probably embracing a wider spectrum than it would connote to modern ears.

Are we a 'snob' school, i.e. one where parents send their sons simply because the name will confer status? This again is difficult to judge, because a school has several reputations at the same time. The public reputation as aired at London dinner-tables among prospective parents is often a few years out of date, or based on some quite casual remark or minor event. The presence of Royalty in a school may confer a cachet to some minds, but be off-putting to others. A good academic record leads to a reputation for not being interested in games – as happened to Summer Fields in a recent publication. Yet over the past few years, we have won more matches than we have lost, but we don't make a fetish of winning.

About 15 per cent of Summerfieldian parents (in 1988) describe themselves as company directors, and about 10 per cent are barristers. After those two, the most frequent occupations are stockbrokers, medics of various sorts, chartered accountants, insurance brokers, merchant bankers, engineers, army officers, farmers, solicitors, investment managers, and some involvement with paintings or art. The less frequent (perhaps because more individual) professions include four writers (and one lexicographer), three architects, three diplomats, two painters, and one each of: actor, ballet-master, schoolmaster, museum curator, restaurateur and clerk in holy orders. Whatever this may or may not say about Summer Fields as part of the social structure of Britain, it is certainly a stimulating mixture.

It may be (to misquote Lady Bracknell) that there is something peculiarly stimulating about the air in this part of Oxfordshire. Boys are prone to be matchmakers, and younger masters have traditionally had their names coupled with those of assistant matrons in romantic terms. But the past two or three years have not needed gossips to invent matches: first, Henry Phillips and Jackie Garton; next, Johnny Bush and Caroline Spicer; and then, the only recorded instance of two of the teaching staff teaming up, Mark Johnson and Jane Butler. If these were not enough, Bill Dixon and Margaret Collinson were married little more than a year after retiring from their respective positions as Bursar and House Matron. Four happy notes on which to end make a triumphant major chord to close the chapter of the recent past ...

210–213. Four 'happy couples': the recent spate of SF marriages: 210. Henry Phillips and Jackie Garton; 211. Johnny Bush and Caroline Spicer; 212. Mark Johnson and Jane Butler; 213. Bill Dixon and Margaret Collinson.

AND THE FUTURE?

As we have been looking at the past, so the future will look at us – possibly with amazement, probably with amusement, and, we may hope, with sympathy. The future holds up a mirror in which to examine the present: Is *this* the way that we are really going? Is *this* what we intended to be doing? So our final short chapter will not be an exercise in prophecy, but will examine present tendencies in the light of their future outcomes.

And always with hope. If *Mens Sana in Corpore Sano* is a good aim for education, *Dum spiro, spero* is an essential rule of life. There have been times when we certainly needed our optimists: in 1914, just after our Golden Jubilee and, even more, in 1939, when JFE's optimism and GB's hard work combined to save the school in the midst of the nation's darkest hours. The centenary in 1964 was the beginning of a very grey chapter in British history, when the obsolescent hydra of trade union domination combined with inflation to suggest that the days of independent education really might be numbered, and the Labour Party gave manifesto commitments to curb, or even terminate, it. The last ten years have given a breathing space, but perhaps no more. What does 1990 have up its sleeve?

Having learned as a nation to live under the threat of nuclear extinction and to go about our daily business rejoicing, those working in independent schools are aware that one day (possibly even in the 1990s) there may be a revolution in which they are an early casualty. This threat began to look quite large in the late 1970s and has now receded somewhat, but it would be idiotically complacent to think of it as gone for ever. Both as citizens of the world and as upholders of private education, then, we may be living on borrowed time.

The effect of this should be to make us wary and self-critical: we need to be certain of what we are doing, and of its implications.

'Above all, I want him to be happy,' say prospective parents, and in many cases it is true. The boys' happiness depends on their being healthy, learning constructive coexistence and periodically experiencing a sense of achievement. 'Periodically' because a full life should not always be a life of doing things. There is a temptation in even the most enlightened of schools to see everything in terms of measurable results, like statistics. A well-rounded boy should be able to face the occasional spotlight of, say, speaking in public, singing a solo, or going out to bat in a match; he should be able to be part of a crowd without losing his unique identity; he should be happy in the company of others, but equally happy when on his own. 'Self-sufficiency' is often used to mean beating the elements, but its real and wider meaning is a quality that any whole person should possess. A boy leaves, we hope, to go on to success at his next school and in Real Life, but not merely the visible success of making an enormous amount of runs or money, of becoming Captain of his House or a Cabinet minister.

Money is something of a two-edged sword, and might well turn out to be a danger to prep schools. There is at present so much of it about. We may laugh at the courteous jostling of heads, who vie with each other in erecting more and bigger buildings. One adds a computer centre, so another plunges into a swimming-pool; X builds a sports hall, so Y overtrumps him with a CDT centre. Each of these things is valuable in itself, but its purpose should not be simply to give the Head something new to boast about on Sports Day. It would be a mistake to think that every school has got to have all of them, or that the school which has the most is necessarily the best. Mere facilities are no substitute for education.

An element that has contributed to the success of many prep schools, and certainly of Summer Fields, has been the presence of such varied individuals among their staffs, leading to a blessed individuality and variety in the pupils. One can endow the past with imagined qualities and think that 'In the old days giants walked the earth', but several characters in this history *have* been larger than life. The school itself has also had an inspiring individuality, and this may become hard to preserve in the face of core curricula and rapidly shifting educational fashions. Just as we believe that there is no such thing as a 'typical Summerfieldian', so one may hope that there is no typical prep school; and, if there were, we should not wish to be it. So we need to stand back from the educational market-place and be prepared to resist selling our souls for fashion. In an envious society, it may be increasingly hard to produce real people rather than clones. If our boys enter the world with only an aptitude for making money, playing squash, sometimes cleverly breaking the seventh commandment but never the eleventh, we shall not have been doing our job properly.

That several people feel that we have been doing the job properly is suggested by the expansion over the past forty years and the fully subscribed entry lists. To keep their numbers up, many schools have had to take more day-pupils; indeed, some totally boarding-schools have become entirely day-schools in the course of twenty or so years. Other schools have turned to co-education. We do not seem likely to make either of these changes in the immediate future; but it is not impossible that all schools may have co-education forced upon them in due course. It would be delightful to have girl-pupils, but there are severe practical difficulties in the way: either we should have to deny boys who seek places, or we should have to become so large as to be very different and, many would feel, a less personal place. The Headmaster has four daughters, and many wondered, when Sarah approached prep school age, whether we would go co-ed; but the time passed, and we still have not taken girls since the early 1870s.

As for the subjects that prep schools offer, these are at present dictated by the Senior Schools – perhaps too much so, not through the fault of either, but because Common Entrance is too complex and too specific an exam. It is now, however, coming under heavy pressure from GCSE, and we must prepare ourselves for an increasing amount of course-work and profiles. There is much to be said both for and against these, but, if they serve to reduce the exam, they will be helpful; the worst of both worlds will be to preserve the exam in all its four days while adding course-work and profiles. Maths and English are reasonably assumed to be essential to our syllabus, but the other subjects are frequent topics for debate.

French, or some foreign language, seems to have a fair claim to remain – though the classicists would argue that Latin gives an unrivalled training for all subsequent language-learning as well as teaching civilization, art, politics, law and culture. It is sad that Latin, by becoming 'elitist', has not remained a *lingua franca*; it would have made the ideal language of the EEC, and comes with the bonus (*bona, bonum*) of a great and valuable literature. Science is rightly a central subject; we do an increased amount of physics and electronics both in and out of school hours, and its biology content overlaps with geography via ecology. Regrettably, history is likely to go into decline, becoming a tele-hobby rather than a serious study, and scripture is going the same way, becoming confused with the racial issue of multi-faith studies – which is exactly what nine-year-olds do not need. They can build a faith on simple stories, clear moral precepts and ritual; some will reject this faith afterwards, but at least they will have been shown something positive and know what they are rejecting.

Craft, Design and Technology (CDT) are at present riding high in educational esteem: they bring together skills that were previously covered in art, carpentry, technical drawing and computing. Being both creative and practical, they present the currently attractive target for many educational aspirations. Over the next years, schools may have to use great care in seeing that they do not merely pay lip-service to the aesthetic and cultural, while becoming more intensely practical – or 'relevant', to use another buzz-word.

From the media's point of view, education is one of the most consistently 'newsworthy' topics, both at the level of serious discussion and in the exploitation of children's charm and the manipulation of their views. This will go on being so; it is, after all, a subject with which everyone is concerned and on which everyone feels entitled to have a say. So, whether we like it or not, a permanent spotlight is fixed on our schools, and the media will do what they can over the years to undermine their stability by keeping education 'controversial' and 'newsworthy'. Techniques for coping with this range from 'adopting a low profile' to 'If you can't beat them, join them'. Judicious use of the media has proved helpful in some cases: the television series about Radley managed to be both controversial and beneficial to independent schools. One or two prep schools have featured in tele-journalism to less advantage, however.

Despite the long-established IAPS and the more recent SATIPS, most prep schools existed in comparatively splendid isolation until the 1960s. This is no longer possible or desirable. We are now members of several bodies who can give advice and help over all sorts of problems as well as presenting a quasi-political front if the need arises. This increasing trend will add yet more literature to the Head's in-tray; by the turn of the century, schools may well need to have a file-keeper, whose working day is spent in filing and retrieving files for the school secretary and staff. Like it or not, the computer has come to control our lives by providing innumerable and valuable short-cuts; it would be hard to get on without it now.

Mrs Maclaren would no doubt have approved, for she was nothing if not thorough, though she might see the potential dangers of so many lives being governed by computers. It must continue to be the people that matter; healthy institutions are those in which the individual is of more importance than the institution itself. Though it is the whole that enables the parts to work, in this case the parts are more valuable than the whole.

215. The way Ahead? Mark Johnson showing the 1988 new boys round.

EPILOGUE

June 22, 8.15 p.m. The end of a near-perfect almost-midsummer day. In their red and white athletics gear, the last stragglers from the tennis-courts stroll in. Sam Owen, keeper of the fields, weighed down by the usual collection of heterogeneous clothing, struggles towards the changing-room. I flop lazily on to one of the Alington benches – though solid teak, remarkably comfortable because so carefully shaped – on the mid-wicket boundary of the sunlit and cedar-shaded cricket field. A rare vision on my left of the pavilion with its north face lit up.

A view of a school. Three crosses silhouetted on the Chapel roof; to its left, the older buildings, vertical, almost Gothic, aspiring to the sky and to God. The highest point of Summer Fields is now a television mast, but not much lower come a chimney – one of the few left – out of which grows an unrepentant elder, and a weather-vane with the school arms, its arrow pointing unwaveringly west-north-west. To the right and in front of this is the new school, horizontal in aspiration: on the level in an egalitarian world.

But these buildings lose themselves insignificantly among the trees planted a hundred years ago: pine, cedar, beech and lime, which still offer a refreshing crown to the hard, gritty, concrete-block landscape of 1980s Summertown.

Beyond the Chapel, St Edward's bell strikes the half-hour. The pavilion blushes a little deeper, as the cricket square grows more steeply streaked and illumined by its cedar tiger-stripes: the pitch where today Ben Prior and Oliver Etridge played innings that they will remember for ever, and a hundred assorted boys and masters of Summer Fields and Winchester House formed an early evening crowd as Charles Churchill demonstrated his new, science-fiction bowling machine.

The run-stealers flicker to and fro. But there are other, older ghosts here, too. Do Hugh and Margaret Alington sit on this bench of a summer evening and applaud the novelties of the school they left fifty years ago? Does GB, even more skeletal than in life, bowl lanky left-arm-round where the nets once were? Does Mrs Maclaren herself walk briefly to the edge of her lawn that has an edge no more? And do hundreds of ghostly boys fling themselves about in summer abandon, like afternoon larks butting the sky?

Bird-song dominates the scene, but one small old-fashioned propeller-plane putts across the blue towards the emerging moon. Two magpies prance on to the turf on my left, and then flaunt noisily along the boundary. A pigeon scuffles from among the small oaks, and a blackbird pecks and hops, hops and pecks at the stuffing from a pad, which looks like bread. The Chaplain comes out to give his dog, Uppity, a last run: her feathery auburn tail turns gold as she hits the sunlight.

The end of such a day always suggests the end of an era, but a contentment in the continuing of the same, for it never is thoroughly finished. Red and white roses nod Tennysonian echoes of the colours that barely flap from the flagpole. A grubby white sun-hat that Sam has missed; no longer red caps everywhere, but still something of a *fête-champêtre*. Perhaps a future laureate was fitfully happy here, yet restless to move on and earn his laurels. Perhaps, even in a jet age, all the fields can briefly be summer, and one can believe, on an evening of sun-warmed bird-song and gentle ghosts, that there is time to spare?

APPENDIX 1

HEADMASTERS AND PARTNERS, 1864–1989

Headmaster		*Partners or Assistants*	
1864	Gertrude Isobel Frances Maclaren		
		1879	Rev. C. E. Williams
			Wallace Maclaren
1896	Rev. Charles Eccles Williams		Rev. E. H. Alington
1918 (July)	Rev. Edward Hugh Alington		Rev. C. A. E. Williams
1928 (Jan)	Rev. Cyril Archibald Eccles Williams		A. F. Alington
		1930	J. F. Evans
			G. Bolton
			R. A. K. Jacques (to 1939)
1939	John Fitzgerald Evans		G. Bolton
1956	Geoffrey Bolton		P. M. B. Savage
1960	Patrick Morris Boscawen Savage		J. P. Marston (to 1970)
			J. L. Bell (to 1978)
		1970	N. Talbot Rice
1975	Nigel Talbot Rice		
		1978	N. E. Aldridge

APPENDIX 2

GOVERNORS

1955, June	The Rt Rev. R. C. Mortimer
	Lt Col. A. M. Borthwick
	Admiral Sir William Davis
	Viscount Lambert
	The Rt Hon. Harold Macmillan
	J. W. Max-Muller
	T. G. Usborne
November	Sir Roger Mynors
	The Hon G. R. St Aubyn
1956, March	D. McKenna
November	J. F. Evans
1958, June	The Earl of Gosford
November	F. E. P. Sandilands
1963, February	J. D. Carleton
June	The Rt Hon. Sir Christopher Slade
1965, February	A. F. Alington
November	The Rt Rev. R. F. Cartwright
1966, March	C. H. Christie
	Sir Kennedy Trevaskis
1967, June	N. C. Pearson
1971, November	Lady Fox
	Sir David Lane
1975, March	W. H. N. Wilkinson
June	M. M. Jones
	The Rev. Canon P. Pilkington
1978, March	J. T. Faber
November	P. M. B. Savage
1979, November	Lady Lloyd
1983, March	Mrs R. T. Fox
1984, November	R. P. Butler
	Sir Zelman Cowen
1986, November	E. Evans-Lombe
1987, March	The Hon C. R. Bailey
	Sir John Riddell
1988, March	R. M. Morgan

APPENDIX 3

TEACHING STAFF SINCE 1864

(a) Complete Chronological List, 1864–1988

Year of arrival precedes the name; year of departure follows it in brackets; an asterisk indicates a guessed date.

1863	Mr and Mrs Archibald Maclaren (1884 and 1896)
1865	Rev. W. W. Jones (1874)
1866	*Tollit
	*Sedding
	*Archie Maclaren (a nephew) New Inn Hall but did not graduate
1867	*J. W. Talboys, New Inn Hall
	*Tremenheere Passingham
	Rev. C. H. Grundy, St Edmund Hall (1871)
	Miss Sarah Williams (1904)
1868	Rev. W. Donne, Wellington College and Brasenose (1875)
	*Miss Wheeler
1869	*Bellamy
1870	Rev. E. R. Massey, Exeter College, Oxford (1874)
1871	Rev. L. J. Chamberlen, Winchester and Brasenose (1875)
1872	Rev. R. B. C. Everard, Marlborough and Brasenose (1876)
1874	Charles Eccles Williams, Swansea Grammar and Brasenose (1918)
1875	Rev. O. J. Dunn, St Edmund Hall (1876)
1876	Rev. D. Cuming, Trinity College, Cambridge (1878)
1877	A. J. de Winton, Sherborne and Merton (1885)
	G. O'B. Alington, Uppingham and Queen's College, Oxford (1885)
1879	E. H. Alington, Westminster and Hertford College, Oxford (1927)
1883	J. F. Crofts, Bedford School and Sidney Sussex, Cambridge (1920)
1884	G. W. Evans, Trinity College, Dublin (1924)
1885	T. J. F. Haskoll, Exeter College, Oxford (1896)
	J. W. H. Maclaren O S, Wellington College and Magdalen (1903)
1886	C. Gathorne-Orr, Charterhouse and Oriel (1889)
	S. S. Savery, Kingswood School and Christ Church (1888)
1887	W. Salter, Malvern and Merton (1896)
1888	*Hatch (1 year?)
	*Partridge (1 year?)
1889	P. C. Joy, Winchester and Oriel (1896)
	H. T. G Alington, Marlborough and Magdalen (1896)

1890 T. S. Morton, Charterhouse and Clare College, Cambridge (1897)
1893 F. P. Penny, All Souls College, Oxford (1927)
1896 Rev. C. H. S. Gmelin, Magdalen College School and Keble (1914)
G. Jenner, Magdalen College School and Magdalen (1902)
1897 C. E. Smyth OS, Charterhouse and Trinity College, Dublin (1924)
E. D. Compton, Lancing and Keble (1903)
C. Willett, Malvern and Brasenose (1902)
1899 C. Edgington, Charterhouse and Magdalen (1901)
1902 G. D. Barne, Clifton and Oriel (1908)
R. G. Pidcock OS, Winchester and New College, Oxford (1909)
D. Hollis, Clifton and Queen's College, Cambridge (2 terms)
1903 Miss Rhoda Hill (1946)
R. D. Slater, Wellington College and University College, Oxford (1909)
W. D. Nixon (1905)
1904 Miss Rankin (5 terms)
1905 Miss Mildred Hill (1946)
J. H. E. Besant (1911)
1908 P. C. Henderson, Brasenose (1915?)
1909 G. H. Alington, Marlborough and Magdalen (1912)
B. M. Barker (1915)
1910 W. S. Case, Winchester and Magdalen (1922)
1912 E. K. Barber, King's Canterbury and Keble (1914)
1914 Rev. C. A. E. Williams OS, Radley and Brasenose (1939)
J. F. Evans, Marlborough and Keble (1956)
Rev. J. A. C. Lysaght, Pembroke College, Oxford (1949)
1915 *Taylor
*Cole
*J. M. Alington
1916 G. W. S. Alington OS, Radley and Magdalen (1917)
1917 L. A. G. Strong, Brighton College and Wadham (1930)
1919 Hon B. B. Buckley OS, Eton and King's College, Cambridge (1926)
G. Bolton, Repton and University College, Oxford (1960)
1921 R. W. G. Robinson, Haileybury and University College, Oxford (1945)
1922 D. B. Davies, Wadham (1 term)
A. F. Alington, Marlborough and Magdalen (1937)
H. R. Annis, organist (1940)
1924 R. A. K. Jacques OS, Harrow and Brasenose (1939)
1926 G. S. Frodsham, Magdalene, Cambridge (1935?)
1927 Ll. H. Jeffreys-Jones, Rugby and Magdalen (1935)
T. E. Whittome, St John's College, Oxford (1 term)
C. Day Lewis, Sherborne and Wadham (1 year)
C. G. Mullins, St Andrew's, Grahamstown and Keble (1 year)

1928 W. R. Clotworthy, St Edmund Hall (1 term)
E. Snell, Winchester and Brasenose (1931)
H. M. Mullins, St Andrew's, Grahamstown and Keble (1939)
1930 C. H. Barnes, Winchester and Pembroke College, Cambridge (1934)
1931 J. P. Marston OS, Charterhouse and Trinity College, Oxford (1970)
1932 J. C. Nixon, Trinity College, Dublin (1 term)
1934 W. J. Fallows, Shrewsbury and Cambridge (1937)
R. M. C. Sanderson, Marlborough and Oxford (1 term)
1937 J. H. Biles OS, Rugby and Balliol (1940)
P. H. Williams, Bradfield and Brasenose (1 year)
1938 J. L. Bell OS, Radley and Worcester College, Oxford (1978)
1939 P. M. B. Savage, Westminster and Christ Church (1975)
E. J. H. Dixon, St Edward's and Christ Church (1940)
J. B. Burrough, Cambridge (1940)
R. C. S. Traill, Cambridge (1940)
E. G. Mansfield, Westminster
E. K. Stephenson (1940)
R. D. Pendlebury (1941)
A. W. H. Thomson (1946)
J. M. Wall (1941)
1940 E. K. Barber returns (1946)
D. V. Mansel-Carey, Uppingham and Magdalen (1946)
O. Jeffreys-Jones, Rugby and Trinity College, Oxford
A. Rau
J. S. Puttock
N. M. Wright, St Edward's and Pembroke College, Cambridge (1946)
D.Standring (1946)
M. P. Dobson (1946)
1941 Rev. H. W. Perry-Gore (1946)
G. A. Fraser OS, Marlborough (1 term?)
I. D. W. MacEwen
C. H. Barber, Radley and Christ Church
D. L. L. Stewart OS, Eton and Magdalen
R. Thicknesse OS, Shrewsbury, Keble and Trinity College, Oxford
J. H. G. Shephard OS, Eton and New College
1942 W. J. V. Tomlinson, Felsted and Emmanuel College, Cambridge (1947)
J. D. R. Hayward (1 term)
R. C. T. James, Westminster and St Edmund Hall (1949)
L. F. O'Connor (1947)
1943 *Miss Walford (1947)
*Miss Glover (1947)
1945 H. W. Clayton, Peterhouse (1968)

1946 Rev. K. Menzies (1949)
Brigadier F. Dickins (1 year?)
*Holder (1 year?)
P. J. H. Johnstone, St Edmund's, Canterbury and Selwyn (1979)
P. Garrard (1 year)
1947 Miss J. Rothwell (1949)
Rev. T. A. Lewis (1 term?)
T. N. Tunnard, New College, Oxford (1949)
D. L. Henderson, St Edward's (1 year)
H. W. L. Hartley OS, Eton and Merton (1979)
1948 T. D. Womersley, St Edward's (1 year)
Col. A. G. W. Joliffe (1950)
C. H. Hossell, St Edward's and Trinity College, Oxford (1956)
Rev. W. H. Jarvis (1958)
A. M. Mackrill OS (1 term)
Mrs Sheila Herdman (1952)
L. B. Fosdike (1 year)
1949 Miss C. J. Romilly (1952)
W. A. Williams, Sherborne and Oriel (1975)
P. Alexander, Eton and Christ Church (1 year)
Wilkinson (1 term)
1950 M. Harcourt-Smith, St John's College, Oxford (1 term)
R. N. Porthouse, Worcester College, Oxford (1978)
J. A. Sadler, Wadham (1955)
1951 F. Prichard, Marlborough and Brasenose (1 year)
F. Jeffreys, Bryanston and Keble (2 terms)
1952 A. M. Loft-Simson, St John's College, Cambridge (1954)
Miss P. Faulkner (1955)
1953 P. F. R. Boggis, St John's College, Cambridge (1954)
Mrs Joyce Johnstone (1956)
1954 Rev. J. E. Ralphs, Merton (1955)
1955 D. J. O. Kidd-May, Eastbourne and Worcester College, Oxford
Miss May Hill (1 term)
1956 T. D. D. Williams, Christ Church (1963)
Mrs Margaret Clayton (1968?)
I. B. Kellie, Bedford and Pembroke College, Cambridge (1959)
S. M. Starkey, Repton (1958)
Miss Pearl Alexander (1963)
1957 D. J. Mordaunt, Wellington College (1961)
C. N. J. Marston, Eton (on and off to 1959)

1958 Rev. J. W. Sherlock (1 term)
C. R. Symmons, St Edward's (1 term)
Rev. D. J. Challis (1960)
A. W. S. Robinson (1959)
1959 D. H. Wilks (1960)
C. J. Saunders, Lancing (1960)
1960 R. B. Blackburn (2 terms)
Rev. R. T. Greenacre (1 year)
D. R. Gatward (1965)
A. J. Corran (2 terms)
C. E. M. Snell, Winchester (1966)
L. A. Rawstorne OS (1962)
1961 J. H. Chatterton (1 term)
H. G. Jones, Grove Park (1968)
Rev. J. O. White, Christ's Hospital (1967)
J. H. Colquhoun (1 term)
J. C. W. Murray, Charterhouse and Lincoln College, Oxford (196)
1962 W. A. Stewart (2 terms)
N. E. Aldridge OS, Eton and King's College, Cambridge (1966)
1963 D. N. Richardson (1970?)
Robert Stéphan (1 term)
C. J. G. Brown, Westminster (1 term)
F. V. Hayes, Wellington College (1 year)
F. H. Larr, Marlborough (1 term)
1964 C. ff. Churchill, Wellington College and Jesus College, Cambridge
J. G. Clifford (1 term)
D. Calvert-Smith OS, Eton (1 term)
N. J. Chapman, Felsted (1967)
1965 N. Talbot Rice, Charterhouse and Christ Church, Oxford
J. F. Blackburn (1 term)
C. R. W. R. Inge OS, Radley (1 term)
C. Mackenzie (1 term)
D. M. Langdon, St John's, Leatherhead, and Royal College of Music
M. A. Rogerson, Eton (1967)
1966 J. O. Lemon (1 term)
M. Vickery (1 term)
R. A. L. Ogston, Oundle and Christ Church, Oxford (1979)
K. M. I. Dunbar (1971)
A. Selwyn (1 term)
Miss P. Boon, Birmingham University

1967 K. L. Best, Brighton (1 term)
H. M. O. Jones-Davis (1972)
C. H. Born (1 year)
1968 Rev. E. S. Wragg (2 terms)
D. H. Ireland, Merton College, Oxford and Cuddesdon (2 terms)
Rev. H. C. Thorold OS, Eton and Christ Church, Oxford (1975)
C. J. Chute OS, Winchester (1 year)
M. P. Featherstone-Whitty (1 year)
Mrs J. M. Lane, Manchester College of Art and Academy of Fine Arts, Istanbul (1973)
1969 R. H. C. Legard, Cambridge (1 year)
R. N. Tunstall (1 term)
G. J. StJ. Steadman (1973)
W. L. A. Pryor, OS, Eton and Trinity College, Cambridge
M. E. Rice, Lincoln College, Oxford, (1972)
1970 NJC returns (1988)
C. H. R. Penny (1 year)
1971 R. E. B. W. Field (1973)
RHCL returns (1 year)
1972 R. A. H. McNeile, Marlborough and St Mark and St John, Chelsea
I. C. Lloyd-Oswell, Lancing and St Paul's, Cheltenham (1975)
T. Slade, Cambridge HS and Imperial College, London (1974)
1973 T. S. Cox, Marlborough and Caius College, Cambridge (1986)
P. R. D. Gould, Sherborne and St Mark and St John, Chelsea (1977)
1974 Mrs C. W. Stoddart (1980)
Mrs M. J. Barrett, Edinburgh University
I. H. Taylor (1 term)
1975 R. S. Orr, Bishop Otter College (1978)
Rev. F. W. King (1980)
Mrs S. E. King (1980)
NEA returns
O. J. Lee OS, Harrow and University College, Oxford (1984)
1977 A. H. R. Finn, King's, Canterbury (2 terms)
M. Rooney, Rossall (1 year)
Mrs J. Z. Andrewes (1979)
1978 S. R. Bullard OS, Milton Abbey (1 term)
T. C. N. Flynn, Harrow (1984)
R. G. R. Balding, Bloxham
A. V. Browne, Keele University (1987)

1979	R. O. Barnes, Uppingham and Westminster College, Oxford (1985)
	M. J. Feben-Smith, Hereford Cathedral School and King Alfred's (1983)
	J. R. Blake (1983)
	M. J. B. Riches, St George's College and University of Natal
1980	Rev. F. B. Capie, University of Auckland and Oxford
	J. H. Bush, Wellington College and Southampton University
	Mrs A. W. Boning, Loughborough and London University (1983)
	Mrs C. E. Hollander, Homerton College, Cambridge (1986)
1983	J. Gatward, Rugby (2 terms)
	G. W. Hannah, Birmingham University and St John's College, Cambridge
	M. R. Johnson, Exeter School and St Mark and St John, Chelsea
	A. E. Grunwell (1986)
	JML returns
1984	S. Mendes, Magdalen College School (1 term)
	B. J. Ogilvie, Morgan Academy and Aberdeen University
	R. H. C. Phillips, Harrow and London University
	Miss J. M. Butler, Queen Elizabeth Girls Grammar, Barnet and Bristol
1985	C. R. F. Proctor, Cheltenham (2 terms)
1986	W. Cash, Downside (1 term)
	J. A. S. Mayall, Malvern and Brasenose
	C. StJ. S. Heinrich, King's School, Worcester; University of Kent
	Mrs B. J. Heinrich, Oakdene, Beaconsfield; University of Kent
	R. H. Bradwell, Royal Air Force College, Hereford
	M. J. Ford, Oxford Polytechnic
1987	B. Cooper, Felsted (1 term)
	Miss M. E. Ellis, Homerton College, Cambridge
1988	B. Russell, Downside (1 year)
	A. Ruxton, Cheltenham (1 term)
	W. Bailey, Queen Elizabeth Grammar School, Ashbourne, and St Luke's, Exeter
	Miss V. H. Gossage, University of Guelph, Canada

(b) In charge of Fifth Form

1864	Gertrude Isobel Frances Maclaren
c. 1880	Charles Eccles Edmund Williams
1917	Edward Hugh Alington
1927	Geoffrey Bolton
1952	James Louson Bell
1978	Nicholas Edward Aldridge

(c) Governesses and Junior Form Mistresses

1867–1904	Miss Sarah Williams
1903–46	Miss Rhoda Hill
1904, January–July	Miss Rankin
1905–46	Miss Mildred Hill
1947–9	Miss Joan Rothwell
1948–52	Mrs Sheila Herdman
1949–52	Miss Cynthia Romilly
1952–5	Miss Patricia Faulkner
1953–66	Mrs Joyce Johnstone
1956–63	Miss Pearl Alexander
1962–68	Mrs Margaret Clayton
1966–	Miss Patsy Boon (becoming in 1976 Mrs Logan)
1975–80	Mrs Suske King
1980–86	Mrs Clare Hollander
1986–	Mrs Belinda Heinrich
1988–	Miss Valerie Gossage

(d) Art

It is not easy to say when art lessons began. Some Old Boys have memories of copying things under the eye of F. P. Penny; and during the 1920s J. Allan Shuffrey clearly made an impression. Gillian Tanner, Mrs 'Bobs' Alington, was generally agreed to have transformed the art, and she was succeeded in 1937 by Miss Tremlett, who may have lasted out the war, after which Phyllis Alden conducted art lessons for some years in the ex-billiard room of Mayfield (now Hades). She was followed by a Mr Wardle, and then:

1965–8	Mrs D'Alby Black
1968 (1 term)	Mrs P. Marston
1968–73	Mrs J. M. Lane
1973–80	Mrs C. W. Stoddart
1980–83	Mrs A. W. Boning
1983–	Mrs J. M. Lane

(e) Music

Was R. D. Slater (1902–9) the first music master as such? He was succeeded by B. M. Barker, who left rather suddenly in 1915; but by then W. S. Case was on the staff, and was his obvious successor. Upon the death of Case in 1922, H. R. Annis acted as both choirmaster and organist until the outbreak of war. Miss Violet Harris taught the piano between 1934 and 1957. During the war, A. W. H. Thompson, an import from Farnborough, did much to improve the choir, and he was followed briefly (1947–50) by T. N. Tunnard. H. W. Clayton held the fort for a year or two, both before and after F. Jeffreys and A. M. Loft-Simson each ran the music for a short spell. During this time (in fact until 1977) Miss Cynthia Hartwell taught the piano.

1959–60	D. H. Wilks
1960–65	D. R. Gatward
1965–	D. M. Langdon

In the early 1970s, David Langdon ceased to be the 'music master' and became the 'director of music'; in 1983, Anthony Grunwell became his assistant director, and he was succeeded in 1986 by Martyn Ford.

(f) Gym Instructors

'Corpus Sanum' was an important element at Summer Fields from the first. Until 1898, the boys went into Oxford to receive instruction at the Oxford Gymnasium. Wallace Maclaren had inherited this from his father, and may well have been in charge of gym at SF until the arrival of various professional instructors. He was certainly overall judge of the annual Gymnastic competition, which started in 1899. Other judges (and therefore possibly instructors) at the turn of the century were Mr Burdett and Mr Raimondi, in addition to Dr Williams and E. D. Compton.

1898	Mr Collins
1900	Mr Wilcox
1902	Sergeant Morley
1937	Jack Morley, his son (also known as 'Sarge')
1961	H. G. Jones
1966	K. M. I. Dunbar
1969	W. L. A. Pryor
1978	A. V. Browne
1986	R. H. Bradwell

(g) Magazine Editors

1897–1903	E. D. Compton
1903–8	G. D. Barne
1908–14	C. H. S. Gmelin
1914–27	C. A. E. Williams
1928–46	G. Bolton
1947–57	P. M. B. Savage
1958–64	H. W. L. Hartley
1964–6	N. E. Aldridge
1966–70	R. N. Porthouse
1971–4	P. M. B. Savage
1975–84	D. J. O. Kidd-May
1985	R. O. Barnes
1986–	N. E. Aldridge

(h) Chaplains

There was no chaplain until 1939, as the previous three headmasters had all been in holy orders.

1939–48	Rev. J. A. C. Lysaght
1946–8	Rev. K. Menzies
1948–58	Rev. W. H. Jarvis
Summer 1958	Rev. J. W. Sherlock
1958–60	Rev. D. J. Challis
1960–61	Rev. R. T. Greenacre
1961–7	Rev. J. O. White
1968 January–July	Rev. E. S. Wragg
1968–75	Rev. H. C. Thorold
1975–80	Rev. F. W. King
1980–	Rev. F. B. Capie

APPENDIX 4

OTHER STAFF

(a) Matrons, Sisters and Nurses

?–1896	Miss Branscombe
1896–1923	Miss Lilwall Peirce
?–1927	Nurse Bright
1923–7	Nurse Hayes
1927–35	Mrs Dennis
1929–39	Sister Parsons
1936–7	An unnamed Matron for five terms
1937–9	Miss Raspin (Matron)
1939–41	Miss Reilly (Matron)
1939–41	Miss Bailey (Nurse)
1939–42	Miss Grant (Sister)
1941–3?	Miss Simpson (Matron)
1941–?	Miss Denniston (Nurse)
1942–57	Mrs Beadon (Sister)
1943–52	Mrs Elizabeth Terry-Bevan (Matron)
1953 (briefly)	Miss Rogers
1953–75	Miss Nancy Lovett (Matron and Sister)
1973–86	Mrs Margaret Collinson (Matron)
1975–82	Miss Rachel Trott (Sister)
1982–4	Miss Gay Salway (Sister)
1984–5	Miss Nicola Trencham (Sister)
1985–7	Miss Deborah Williams (Sister)
1986–8	Miss Tamsin Rawlins (Nurse/Sister)
1987–	Mrs Sue Balding (Matron)
1988–	Miss Katherine Prior (Sister)

(b) School Doctors

1884–1927	J. C. R. Freeborn
1927–59	F. G. Hobson
1959–60	B. Juel-Jensen
1960–79	D. H. Richards
1979–	R. A. E. Spilling

(c) Housekeepers

*1867–96	Mary Anne Branscombe
1896–1915	Mrs Paine
1932–45	Miss Bell
*1945–7	Miss Balkwill
1948	Miss Burdett
1949	Mrs Hebdon
1949–50	Miss Bradbury
1950–54	Miss Johnson
*1954–60	Miss Craig
*1960–70	Mrs Dawson
1970	Mrs Taylor

(d) Bursars and Bursar's Secretaries

1952–3	Colonel O'Leary	
1959–63	Major G. W. Acworth	
1963–75	Commander E. E. Hitchens	Mrs Sarah Aitchison
1975–86	Group-Captain W. M. Dixon	Mrs June Bayliss
		Mrs Anne Hawes
1986–	Major A. N. Lane	Mrs Sylvia Harris

(e) Secretaries and Assistant Secretaries

1930–61	E. F. Bowtell	
1961–4	Mrs Jean Maltby	
1964–76	Miss Lois M. Hey	
1976–8	Miss Janet Macpherson	
1978	Miss Rosemary Cox	Mrs Sybil Blake
		Miss Arwen Warmer
		Mrs Lorna Woods
1986	Miss Annabel Arnold	Miss Sophie Wallis

(f) Booty and Maintenance

–1897	Mr Paine senior
1897–1931	C. H. Paine
1931–58	L. Hill
1959–80	'Jack' Edmonds
1980–85	Ernie Watson
1985–	Michael Dale

(g) Groundsmen

1880s–1951	Charlie Fathers
1918–82	Charlie Simms
1950–83	Frank Ricketts
1963–	Roger King
1965–	Ray Bennet
1966–	Graham Person

(h) Carpenters

1897–1931	C. H. Paine
1935–78	Tom Allsop
1978–82	Keith O'Connor
1983	Peter Sarak
1983–	Alan Allmond

APPENDIX 5

SCHOLARSHIPS WON SINCE 1960

(Scholarships up to 1960 are given in the Summer Fields Register, 2nd Edition)

1961	N. J. G. Beer	5th Stowe
	P. I. L. Maxwell	Marlborough
	P. T. W. Hudson	Clifton
	G. D. Chamier	Eton
	P. S. S. Macpherson	Exh. Fettes
1962	J. B. Mynors	3rd Marlborough
	A. M. F. Cartwright	8th Marlborough
	C. C. Osborn	Eton
	J. St J. H. G. Wormald	Eton
	M. I. Dyer	Oundle
1963	J. St J. H. G. Wormald	2nd Eton
	N. R. H. Bailey	Eton
	A. D. Roberts	Eton
	M. O'B. Acheson	St Mark's, Southborough
1964	M. P. R. Wormald	3rd Eton
	A. E. E. Webster	Eton
	O. J. Lee	Harrow
	N. D. E. Inge	Exh. St Edward's
1965	C. P. Dobbin	2nd Radley
	D. L. Natzler	3rd Eton
	N. V. C. Polunin	17th Eton
	S. A. Weinstock	19th Winchester
1966	C. B. Mynors	6th Eton
	C. J. H. Woodward	7th Eton
	R. E. B. Burrows	9th Eton

1966 (cont.)	Hon. A. W. R. Morrison	17th Eton
	E. H. Lee	5th Harrow
	D. C. Collard	Exh. Radley
1967	H. J. Kharas	Eton
	F. Dinshaw	Eton
	A. J. L. Burrows	Anna Shaw, Eton
	J. E. P. Hodson	Marlborough
1968	R. Tylden-Wright	8th Eton
	Hon. M. E. P. Piercy	Exh. Shrewsbury
	A. Penny	Flett Bursary, Fettes
1969	D. H. Shaw-Stewart	3rd Eton
	J. N. C. Gaisman	Eton
	A. G. H. Lane	Eton
1970	R. F. Trew	Eton
	A. Nicholson	Eton
	M. S. Fox	Eton
	J. N. Bray	Marlborough
1971	J. W. M. Lane	1st Eton
	G. A. R. Leggatt	5th Eton
	A. R. I. Gardner	15th Eton
	J. P. Slot	Music Sch. Eton
	M. S. A. Wade	Music Sch. Eton
1972	H. T. D. Morris	17th Eton
	M. P. Drew	Judd Sch. Tonbridge
	A. C. Bedell	1st Bromsgrove
	P. F. Noel-Baker	Minor Sch. Leighton Park
1973	P. W. Morris	9th Eton
	C. P. Burrows	Music Sch. King's Canterbury
1974	A. N. M. Cheetham	Eton
	S. J. Dent	Harrow

1975	M. Q. Choyce	5th Eton
	P. R. Messum	3rd Charterhouse
	P. A. Bacon	4th St Edward's
	C. D. Tatham	Exh. Winchester
1976	P. G. H. Dillon	5th Eton
	E. S. G. A. P. G. O'Meara	9th Eton
	J. A. G. H. Stewart	Exh. Harrow
1977	G. T. S. Davson	2nd Eton
	R. A. Carless	8th Eton
	L. S. Clow	15th Eton
	D. W. D. Chamier	19th Eton
	S. E. Morris	7th Marlborough
1978	T. J. Webber	4th Marlborough
	R. P. Lea	10th Eton
	L. S. Clow	12th Eton
	P. R. H. Starey	Music Exh. Radley
1979	N. E. Evans-Lombe	3rd Eton
	P. A. Wolrige Gordon	11th Eton
1980	P. G. C. de May	11th Eton
	J. A. D. Carr	14th Eton
	J. F. Bruce	18th Eton
	H. E. Powell	24th Eton
	J. P. C. Edwards	Thompson Sch. Radley
	S. R. Gardiner	Exh. Radley
	R. M. Middleton	Exh. Radley
	M. M. Flynn	Exh. Stowe
	P. Gilardini	Exh. Downside
1981	M. L. N. Wilkinson	15th Eton
	A. Manisty	18th Eton
	J. F. Pelham-Burn	Major Sch. Radley
	R. D. R. Stark	Exh. Radley
	W. St G. A. Cazalet	4th Uppingham
	P. I. R. Zvegintzov	Art Exh. Sherborne

1982	W. B. M. Coley	4th Eton
	E. A. Hansen	10th Eton
	J. M. Daniel	14th Eton
	S. D. P. Welsh	15th Eton
	A. Manisty	Music Exh. Eton
1983	R. F. J. Brown	3rd Uppingham
	J. C. D. Henchman	Thompson Sch. Radley
	J. C. F. Heynes	Exh. Radley
	J. C. S. Rodesano	Exh. Radley
	J. C. S. Rodesano	Music Exh. Radley
1984	O. H. B. Page	1st Radley
	B. J. G. W. Grist	4th Eton
	A. Sohmen	14th Eton
	L. S-K. Fung	Music Sch. Eton
	A. Sohmen	Music Exh. Eton
1985	W. J. Cowan	1st Radley
	W. D. T. Heynes	Exh. Radley
	R. T. G. Nash	7th Winchester
	N. J. I. Kind	7th Eton
	A. J. Walford	13th Eton
1986	H. T. D. Boyd-Carpenter	1st Ampleforth
	H. B. Gibbs	10th Ampleforth
	T. A. Donaldson	11th Eton
	T. A. M. Cobbe	16th Eton
	J. N. B. Page	2nd Radley
	R. S. T. Henchman	Minor Thompson, Radley
	J. E. D. Robson	Exh. Radley
	A. J. Mellanby Lee	Exh. Marlborough
1987	M. B. Swire	6th Eton
	A. C. B. L. Payton	20th Eton
	F. R. Farquhar-Oliver	5th Radley
	T. D. Soper	Bradfield
	J. A. E. Spilling	Music Sch. Winchester
	A. B. Liddell	Choral Exh. Radley

1988	C. A. C. Smith	5th Eton
	J. A. G. Carew Pole	10th Eton
	A. T. Leathers	12th Eton
	L. Cadogan	Major Sch. Harrow
	J. D. P. Carter	Major Sch. Radley
	C. A. Lesser	2nd Downside
	E. Morton Jack	Music Exh. Eton

BIBLIOGRAPHY

(a) Works which specifically mention Summer Fields

LETTERS from Rev. C. E. Williams to Austin Anderson, 1882–1940.

THE SUMMER FIELDS MAGAZINE, 1897–1988.

THE SUMMER FIELDS REGISTER, 1st Edition, 1864–1929.

——2nd Edition, 1864–1960.

A CENTURY OF SUMMER FIELDS, ed. Richard Usborne, Methuen, 1964.

REFLECTIONS BY AN OLD PEDAGOGUE (upon Preparatory Schools, especially Summer Fields), by Rev. C. E. Williams, unpublished *c.* 1928.

MICHAEL, 1910–1931, printed by the Nonesuch Press, 1932.

PACK CLOUDS AWAY, by Bernard Darwin, Collins 1941.

THE WORLD THAT FRED MADE, by Bernard Darwin, Chatto & Windus, 1955.

ALONG THE ROAD TO FROME, by Christopher Hollis, Harrap, 1958.

RONALD KNOX, by Evelyn Waugh, 1959.

THE BURIED DAY, by C. Day Lewis, Chatto & Windus, 1960.

RECOLLECTIONS OF SUMMER FIELDS, by Geoffrey Bolton, unpublished *c.* 1960.

CROWDED CANVAS, by John Spencer Churchill, Odhams 1961.

GREEN MEMORY, by L. A. G. Strong, Methuen, 1961.

A TEACHER'S STORY, by Guy Boas, Macmillan, 1963.

HEADMASTERS AND OTHERS, by Hugh Stubbs, unpublished, *c.* 1964.

APPROACH MARCH, by Julian Amery, Hutchison, 1973.

THE KNOX BROTHERS, by Penelope Fitzgerald, Macmillan, 1977.

SUMMERTOWN SINCE 1820, by Ruth Fasnacht, St Michael's Publications 1977.

TALL, DARK AND GRUESOME, by Christopher Lee, W. H. Allen 1977.

PRELUDE, APOLOGIA, ANECDOTES AND ABOLITIONS, by Patrick Savage, unpublished, 1988.

BLIND IN ONE EAR, by Patrick Macnee, Harrap 1988.

(b) Other Related Writings, inevitably only a selection:

BIBLIOTHECA CLASSICA, BIBLIOTHECA THEOLOGICA and other Bookseller's Catalogues issued by D. A. Talboys, 1822–1838.

THE OXFORD CHRONICLE, May 1840.

THE GENTLEMAN'S MAGAZINE, June 1840.

THE ADVENTURES OF MR VERDANT GREEN, by Cuthbert Bede, Longman, 1854–7.

CROCKFORD'S CLERICAL REGISTER, 1861ff.

A MILITARY SYSTEM OF TRAINING FOR INSTRUCTORS, 1862;

A SYSTEM OF FENCING, 1864;

TRAINING IN THEORY AND PRACTICE, 1866 – by Archibald Maclaren.

PHYSICAL EDUCATION, edited by Wallace Maclaren, 1895.

THE FAIRY FAMILY, by Archibald Maclaren and Edward Burne-Jones, Longman, Brown, Green, Longmans and Roberts, 1857

——introd. by John Christian, Dalrymple Press (London) 1985.

MEMORIALS OF EDWARD BURNE-JONES, by Lady Burne-Jones, 1907.

THREE PLAYS FOR SCHOOLS, by Geoffrey Alington, Bell, 1913.

REMINISCENCES OF MY LIFE, by Henry Holiday, Heinemann 1914.

EVER AFTERWARDS, 1917; THE EMERALD, 1919; MOONSHINE, 1921, by Cyril Williams and W. S. Case, unpublished.

CHAYTOR'S, by Adrian Alington, Chatto & Windus, 1933.

A QUESTION OF PROOF, by Nicholas Blake, Collins, 1935.

THE LAST ENEMY, by L. A. G. Strong, Gollancz 1936.

A VICTORIAN SCHOOL, a History of Wellington College, by R. St C. Talboys, Blackwell, 1943.

A HISTORY OF WELLINGTON COLLEGE, by David Newsome, John Murray, 1959.

MY GRANDFATHER, HIS WIVES AND LOVES, by Diana Holman-Hunt, Hamish Hamilton, 1969.

A SHORT HISTORY OF BRAMCOTE SCHOOL, by various authors [no date].

INDEX

Numerals in *italics* refer to pages on which illustrations occur